977733

# Best Short Stories 1988

# Contents

# Introduction

ONCE AGAIN WE are proud to present the best of recent output in the short story, in the British Isles, the Commonwealth and anywhere creative English is written except America, which has annuals of its own.

The best? Despite our justification for the superlative in our introduction to last year's volume, this word still appears to irk critics: what are our criteria? In a review of that selection we were gently chided for playing our editorial cards too close to our chest. But surely the definition of best is simple enough, because so entirely subjective. It is what we as readers liked most without having to know why, what we most wanted to share with others, what seemed to us to add more to the savour and relevance of life than countless other very good stories did. Both of us in our separate searches have looked for certitude of vision, no matter how expressed. Even a writer imprisoned in verbal platitude or besotted by an excess of felicity belongs forgivably to the best if he or she unlocks feeling. Ordinary words in easy patterns often produce the eloquence we sought.

Part of the pleasure of a fine story lurks in the twinge of disappointment when it ends. Couldn't it have been a bit longer, you say, give us more of this character's oddity, more than just a glimpse of that landscape? The answer is invariably no. These stories are chosen because their length is exactly right, even if you long to explore further the worlds they conjure up. Far more than a novel, intended to engulf you for hours, does a story you read in minutes reverberate in the imagination for days. But only if you take them slowly, at leisure, one at a time.

As usual we have read widely in weeklies, monthlies and quarterlies as well as newspapers to ensure that no story worthy of inclusion passed us by. We are delighted for the first time to include stories that appeared in *Granta,* the *London Review of Books, Fiction Magazine, Vogue* and the recent Northern Irish periodical *Passages.* As usual, too, we append a set of notes on the authors, who, as their subject-matter reflects, come from places as far apart as India, Canada, Trinidad, Pakistan and South Africa, and, of course, throughout the British Isles.

The best? All we can say in the end is that these are the stories that most touched, amused, shocked or attracted us, and won their place in these pages after a tough fight.

Giles Gordon and David Hughes

# Angelo's Passion

## CHRISTOPHER BURNS

'WHAT ARE YOU reading?'

At first I ignore her.

'I asked what are you reading?'

She walks over to the bed. I try to be still but my instinct is to curl away, protecting the book as if she had nothing to do with it.

'Pliny,' she says, twisting the name with her English tongue.

'Pliny,' I tell her, using the Italian pronunciation. 'You recall that you bought it for me in Venice. In English it would be called *Natural History*.'

'Renaissance?'

'He died in AD 79. You will, of course, know what that year means.' I half-expect her to have forgotten.

'Yes,' she says, 'I liked Pompeii.'

Rose is wearing expensive underwear of black lace. There is a subtle, erotic sheen to it. I can think of half a dozen girls straight away who would look alluring in it. Not Rose. She belongs to the age of white underwear – slips and stockings; the kind of things you see in old films from the fifties and early sixties. After all, this was her time.

She leans over me and places a finger on the text. 'It isn't Latin?'

1

'I wish I knew enough to read it in the original. It's a translation into modern Italian.'

'*In the middle of the Ptone . . .*'

I translate. '*Among the Ptonebari and the Ptoemphani, upon the coast of Africa, the dog —*'

'Tell me about it.'

So I tell her what I know about Pliny. About his imaginative vision of the world, his bizarre statements, his odd names. How he had taken the bare physical facts of life and transmuted them into the wondrous, the magical, the divine.

She nods. I can see her storing it all in her memory. She'll take away more than just photographs.

There are two books by Rose's side of the bed. One is a colour guide to Italy. It has lots of photographs, all taken in bright sunshine, all with colours that are too intense. Fortunately it does not go into very much detail about the history and culture of the country. For that I am invaluable.

The other is a sex manual. Printed in America but sold in Britain. There are pages of description, references to sexologists and poets, libertines and artists. There are cutaway diagrams, sketches of genitals in various stages of excitement, photographs of couples making love. In one drawing it is as if the lovers have been sliced, neatly and bloodlessly, by a huge blade. All the anatomy of sex is as bare as an opened corpse. There is, it says, no book better.

Rose leans forward again and takes my ear between her teeth. I can feel the pressure, gentle but scary.

'Let me just finish this chapter.'

She sits up and takes the book off me. I give a heavy sigh of exasperation but she takes no notice. 'But it's *pages* long.'

'Really?'

She puts the book face down under the bedside light.

'Bedtime,' she says.

I sink down in the bed. She strips at its foot. The underwear leaves lines across her skin.

Rose plunders the manual. She wants no possibilities left. She wants the subject squeezed dry. So she coaxes, cajoles, shames me into aping its illustrations. She wants to exhaust hedonism. We couple like dogs, with me high above her haunches, hands on her flanks. I dream that she might dry and, like dogs, we will be glued into an absurd, horrifying embrace.

Afterwards she talks her mad fantasies of taking me back home as a lover, pet, the envy of all her friends. 'We'll be the talk of Herefordshire,' she laughs. 'Rose and Angelo.'

We both know this will not happen. But we will get value from each other while we can.

I feel tired of it all. I feel bored and disgusted at myself. But I'm too much of a professional to let things go before their time. Rose and I have several weeks together before the end must come.

I allow myself moments of petulance. For Rose, this too is part of my Latin charm. For just as she loves me to be the smooth talker, the sharp dresser, the cultivated guide, the accomplished lover, so she expects me to be the moody boy, beautiful but selfish, jealous and adolescent. She *imagines* me. And I support her image of me.

But she also imagines herself. She gives herself a race, claiming to be a Celt. Her red hair proves it, she will say, and I think that when she was a young girl it would, indeed, have been full red. I have tried to find out more about the Celts from her, but they seem to have left little behind them. I have no interest in barbarians.

In the end, it all comes down to our postures on the bed, and her hissed commands to me, her reiteration of my name.

In the early morning, just as the sun comes up, she finds me in the hotel bathroom. My head is tilted back and the back of my head is floating on warm water. I feel like an unborn child, only vaguely conscious.

'Are you all right?' she asks, half-asleep but concerned.

I nod.

'Isn't it a strange time to take a bath?'

Soporific, I merely shake my head.

Only when she has gone back to bed and I have climbed naked from the bath do I realize how badly my shirt has been damaged. Blood has covered one sleeve and spotted the front.

I put it in a plastic bag for disposal later. I'll hide it in the car boot and dump it in some roadside waste bin.

I breakfast on the terrace. Already the sun is warm, and only the faintest of breezes stirs the newspaper. I can hear noises from the kitchen. When the heat has made the hills disappear in haze I put on my dark glasses and hide behind them.

When Rose appears she seems refreshed by the night. She has washed her hair and – I admit it – it looks good. But the lines are deeper at her mouth and eyes, looking as if they are a sculptor's knife incisions on a clay model. And she wears a scarf around her neck. Several times she has caught me looking at her neck and must have noticed some change in my expression. The scarf is red, as bright as blood, but it hides the age that has her by the throat. She would be attractive to an older man.

Like a Caesar, I motion her to sit.

'An interesting edition?'

I grimace.

She leans forward confidentially. 'You were good last night.'

I do not know if I should be irritated or dismissive or proud. I pretend to be proud. 'To be good one must have a good partner,' I say, and hide behind the newspaper.

'But Angelo, you were wonderful.'

I smirk.

The waiter serves her breakfast. He looks at me with that mixture of disgust and envy that I've grown used to over these past few months. And before that, before Rose found me. The waiter thinks he can read our relationship like a book. He would be a fool if he did not see that I can see his jealousy.

'Much news?'

I shrug.

'You look good in that shirt.'

'Thank you.'

'That's the one I bought you in Milan, isn't it?'

'You know it is, Rose.'

'You've changed.'

'You are observant.'

'You change your clothes as often as a woman. That shirt you put on last night was clean.'

'It felt dirty. Even this far north there is still a lot of dust in the air. And possibly this hotel is not as clean as it should be. I must satisfy my vanity.'

'I wouldn't want you any other way.'

I turn a page. The breeze catches it and folds it back. The waiter moves across the terrace, orange juice held high on a silver tray. There are the noises of distant radios, the chambermaids at work, of washing in the kitchen.

'Are you going to wear your suit to the church? Your powder-blue one?'

'Yes, I think so. With the sports shoes.'

'The trainers? Angelo, you can't wear trainers with a suit.'

'Only the very fashionable wear them. I have seen a photograph of Mick Jagger dressed very like me.'

'Are you sure?'

'There are certain things I do very well. One of them is dressing fashionably.'

'Of course, lover, of *course*.'

Your lips are too red, I want to say, they make you look old.

But if I want to keep her I cannot be so direct. I have to go about things in a roundabout way. It is only because of her that I can travel in this way. She pays for the hire car, the hotels, the petrol, the food. She paid for my expensive haircut in Florence, my pre-war-style white slacks, the shoes I'll wear if I take her out tonight. She even bought me the crocodile-skin wallet which I keep full of her money in my breast pocket.

But in St Peter's she stood before the Pietà and said that the woman was out of proportion, that if she stood up she'd be two feet taller than the Christ. I raised my hands in despair. She looked up at me, almost as if she was scared. 'Tell me,' she whispered. It was like a panic of deprivation. '*Tell me.*'

So I told her all about Michelangelo and the technical problem of the seated figure and how it was solved by the basic pyramidal structure; how, at the end of life, he did the Rondanini Pietà, where the forms of the dead Christ merge with those of his mother; how one should look, not for

5

physical anomalies, but for achievement. For grief and dignity and passion.

'Passion.'

'In the Biblical sense,' I said, slightly exasperated.

She nodded dumbly, like a child.

'You look,' I said, 'at how the agony is made beautiful. The whole thing is a metaphor for transcendence. That is what it is about.'

So it was during the rest of our extended wandering around the country. I would take her to ruins and panoramas and historical sites; to galleries, piazzas, churches, opera houses. I told her about Ovid, Dante, Leonardo, Verdi, Bernini. I suggested we divert by certain roads, visit less well-known places, linger a day or so at small hotels. I would read up beforehand and sometimes have to invent little details, but overall I am an honest guide. I have found out a lot of things myself. I'm sure I could make a living out of it.

On the road between Positano and Amalfi she said, 'But this isn't the real south. This is the tourist south.'

'I agree. The north is much more interesting.'

'You don't understand. I want to see the real south. The peasant south.'

'There is nothing there to interest either you or me. There is nothing down there to make any civilized person stop and look.'

'I think we should go. It'll be an experience.'

It was. Its people were suspicious and withdrawn. They disliked people such as us. They thought it was immoral for Rose to keep me. They still believe in darkness and brutality – we saw charm signs on the walls – and they mistrust foreigners. Not even their faces are modern. They belong before the Renaissance.

Rose found them fascinating.

'They are like your Celts,' I sneered, 'with nothing but superstitions to leave behind them.'

I saw them as unexciting but dangerous. She saw nothing sinister in groups of men in dark colours, their boots covered in dust, standing just looking at us across powder-bright town squares. She thought it was all somehow *real*. 'But these people are nothing,' I said. 'There is no individuality in them. They are the same, generation after generation. There is no reality in them.'

A goat had been tethered outside one of the houses. It grazed a barren circle. One day it was found butchered. It had been degutted; it lay with its head thrown back in the middle of a black riot of flies. Rose was a foreigner; suspicion fell on her. They would not serve us in the shops, they spat after us in the street. They made the sign of the evil eye when we passed. A policeman, surly and threatening, visited us in our tiny room at the town's solitary hotel. He talked about the fear of witchcraft and said it would no longer be possible to protect us. We left within the hour.

I felt easier when I had put miles between us and the village. 'I hated it there,' I said.

'Why?'

I sought for reasons. 'It's too hot. Too barren. Too near Africa.'

When we stopped I walked around the car and realized that someone had taken a knife along the side.

'All right,' I said, 'Foggia, Pescara, Ancona. I shall feel happier the nearer we are to civilization.'

Sitting here this morning, reading my copy of *Il Giornale*, digesting my breakfast, I feel a lot more comfortable than I ever did in the south. This is what I was made for, I think, and start to read an article about Venice.

'We're going this morning?'

'To the church? Yes. The frescoes are damaged a little, I think, but still worth looking at. In England you will never have heard of them. Italy is so rich that only a very few things are known about abroad.'

'Angelo, you'll make them come alive for me. You always do.'

'Where shall we go after this? I think it is time we began to move on.'

'But yesterday you said you thought we should stay a few more days. Have you changed your mind?'

'I thought about it overnight. In the bath. There are so many things to see. I want you to have the best of all possible times.'

She leans forward and grips my hand. I give her my special smile. Not for nothing did I have some teeth capped.

'Just let me finish this,' I say, 'and then we will go.' Sooner or later I will pass through Venice again, I need to know the news.

From behind me I hear a high, distressed voice. It carries through the sunlit morning with surprising clarity. I know who it is. Ever since we arrived here a fat woman with dyed black hair and a loud reedy voice has insisted on demonstrating the affections of her cat. She carries it around in a wicker travelling box. She feeds it from her table, talks to it, tells people about its health and habits and intractable sexuality. The waiters, sensing money, humour her. They pretend to be amused by it. They even offer it special food, slices of veal or fish. They are fascinated by it, but it is obvious to me that they hate it. The cat, which is black and furry and groomed, remains sharp-clawed, thoughtless, unapproachable. It opens its black jaws to reveal a mouth of moist, glistening pink, and sharp white teeth.

'What's all the noise about?'

'A missing cat.'

'That woman with the pet cat?'

'Someone must hate it. A waiter, perhaps. One can only take so much.'

'What's happened?'

I shrug as if uninterested and raise the paper to cover my mouth. 'It has been killed. Not in an accident, but by someone.'

She looks at me with a steady uncritical gaze. The cat owner's voice subsides into tears. I can hear the sympathetic lying staff console her. They cluck around her.

'The walk to the church will be lovely,' Rose says.

'Yes,' I say, seeing the lifeless cat placed carefully back in its wicker carrier, blood sticking its fur into tufts.

We don't say much during our walk. The sun is very pleasant, not too hot, and there is little traffic. No one joins us.

★

The church is pleasant but unexceptional, its importance over-emphasized by the local guide book. But it is quiet and cool and old, empty enough to give hollow reverberating echoes. It is easy to feel part of a less flippant, more accomplished age. I don't like their crucified wooden Christ, which is of too recent a date. It is too disturbingly physical for the quiet seriousness of the church. There seems to be no resurrection hidden within.

'Is this good?' Rose asks.

I pull a face. 'If you like that sort of thing.'

'It reminds me of something I once saw. I think it was in Germany.'

'Protestant Art. There is no glory in it.'

'You see no achievement?'

'I see no spirit.'

We walk round to the frescoes. They show Christ borne by angels to heaven, whilst sinners and unbelievers suffer in hell below. The hell is still in good condition, its torments vivid and bizarre, but mould has crept across the heaven. The angels and the Christ have begun to disappear, like something delicate that has been passed over by a flame.

'But this is terrible.'

'Really?'

I haven't heard her. I feel like reaching across and touching the Christ, as if the hand of a believer will somehow cure this sickness and decay. But I know I would only touch stone and the powdery fungal specks of dead paint.

'Look at this. It's a scandal. Public funds should be given to protect it. It is no masterpiece, but it is *real*. Now all the lightness and sureness has gone. The Christ is almost destroyed. It has a few years. Maybe five, but no more. Perhaps it is already beyond salvation.'

'It must end shortly.'

I smack my hands together. The noise echoes down the church. 'What are we if we cannot look after our own greatness?'

She nods. 'Yes.'

All of a sudden I realize what she's talking about. 'Shortly?' I ask, shocked.

She smiles.

'You mean I'll have to earn my own living?'

Rose walks along the frescoes. 'You've opened my eyes to things like that. You really have, Angelo. I couldn't ever forget our time together. And I've learned so much. About all sorts of things.'

I follow her down the church, meek as a slaughterhouse lamb.

'It's terrible about the paintings. You're right. We have a local church with carvings that are hundreds of years old. Done about the same time as these, I suppose. But we had very different styles.'

'Rose,' I say.

'They're very strange. Offensive, even. Not the kind of thing someone like you would expect in a church. I grew up with them, so I don't have that problem. And they've lasted far better than these poor angels. One is a sheela-na-gig. You've heard of such things?'

'Rose.'

'What a pity. It's a very old word. It means a carving of a woman. Holding herself apart. Do you follow me?'

Our footsteps echo in the cool, centuries-old silence.

We spend the night at a hotel two hours' drive away. Rose gives me a present. I can tell that it is a thick, heavy book. I wonder if this is as a farewell.

I unwrap it.

'Michelangelo.'

'You like it?'

I open it up. It is beautiful. 'Yes,' I say, 'very much.' I turn the pages. 'It must be one of the best.'

'*The* best.'

I find the Rondanini Pietà. It is photographed from several angles in different kinds of lighting. The forms sink back into the stone, unable to escape. It is as if holiness has escaped even them. They fall back into the world, like animals without souls.

Three days after we part and I have found Elizabeth. Elizabeth has dyed her hair ash blonde but I can tell what colour it should be by looking at the roots. She is overweight. And she is half-embarrassed by the attention I pay her. But also she is half-excited.

I am a lot younger than she is.

She pretends to try to reject me, but I persist. It is, after all, what she hopes for.

I promise to take her to see the land of Bernini, Dante, Giotto, Tasso, Pliny. Lights of ambition shine in her eyes.

'I'm too old for new ways of doing things,' she tells me later.

'Nonsense,' I say. 'You are a very attractive woman.'

But when we couple like dogs, I sense the same fear that gripped me when I was with Rose. I am trapped by flesh. Dizzy, scared, I finish the operation in a cold sweat and fall on the bed shaking with fear. She does not notice.

Among the Ptonebari and Ptoemphani of the African coast, the dog is worshipped as king. Priests study and interpret every movement. Each twitch or scratch, each lift of the nose or tilt of the head, each emptying of bladder or bowels, each wag of the tail or closing of the eyes, each sniff or bark is taken as a commandment.

Each of these commandments is followed religiously.

# 'Night in Paris'

## PATRICE CHAPLIN

FOR CHRISTMAS 1950 when Lucy was eleven, Aunt Ethel sent her
a bottle of perfume. It was called 'Night in Paris' and was
packaged in a blue box with an Eiffel Tower and a half moon on
the front. It was Lucy's first glamorous present and she was so
thrilled she wanted to keep it forever. That was her first mistake.
Her second was standing it on the dressing-table next to the
glossy postcard photographs of her filmstar favourites, Lauren
Bacall and Robert Taylor. Since she was six she'd wanted to be a
filmstar. The 'Night in Paris' perfume seemed to help that along.
Enclosed in the wrapping paper was a note from Aunt Ethel. 'To
my Darling Dearest Little God Daughter. Auntie's so proud
you've won a place at Grammar School.'

In those days Lucy had a shilling a week pocket money
invariably spent in Woolworth's at the make-up counter. She
could buy a small bottle of Eau de Cologne for tenpence or a
mirror and powder puff in a plastic case for fourpence.
Colourless nail varnish was a shilling, face-powder ninepence.
The 'Night in Paris' perfume adorned Woolworth's counter in
many sizes. The deluxe bottle cost two and nine. After the
glamour shopping she went to Saturday afternoon pictures at
the Odeon. She'd earned the one and three ticket money
washing up in the High Street café.

That Christmas, 1950, her mother received a stiff mauve folder with a satin bow on the front. The writing paper and envelopes inside smelt of lavender. Lucy had seen the present in Woolworth's at three and six. Her mother opened the folder. 'Good. Ethel hasn't written in it. I can give it to your Auntie Vi. I don't need posh stuff like this.' And she put it away in the dressing-table.

Auntie Vi arrived Boxing Day and brought not only a present but her daughter, young Violet, also bearing a gift. Lucy's mother rushed into the bedroom and got out the writing paper. She turned the mauve folder over to scribble a greeting on the back. The price, five shillings, was inked boldly in the corner.

'But that isn't right,' said Lucy. 'It's only three and six. I've seen it in Woolworth's.'

'They don't ink in the prices either. That's your Aunt Ethel. Swank as usual. We'll have to give young Violet something.' Her mother looked around wildly. 'Give her the scent. Come on. You can always get some more.'

Lucy was appalled. 'But it's too good even to use.'

'All the better. Not been touched. They can see that. Come on. Hurry up. They've come all the way from Gosport.' Lucy's mother always got her way in those days.

Reluctantly Lucy wrote on the back of the box. 'To my Cousin Violet with love, Christmas 50.' In exchange she received a doll's hood.

In 1952 Lucy again received a bottle of 'Night in Paris' perfume for Christmas. This time it came from the Reverend Maude and his wife who lived at Weymouth. Lucy wouldn't have thought twice about it if she hadn't seen, faintly scratched on the box, 'Cousin Violet . . . 50.'

Her mother said for all the Reverend Maude's snobbery he was a cheapskate. 'But how did they get my present that I passed on to Cousin Violet?'

'Your cousin was made to send it on to the Reverend's wife, that's why. Your Aunty Vi wouldn't let her daughter use that muck. You know the sort who use that.'

That year Lucy had started wearing 'Californian Poppy'

perfume, Woolworth's one and six a bottle, so she decided to put the present in her drawer until the other was finished. When she came to use it, however, it had gone. Her mother had sent it to Aunt Ethel for her birthday. 'But she sent it to me originally!' Lucy was outraged.

'She won't know. She ought to be glad to get anything. Mutton dressed as lamb.'

The photographs of Lauren Bacall and Robert Taylor had gone too. So had most of Lucy's filmstar collection which she kept in a shoebox in the wardrobe. She hadn't noticed because she was so passionately in love with Mario Lanza after seeing him in *Because You're Mine* and *The Great Caruso* that only pictures of him adorned her room.

Her mother admitted she'd given them to Cousin Violet. 'You don't want those old photographs. She's only a kid. Gives her something to look at.'

Lucy realized her mother, along with Aunt Ethel, had no respect for possessions. The filmstars had taken years to collect. She'd written to the stars care of the studios and usually got a signed glossy photograph in reply. Vera Ellen, Cornell Wilde, Lana Turner, Ava Gardner, Humphrey Bogart, Phyllis Calvert – they'd given dreams and brightened up her dreary schooldays in the suburbs. She tried to explain that to her mother.

'Give all that up. You're not a child. You're nearly fourteen.'

'But I want to be one of them.'

'Make believe. You've got to get on with the real world.' Her mother wanted Lucy to become a private secretary. That's where the status was. Filmstars played no part in that job.

The next Christmas Lucy received a stiff mauve folder of writing paper from Aunt Ethel. Written inside in blue ink was, 'To my Darling Little God Daughter with heaps of love and affection for Christmas 1953. P.S. Only a little gift darling but you can write more letters to your Auntie.' A gummed label on the top right hand corner marked the price. Twelve and sixpence. Lucy tore it off and underneath was inked five shillings, the price Aunt Ethel had originally marked it up to when she'd sent it, all festive and indisputably new, to Lucy's mother in 1950. Lucy sniffed the folder. The lavender smell had gone. The mauve silk bow was flattened and frayed and Aunt Ethel had disguised its age by sewing on a cloth rose.

'What a cheek!'

'Doesn't matter.' Lucy's mother grabbed the folder. 'We'll try and scratch the price out and send it to the Reverend Maude and his wife.'

'But Ethel's written in it!'

'They'll never know. They're half blind. I'll stick a label over the message. Ethel's a nuisance, writing all over the presents like that.'

Lucy got an expensive gift from the Reverend Maude and his wife. A bottle of Coty 'Chypre' fragrance in an un-tampered box. Lucy hadn't seen it in Woolworth's – it was out of that price range.

'I wonder who gave her that,' said Lucy's mother. 'She can't stand scent, old Maude's wife. That's why you've got it.'

By Easter the Mario Lanza pictures were down and the bedroom wall was bare. Lucy had a crush on her gym mistress and was longing to give her a token of the passion. The Chypre fragrance was undeniably right. A memorable gift of love. Lucy began the accompanying note and her mother picked up the bottle.

'Where's this going?'

'To my teacher. It's her birthday.'

'Rubbish. These are Christmas presents. You don't touch these.'

'But it's valuable.'

'All the better. Do for Aunt Ethel. She's come up in the world. She's going to manage a hotel in the Isle of Wight.'

'But it's mine.'

Her mother kept her hands on the Chypre. 'But they're sent out at Christmas. You don't use them.'

Lucy longed for revenge. What better than an incorruptible present, the transitory kind. Next Christmas she'd send out a batch of live things that died. Plants. Unheard of in the

Christmas chain. She even considered perishable things like homemade cakes covered in hundreds and thousands or blancmange packed in ice.

Lucy loved Christmas. She loved cards and carols, crackers, coal fires, party games. From the end of November each year she went carol singing with her friends and they saved the money to buy presents. Lucy enjoyed wrapping them, decorating the packages with holly and tinsel. The professional presents upset her.

In the late forties a special present had gone into circulation but it didn't reach Lucy until the mid-fifties. A small tin of Snowfire vanishing cream, Woolworth's one and three. It was considered a suitable professional gift because the tin couldn't be marked and by lifting the lid it was obvious it hadn't been used. It was passed on to Aunt Ethel for Christmas '55 and she recognized its pedigree. In the same wrapping it was despatched to little Beryl in Folkestone. Aged ten, the girl was delighted. Her mother took it away. 'Whatever is Ethel thinking about? You don't want to put much on your face at your age.' She rewrapped it immediately and sent it to Lucy. 'A late present for my pretty niece.' If she put that old cream on her face, Lucy reflected, the adjective might cease to apply. It lay in the darkness of her dressing-table for years. Before they moved in 1959 her mother removed it from the box of jumble. 'Wait a minute. This stuff's never been used. It might come in for someone.' Aunt Ethel got it with a tin of tea the following Christmas.

Lucy had rejected the secretarial path. After school she'd worked in the local rep as A.S.M. and made her way up to juvenile lead. She was glamorous and earned extra money fashion modelling in London. She no longer shopped at Woolworth's. In 1960, after she'd failed to get a small part in a West End pantomime, she was obliged to visit Aunt Ethel. The Reverend Maude and his wife were also staying. It was a subdued Christmas but she did get one laugh. When Aunt Ethel opened her presents Vi and young Violet had sent a folder of writing paper and a slightly battered box of 'Night in Paris' perfume. Fourteen and six was inked outrageously on the side. Aunt Ethel grimaced but her voice was bright. 'How nice. They don't always have such taste about present giving.'

Both the satin bow and cloth rose had gone from the folder and the gluey scar was covered by a handmade paper doll that leaned forward when the folder was opened.

'How original,' said Lucy mischievously.

Aunt Ethel's mouth tightened. 'Yes. Young Violet was always good at craft.' The Reverend Maude's wife received the Snowfire vanishing cream. It was the first time she'd got that. The Coty 'Chypre' fragrance had gone into hiding.

Lucy gave them a completely innocent present. It could not be corrupted. She laid the plucked goose onto the table. They pretended to be grateful but they were very disappointed. Didn't Lucy know the meaning of Christmas?

All three long-term festive missiles ended up in Aunt Ethel's care. She let them freshen up in her dressing-table pungent with the smell of old Christmas soaps and thirties lavender bags for two years. Then she took the 'Night in Paris' scent and removed it from its box. She wrapped it in an Irish linen handkerchief (Christmas '37) and sent it to young Beryl in Folkestone. She removed the handmade doll from the stationery folder, stuck a Christmas label over the glue mark and wrote right across the front of the folder in indelible red pen, 'Happy Christmas.' In a moment of spite she added '1967'. She gave it to the Reverend Maude. He was ninety-four and had a short memory. So did she it seemed in '68 because she gave the Snowfire cream to Lucy for her birthday. She arrived unannounced in the dressing-room of the West End theatre while Lucy was on stage and left a note. 'Just dropped in on a flying visit with little gifts for my clever God-daughter.' Lucy kept the tin in the dressing-room and the other actresses were intrigued by its age, its nostalgia.

The second 'little present' was the filmstar collection which Lucy had so loved as a child. 'I thought you might like these. I got them for you especially. They're very valuable darling.'

More than Aunt Ethel could know. How she'd got them from Cousin Violet and what circuitous route they'd travelled, Lucy could not guess.

There was an outbreak of the professional presents in 1971 but by then Lucy was in Hollywood. 'Night in Paris' was still going strong. It travelled around as part of a Boots toilet selection. The writing paper had had to come off the circuit in '68. Lucy's mother had received it from the Reverend Maude and the seven of sixty-seven had been changed to a spidery eight. Lucy's mother was licked. She kept it in the dressing-table until she could think of something to do with it.

Aunt Ethel wrote to Hollywood where Lucy was playing small parts. 'We so missed you at Christmas but if you do get back to England there's a little welcome home present waiting at your mother's. It may come in useful for your busy career. We're so proud of you.'

When Lucy finally returned in 1976 after her mother's death, she found the little gift in the sideboard. She lifted off the soft blue crepe paper and on a nest of green nineteen-fifties taffeta lay the bottle of 'Night in Paris'. She hadn't seen it for years. Its smell took her back to her school days, Mario Lanza, the crush on the gym teacher, carol singing. It also reminded her of the Christmases of the war. Waking up early in the cold with the blackout still up and under the dim torch light unwrapping a small packet of perfumed crayons, six colours and a drawing book, some nuts wrapped in silver paper, a packet of Cadbury's chocolate with purple wrapping, a monkey up a stick, an apple, an orange. One year there was the magic of a kaleidoscope. She remembered these as being the happy Christmases.

She took the folder of writing paper from her mother's dressing-table, smelling of mothballs. She tore off the two strips of satin ribbon and took out a yellowing envelope and sheet of paper. She wrote,

'Thank you Auntie Ethel for all the Christmases.'

# The Death of the Tribe

## JIM CLARKE

*For John Rafferty and Jim McSherry*

AS FAR AS Murdach could judge, by viewing the sky through the chimney hole in the roof of the hut, it was about two hours before dawn, or thereabouts. He swallowed down another mouthful of ale from the tankard before him, determined to reduce himself to a drunken stupor before Gerg, the bard, began to sing the praises of those present in the Taoiseach's round hall. His sister's wedding had been a christian ceremony, sure enough, but Patrick had not purged the island of all its pagan beliefs. As was customary, the Taoiseach had called for a mighty feast and an evening of merriment to commemorate the wedding of Padraig and Bride. An appropriate name too, chuckled Murdach.

The droning voice of Gerg whined on and on, and Murdach soon tired of drinking ale. As always happened when he was bored, his thoughts turned to Niamh. Niamh . . . her very name meant 'Heaven' and when he considered her exquisitely beautiful face and flowing black hair, Murdach could not help but agree. She was by far the most sought after woman in Ard na Bhfuinseoge, the hamlet that Murdach professed to call home. That was all changed now, however. Already Niamh was carrying his first child and he did not intend to wait long before marrying her, once the baby was born. Theirs would

19

probably be the next wedding he would attend, he mused. He rubbed the alcohol-induced fatigue from his eyes and focused hazily upon Bride, his sister, and her new spouse. Padraig was a likeable man in his own gentle way, and the muscles he had built up working in his forge ensured that no man picked a quarrel with him. He was tall as well. At five feet and eleven inches, he stood head and shoulders above nearly everyone in the room, except for old Conor, the Taoiseach, or chieftain. He was over six feet tall if he was an inch, Murdach judged. His eye passed around the hall, and alighting upon no one else of even passing interest, he settled down again into his half-slumber.

He awoke suddenly. He was a light sleeper, and as soon as Gerg, the bard, had mentioned his name, he had pricked up his ears and levered his head off the ale-sodden table. It was disrespectful to sleep during the bard's rendition of your finer qualities. He sat up, and feigned extreme interest, as Gerg began. His bloodshot eyes focused on him and Murdach could not help but notice that behind the bard, at the far side of the hall, most people were asleep. As an outsider in the village, there only because of his blood-tie with Bride, Murdach came very low down on the list of those worthy of Gerg's praise. A quick glance upwards confirmed his suspicion; already the sky was reddening with the rise of the early morning sun. He suppressed another wave of boredom and decided to at least try to listen to Gerg.

> 'And Murdach, brother to Padraig's new wife,
> is one worthy of our praise.
> For he has proved his courage in battle
> against the Northern invaders.
> In his home, Ard na Bhfuinseoge,
> The women clamour for his attention.
> But in vain, for he has eyes only
> for Niamh, the village whore.'

Those few still awake laughed hollowly. Murdach's face hardened and he clenched his teeth but he said nothing. To gainsay the words of a bard was to challenge the Taoiseach himself. Obviously, Gerg did not like him for some reason. He wiped ale from his stubbled mouth, and listened to the second verse.

> 'Murdach is also tall and strong
> and always wins in contests.
> See! even tonight he wins.
> He has drunk more ale than us all!'

Murdach cursed under his breath. 'Pitis!' he swore. 'A friendly bantering of jokes I can take, but not this slander.' He was preparing to challenge Gerg, when a voice came from the far side of the hall.

'Conor, taoiseach of myself and my village, will you sit in your high chair and ignore the insults of your bard to a most revered guest, Murdach, my new brother-in-law?' The voice was Padraig's. He was raised to his full height, and his open brat, woollen cloak, revealed his rippling muscles. The challenge had been laid down.

Padraig's booming voice had awoken most of those previously asleep, and suddenly there was a hubbub of noise, everyone wanting to know what had stirred Padraig to such anger. Slowly, the white-haired man on the high seat rose to his full six feet.

'What is the problem, Padraig? This is your wedding feast is it not? Gerg was simply instilling a little mirth into the evening. I'm sure our esteemed visitor took no offence, for none was intended.'

The look that Gerg threw at Murdach was so arrogant and smug, though, it spoke the truth of the matter in volumes. Conor turned to Murdach.

'Well, my friend, is any offence taken?'

There was more than a hint of steel in his voice, and despite this and the warning glance that Padraig gave him, Murdach stood up and proclaimed in a loud voice, 'Yes, there bloody well is.'

For an awful moment, all was still and silent. No one

moved, or even breathed. Then everything happened at once.

'Seize him and bring him to me unarmed!' bellowed Conor, his face purple with rage. As two drunken men struggled to obey their taoiseach's command, the aged taoiseach beckoned to Padraig and Gerg to approach him. Padraig bore an anxious expression. The sight of the red-haired giant and the bald, weasel-faced bard seemed so ludicrous to one young girl, that she laughed aloud. A cuff on the ear from her disapproving father quickly silenced her mirth.

Shortly, the three men stood before Conor. The old man turned to Murdach first.

'What offence do you take, Murdach of Ard na Bhfuin-seoge?'

Murdach was not naturally an eloquent man, and he stumbled, trying to find the right words. Eventually he answered.

'The first offence I take is that my betrothed, Niamh, is the village whore. It is true that she tried other men before me, but never for payment, and she is with my child, she is my fiancée, and I must defend her honour as I would, were she my wife.'

'There will be no combat in the round hall,' pronounced Conor. 'Is that the only offence you take?'

Again Murdach paused before answering.

'No, O Conor. The second and final offence that I take is that I have drunk more ale than any other man in this hall.'

As soon as he said this, all around the hall could be heard the sound of metal on wood, as men hurriedly forsook their tankards.

Conor pondered this, scratching idly at his white beard. 'The first, I will accept, Murdach, and Gerg will retract it. The second is yet to be proved, so I withhold judgement. Should it be found to be legitimate also, Gerg must forsake his bardship. Will you still press this offence? If you are wrong, it would be right for me to punish you for slander.'

Murdach's eagle eyes narrowed. 'I will press the offence.'

Conor nodded in obeisance. 'Deidre!' he called to his niece, who was a serving girl at the feast.

The girl hurried over to her taoiseach immediately.

'Yes, my taoiseach and my uncle?' The dark brown eyes of the girl met Conor's.

'Deidre,' he continued. 'You served Murdach tonight. How many tankards of ale has he consumed?'

The tawny-haired girl paused, mentally accumulating the number. 'Ten,' she replied firmly, 'and one half-drained.'

The old man nodded, smiling encouragement at his young niece. 'And has any man in this hall exceeded that amount of ale on this same night?'

The girl blushed, her cheeks assuming a deep scarlet hue. 'Well, one has,' mumbled Deidre eventually.

'Out with it, girl!' demanded Conor. 'Who was it?'

The girl looked downwards to hide her embarrassment. 'You, Conor.'

Both angered and humiliated in front of the complete townsfolk, Conor waved his hand, as if shooing the girl away, then scratched his beard, and thought again. After yet another uneasy silence, he spoke.

'Gerg, for your slander and for humiliating your taoiseach, I strip you of your bardship. Go! Leave the village and do not return. Consider yourself exiled.'

Gerg stared incredulously at the old man towering over him, then, at another barked command, he fled from the hall.

The old man's voice dropped to barely above a whisper as he addressed Murdach and Padraig.

'You win this time, Murdach, but remember that both Gerg and I are men not easily slighted. It would be better if you did not stay overly long in Muirthemne, but returned quickly to Ard na Bhfuinseoge, for they tell me you have been absent for five months, fighting the Norsemen. Gerg, I would warn you, is cunning and he seems to have taken a dislike to you. You would do well to avoid him, should you come across him on your return to Ard na Bhfuinseoge.'

Murdach cleared his throat of the cloying ale, and spoke.

'I will leave before this morning is out, great Conor. I wish only a few hours' sleep before I go.'

Conor nodded his agreement.

'Yes, that would be best. And if you wish to see your sister again, invite her to your hearth. You have angered their bard and humiliated their taoiseach, and these people are the sort to bear a grudge!'

Murdach sighed. The visit had not turned out well at all. He knew without turning around that it was Bride who was sobbing. He still had no idea why Gerg had acted so, but he knew that the actions of the conniving bard had ruined, not only his sister's wedding, but also the relations between Muirthemne and Ard na Bhfuinseoge. On a diplomatic basis, Padraig's marriage to Bride might as well not have existed.

Conor then addressed Padraig. 'Keep an eye on Murdach before he leaves. See he doesn't get into any trouble, and drive him as far as Dun Dealgan in your chariot.'

Padraig agreed, 'I will, O Conor.'

The taoiseach was then about to dismiss them, when a young boy, no more than fifteen, but tall for his age and scrawny, burst into the hall and ran up towards the firepit in the centre of the round hut. There, he stopped and bowed at Conor, then he walked around the pit and strode up to the high seat.

'Well, boy?' boomed Conor Mac Niall in his most commanding voice.

'G-great Conor,' he wavered, 'I have just returned from Dun Dealgan, where I heard tell of a new wave of raids by the Vikings. One man from Tara told me that they are even progressing inland as far as ten miles! And it seems that the Danes and Saxons cannot hold them in check. Already they have burnt and plundered the abbey at Ard na Doire.'

Murdach gasped. 'Ard na Doire! The hill of the oak grove! It is barely a mile from the hill of the ash trees, my own Ard na Bhfuinseoge!' Quickly he gathered both his thoughts and the few items he had with him together.

'Conor, I must beg your leave. I must return to Ard na Bhfuinseoge immediately.'

The taoiseach assented. 'You may depart, Murdach. God speed to you. I am only sorry that I cannot allow Padraig to go with you now. Should the Norsemen attack us, all our men must be ready to defend Muirthemne. God be with you, Murdach.'

Murdach protested vigorously, but to no avail. He was quickly ushered out of the hut, handed his weapons, and led to the east gate of the village. They almost pushed him through the wooden gate, and then shut it tight behind him. Murdach looked up at the ten-foot wooden poles, bound together and driven into the ground to form a wall, and realized the futility of it all. The Norsemen would burn their painstakingly built wall to the ground. In spite of his solemn mood, he laughed. Then his thoughts turned to Niamh again and he set off towards the dirt track that led to Dun Dealgan. As he strode along a thousand questions sprang to mind. What if Gerg had not been at the feast? What if Conor had summoned his brehon, or laughiver, instead? What if . . . He suppressed them all. He was a week, maybe ten days' journey from Ard na Bhfuinseoge and his family and friends. To him, that was all that mattered now. It had been a bad day indeed.

## A Week Later

Murdach awoke on his fern bed to the sound of crying curlews far above. For the past seven days, the weather had not been kind to him, hampering his journey south with rain and fog, but already he had reached Wicklow, and was not far from the hilltop of Ard na Bhfuinseoge.

He began the day with both apprehension and exhilaration. The sky was a deep azure, and the heavens were clear of all grey, puffy blemishes. This would be a glorious day, Murdach promised himself.

He polished off the last of the food he had bought in Tara, and washed down his meal with water from a stream which babbled incessantly just beyond the waving poplar trees, under which he had sheltered the night before. He gathered his belongings together and, strapping on his sword-belt, set off.

Murdach had been walking three, maybe four hours, and the sun had almost reached the zenith, when he caught sight of a ragged figure staggering across the vale into which he had descended. As he got closer, Murdach could discern that it was a monk, and over his shoulder he bore a heavy hessian sack.

25

'Pitis!' murmured Murdach. 'He's from Ard na Doire!'

At Murdach's shout, the man glanced upwards, the hope visible in his eyes even from twenty yards. When the monk's eyes caught sight of Murdach's blade, however, the hope faded and the man made a peculiar whimpering noise. He fumbled about his cassock, then laying down the sack carefully on the springy grass, he produced a jewelled crucifix.

'Put your holy cross away, brother,' called Murdach, smiling. 'I am no demon to shy away from it, but a christian man, baptised like yourself. My blade is my only defence against the heathen Norsemen, who ravage our fair isle again. I was serving under my grandfather, Ciaran Mac Niart, in Emhain Mhacha, to learn scrivening and the art of combat, when the Vikings attacked the northern coast, and we were called to defend it. I am now returning home to Ard na Bhfuinseoge, to marry my betrothed, Niamh.'

All the time he had been speaking, Murdach had been tentatively stepping towards the monk, and now he was barely three feet from the cowering man. The hooded figure peered closely at Murdach then laughed aloud and clapped him on the back.

'If it isn't Murdach Mac Labres! I know you now, my son. It was you who used to bring extra milk to the abbey during the winter months with your sister. She's to be married, so one of my brothers heard.'

Murdach nodded, grinning foolishly. He had always liked the kindly hooded men of the abbey and he felt the urge to pour out his worries, his joys, his tears and anxieties to the old man, as he was wont to do as a child. But he did not.

The monk's face suddenly assumed a solemn expression. 'They pillaged the abbey, Murdach. All the monks . . .'

He paused and tried again.

'They killed them at prayer, Murdach. Those northern heathens defiled our chapel with murder!'

The old man was deeply upset, for Murdach could plainly see the tears streaking down his face. He sat the monk down on the ground.

'How did you escape the slaughter, Brother Enda?'

The old brother smiled ruefully, the tears on his cheeks glinting in the noon-day sun.

'I slept in. I was still in my cell when the defilers came. When I saw them, I went to hide in the sacristy. That's where I gathered these.'

He indicated the sack that lay, blood-soaked, on the grass.

Murdach opened the sack and gasped as all the treasures of the abbey spilled out onto the grass. Beautifully embellished books of scripture and jewelled chalices and crucifixes, encrusted with gold, all poured out onto the ground. Murdach's eyes widened, then he looked up and his eyes met with Enda's.

'What are you going to do with all this?' His waving gesture was reverent, awestruck even.

'Take it to one of the bigger monasteries, I suppose,' muttered the monk grimly. 'Monasterboice, most likely. Father Abbot was taught there. You said you were going back to Ard na Bhfuinseoge?'

Murdach muttered agreement. 'Mmm. How does the village fare?'

Brother Enda's sombre mood softened slightly. 'You know the forest as well as I, Murdach.'

The young man nodded vigorously, smiling. The forest in southern Wicklow was so dense in places as to make travel impossible. If you did not know the territory, you could be lost for weeks in the undergrowth. It was probably by chance that the Norsemen had come across the abbey at Ard na Doire.

'I think, God willing, that the raiders will not discover the hill of the ash trees, Ard na Bhfuinseoge. But the forest was teeming when I left, Murdach. They were looking for survivors to take into slavery, no doubt. I would not attempt it, my son,' continued the monk.

Murdach looked at the dense, foreboding forest, then smiled wryly.

'It is a gaes to me not to defend my betrothed and my home, brother. Even if I were not required by duty, I would go out of love.'

'Well said, Murdach!' smiled the monk gently. 'I will not

hold you back, then. Fate has dealt us both perilous cards, and I only pray to God that we will both pull through unscathed. Dia Deifer! I must hasten from this place for fear that the heathens are chasing me. May God be with you, Murdach.'

The old man gathered all the treasures into the sack, then paused. 'Here, Murdach,' he said in a fatherly tone, handing him a jewelled golden crucifix, 'it is not right that all the abbey's treasures leave the hill.'

And with that, the monk heaved the bag onto his shoulder with a heavy grunt. Murdach simply stood and watched as the saintly old man slowly trudged off into the distance. Again he felt the feeling of futility rising in his chest, but this time he did not revel in it. He realized that Enda would not get more than about three miles before being robbed, bludgeoned and left for dead by some gold-greedy foreigner from the Danish settlement at Dublin. He swallowed down his emotion and prayed he was wrong, but in his heart, he realized he was right.

After about ten minutes' walking, Murdach entered the ruffled mantle of green that was the forest of Wicklow. 'Enda was right,' he mused. 'No Dane or Saxon or Viking could possibly find Ard na Bhfuinseoge without a guide.' With this assured comfort he consoled himself.

For the remainder of the daytime hours he neither stopped nor slackened his pace, and he was ever wary. Twice he was forced off his chosen route to avoid a sluagh of Norsemen prowling the wood, but now he was getting near. If luck was with him, he could be there before the end of the first night watch, Murdach judged. Gradually he wound his way through the familiar maze of trees and undergrowth, until he was in the sheltered vale below the hill of the ash trees, surmounted by the habitation of Ard na Bhfuinseoge. Home.

It was twilight when Murdach finally began the final ascent up the craggy, forested hillside to the village. The glow of the dying sun held him in a buoyant mood and his spirit exulted at the thought of being with Niamh at the fireside once more. 'Five months is long in any man's life,' he thought. Murdach was guessing at just how long it would be before Niamh gave birth, when he slipped.

Earth, trees and sky whirled around in a lightning blur and when all was steady again, Murdach discovered that he lay flat on his back and his left leg throbbed with a dull, pulsating pain. After a few seconds to regain his composure, he levered himself up into a sitting position. His lower shin was bleeding profusely from where he had gashed it on a rock.

'By the holy Bridget!' he snarled. 'Am I ever going to get home at this rate?'

Dragging his leg slightly, he staggered a little way up the hillside to a small cave. He knew its position well – many were the times he had hid in it with his brother Eoin from their father's wrath. Today, he hid from the Norsemen. He sat there in the foreboding gloom, and bound his leg with a strip of his brat which he had cut with his knife. As he sat, he watched the sun sink slowly but surely behind the hill of the ruined abbey, Ard na Doire, and he thought. He thought of his brother Eoin, afflicted with some pestilence at birth that had left him without any hair.

Baldy, they had called him, until that October day about fifteen years before. One dead and five wounded before Labres, the big, hulking man they both called father, disarmed Eoin of the sword. He was never called names again, save once. Eoin was skilled in the art of clever speaking, and thus perfectly suited for training as a bard. That was his undoing though. At play one day, Cullen, the taoiseach's son, accidentally struck Eoin with his hurley stick. Eoin turned and retorted with a disgusting epithet referring to Cullen's eating habits. Cullen, not known for his father's subtlety, had simply stated aloud, 'At least I've got hair, baldy.' At that, Eoin had raised his ash-wood hurley stick and battered Cullen to death. It had taken both his father and himself to drag Eoin from the body that time, Murdach mused. Red blood and red sky.

Eoin had been exiled, of course. But for the intervention of Labres and Ciaran Mac Niart, Murdach's grandfather, who was visiting, Eoin would have been ritually sacrificed. Nessa, the taoiseach of Ard na Bhfuinseoge at that time, was one of a dying breed – he was a pagan. Five hundred years after Patrick there were still pagans and pagan sites to be found in Ireland, but they were very rare. With the death of his son, and then his wife and brother a few years later, Nessa was the last pagan in Ard na Bhfuinseoge. When he died, Labres assumed taoiseachship.

It was now night. Murdach prepared his brat like a sleeping bag, and lying down, he prayed to God he would be fit to walk in the morning.

His sleep was fitful, and at times he thought he heard agonizing screams. He tossed and turned through the night and a sudden flash of a dream awoke Murdach just before dawn, at the paling of the sky.

He was sweating feverishly and shivering uncontrollably. He realized he could not accept what he had just discovered. Gerg the bard in his dream had merged with Eoin Mac Labres. They were one.

Staggering to his feet, Murdach wrapped his brat around him and gathered his belongings together. He must tell someone this. He realized now the reason behind Gerg's action at the banquet. He resented still everyone in Ard na Bhfuinseoge and the sight of his brother and sister present in his new home must have enraged him sufficiently to do what he had done. Yet what had it gained him? He was exiled again.

Gritting his teeth against the biting pain, Murdach slowly trudged up the hillside. The air smelt smoky. 'They must be smoking yesterday evening's salmon,' pondered Murdach, his mouth salivating at the thought.

He finally reached the top of the hill and looked down into the vale beyond, towards Ard na Bhfuinseoge. It was a desolation. Smoking huts and a smouldering fence were all that remained of the village. 'The Norsemen!' he growled. Ignoring the screaming protests of his leg, Murdach ran towards the scene of disaster, choking on his anxiety and the smoke. He stopped in front of the hut of his father, Labres the taoiseach, and peered inside. His father and mother lay gutted in their beds, blood-soaked blankets the only remaining witnesses to the carnage. As he staggered, numb, from one hut to another the scene was the same in each one.

Suddenly, a terrible fear grabbed at his heart. Murdach

sprinted for his own hut, his breath fast, and his left leg all but forgotten. With a desperate fury, he burst into the hut. It was empty, but the shambles before him confessed a scuffle had taken place. Only one thought possessed Murdach now – where was Niamh?

As he staggered around the ruined village, Murdach realized with a sudden start. This was the deireadh an tuath, the death of the tribe.

But to Murdach, the tribe, his parents, his friends and his village no longer mattered. He wanted to find Niamh. Just beyond the west side of the fence, Murdach found her. And he retched. And retched again.

On a flat slab of stone lay the body of Niamh. She was naked, and face down. Her back had the blood eagle cut into it. This horrific form of sacrifice to Odin entailed cutting slits down either side of the spine, then breaking the rib-cage and pulling the lungs through the holes like the wings of the eagle.

Trembling violently, Murdach knocked her body over. She rolled over, now face upwards. He retched again and then a fourth time.

Her womb had been cut out. Murdach looked away from that bloody hollow and his eyes rested on a red mound a short distance away. He focused on it, then retched a fifth time.

It was the foetus of his son.

Murdach slowly rose to his feet. His tear-streaked face looked up to the sky and he opened his mouth.

He screamed, 'Why?' and his agonized wail reverberated around the vale, then soared up to the heavens. But there was no answer for him there.

In the forest, in the camp of the Vikings sat Eoin Mac Labres, Gerg the bard. He heard the terrible wail of his brother and smiled briefly, though he found no real joy in it. Revenge was not as sweet as he had heard tell. But at least he had brought about the deireadh an tuath. In that he was pleased. Muirthemne was next.

He felt a slight spattering on his face, and looked up. It was starting to rain from the grey clouds that had accumulated throughout the morning.

'Pitis!' he thought. 'It's going to be a bad day after all.'

# Autumn Rain

RICHARD CRAWFORD

IT WAS A grey, wet, autumn afternoon. Great heavy raindrops fell from the low sky and slapped monotonously on the car roof, and across the estate the dark bulk of the Black Mountain was nearly obscured by drifting veils of rain. In the front passenger seat Eliot fiddled nervously with the buttons of his damp reefer jacket, buttoning them and then unbuttoning them again. He was afraid, a deep, wrenching fear that pulled and tugged at his guts and crawled like a live thing in his stomach.

Beside him in the driver's seat Hunter pulled lengthily on the stub of a cigarette, exhaling carefully through his nostrils, savouring it. He stared thoughtfully straight out of the windscreen down the rainy street. In the back Neeson was hunched over, picking at his nails, and beside him Tate played with the safety catch on the pistol, clicking it on, then off, on, then off. The car smelt of cheap cigarette smoke and the extra-strong throat lozenges which Tate always sucked.

'The fucker's late,' said Tate.

'He's usually here by now,' Neeson replied, as if it was a slur on his character. 'I watched him every day last week.'

'We'll give him another fifteen minutes and then we'll head

on. I've got more important things to do than to wait for this cunt.'

Tate was the worst. He was the one with the real badness in him. It showed in his tiny lizard eyes behind the thick National Health glasses, eyes that swivelled and turned almost independently of his head as if they had a life of their own. He would be sitting talking to someone else and then the eyes would slip around and fix their gaze on you, linger for a while, and then go smoothly back to their original position.

Neeson wasn't so bad, he was just stupid, and would suspend his own personal scruples and morals if ordered to. And Hunter, he was hard to figure out. He wasn't quite the same as the rest of them, more intelligent somehow, and he had an appearance of someone who thought a lot. Wide, open forehead and brown hair brushed straight back, reminiscent of one of the romantic poets, and a firm jawline under the stubble. But then appearances can be deceptive, Eliot reminded himself, watching as Hunter finished his fag end and jammed it into the overflowing ashtray.

'You want to give that up, it's a disgusting bloody habit,' observed Tate sourly from the back.

'Yeah,' said Hunter.

'I mean, do you know how much damage nicotine does to your lungs?'

'Surprise me.'

'It blocks them up. Shrivels them. They end up like wee bits of coal.'

'Well, they're my lungs, aren't they?'

Eliot leaned his forehead against the cool glass in the side window and looked at the man's house across the street. It was a small, nondescript house, one of a grey-painted terrace, no different from the rest. On the overgrown front lawn a child's tricycle lay broken and rusting. The venetian blinds were down but open and every now and again he could discern movement behind them. He imagined what his wife would be doing; getting the dinner on, clearing up after the kids, maybe phoning a friend. Normal, everyday events in the calm before the storm.

'You going anywhere for Christmas, Joe?' Hunter asked Tate. He was the only person who ever called Tate by his first name, if indeed that was his first name. Neeson had tried it once and was casually ignored until he used the correct form of address: Mr Tate.

'Nah. I was thinking of taking the kids down to Fermanagh over the holiday, but there's fuck all for them to do down there. They'd drive me up the fucking walls.'

'What were you going to stay in, a caravan?'

'Aye.'

'How many kids have you got, Joe?'

'Two boys and a girl.'

Hunter shook his head. 'I see what you mean,' he said.

Eliot noticed a figure coming towards them, up the street, bent almost double against the rain. His stomach flipped. God, is that him? Jesus. Jesus!

'Here he comes,' said Neeson, who had seen him too.

'You sure that's him?' Tate asked him harshly.

'Aye, I think so . . . aye, that's him, he always wears that parka.'

'Right,' said Tate, in a commanding tone of voice. 'We'll take him as he turns into the garden, okay? Eliot, you take his right and I'll go for his left. Get him inside the house as quick as you can. Neeson can do anything else that should need done.'

The mood had altered completely, they were all tense now, all concentrating on their individual tasks, each one going over in his mind what he would do. The waiting was over and the action was beginning. Eliot fought to control his bladder as his heart thumped hollowly in his chest like a hammer on an empty bucket. So this is it. Jesus. His mind was racing, sucking in details and magnifying them out of all proportion: the silver globules of rain hanging like drops of mercury on the car windows; the heavy metallic clicking sound of the pistol in the back seat being cocked; the little plastic sticker on the dashboard above the glove compartment which said 'Fasten your seatbelts' in bright red and gold. Fear rumbled in his stomach, the tingling, grinding fear of impending crime. I could stop now, he thought suddenly. I could get out of the car and run and leave them to it, it's not too late; I haven't done anything really serious yet, but in five minutes I'll be committed, I'll be in for good, no way out but a prison cell. Or a bullet in the head.

Hunter started the engine and in the back seat Tate opened the door catch, holding the door closed with one hand. The man was almost level with the car now, the fur-lined hood of his parka pulled close around his face, obscuring it, but Eliot noticed the patched faded jeans and down-at-heel cowboy boots. He arrived at the path leading to his front door and began to turn down it and Tate yelled 'Now!' then they were out and running and the rain was cool on their faces. The man saw them, the fear showing in the wide eyes above a thick black moustache, and tried to run but it was like slow motion and Neeson slammed into his back, throwing them both to the ground. Tate grabbed the man by the arm and began to drag him towards the front door of his house, as Eliot moved round to avoid the kicking feet, and moving as if in a dream, took the hood of the parka and began to pull on it. Then there was a splintering of glass as Neeson kicked the door in. Inside a woman screamed.

'Quick, get the fucker inside!' Tate was yelling and pointing at Eliot and the struggling man. Eliot felt somewhere far away, as if he was watching a film in which he played a leading role, observing but not comprehending. They dragged the man into his hallway over the shards of glass from the door. He was screaming, crying.

'Oh, God, please, please, help, oh God, it wasn't me, I've got nothing, Jesus Mary God help, no, no!'

Neeson had a big hand tangled in the man's hair and he hauled him up roughly, slamming his back against the pastel-coloured wallpaper. The man was struggling and crying and he looked at Eliot with a desperate urgency in his face, then nausea surged up in Eliot's stomach and he looked away. Details were crowding in again, the blood donor badge on the man's parka, the sound of a television somewhere in the house, and the smell of frying bacon coming from the kitchen.

'Bastards!!!!' The scream was high-pitched and feminine and

the woman rushed down the hall only to be caught by Tate
and slapped violently across the face.

'Leave him alone, you bastards.'

'Shut up,' Tate shouted.

'Leave him alone, he's done nothing.'

'Fucking shut up!' Tate threw her against the wall and she
fell down on the floor with a little sob as the air left her lungs
and then Tate kicked her hard in the side. She curled up in a
ball and whimpered softly on the carpet. The hall was
suddenly quiet except for the woman's heavy sobbing and the
man's terrified panting. Tears of rage and frustration and fear
were streaming down his face.

'Bastards,' he said, in a twisted, fearful little voice, and with
a sudden movement Tate swung the barrel of the pistol in a
wide arc and smashed it into his face. There was a sickening
crunch of metal on bone and Eliot felt his legs start to buckle as
the dark blood spurted from the man's mouth, dropping onto
his shirt and jacket. Neeson punched him in the stomach for
good measure.

Now Tate was standing in front of the man, his back against
the opposite wall of the narrow hallway. His nostrils were
flaring and his face was red and Eliot was reminded of a
schoolboy with a dirty magazine until he saw the dead eyes
behind the heavy glasses. He motioned to Neeson who pulled
the man's head back by the hair.

'You've been a bad boy, Conor, and you know what we do
to bad boys, don't you?'

The man began to cry again and tears mingled with the
blood on his face.

'Well, fuck you.' Tate's teeth were clenched, his eyes wide,
his breath coming in gasps in an almost sexual excitement. He
held the heavy pistol in both hands and he slowly dropped the
barrel until it was three or four inches from the man's right
knee. The man suddenly realized what was happening and he
began to struggle with a desperate strength, nearly pulling
himself out of Eliot's grip.

'No, no, no, not that, Jesus Mary no, oh God, no.' He was
crying and sobbing and his wife had begun to scream and Eliot

wanted to look away but his head wouldn't move and his eyes wouldn't move and then there was the deafening bang as Tate pulled the trigger and the man screamed and blood and white shards of bone spattered the pastel wallpaper. Eliot felt him sag in his grasp, heard the tinkle as the ejected case bounced off a wall, felt the vomit rising in his throat. The man's knee had disappeared, transformed in a moment into a dark red spongy mess in which the shattered bone lay like splintered ivory. Neeson let go of his hair and he slumped onto the floor, moaning quietly.

They stood for a moment with the sound of the shot ringing in their ears, frozen in contemplation of the crippled wreck before them. The man's wife crawled over to him and put her arms around him, her face contorted and reddened with the crying.

'All right, let's go,' said Tate, suddenly running out through the smashed door, his feet crunching on the broken glass. Hunter had the car doors open and they piled in quickly, then he revved the engine and let out the clutch and with the back end spinning wildly they took off down the street.

In the back seat Tate was laughing. 'Jesus, did you see that? His fucking knee exploded! Fucking hell!' He slapped Neeson on the knee and Eliot heard the pistol being unloaded.

'Fuck me, Hunter, you should have seen it,' Tate went on. 'Fucking magnificent!'

'Yeah,' Hunter said out of the side of his mouth, concentrating now on the busy rush hour traffic. He had lit another cigarette which he held clamped between his lips so that it poked straight out in front of him.

Eliot lay slumped in the front seat, trying not to be sick. He felt the nausea coming in waves, bubbling up from his tortured gut. With half a mind he watched familiar sights glide by outside; the graffiti-daubed Busy Bee shopping centre; black taxis glistening in the rain; the wire and tin fencing of the police station. So familiar and yet so changed, made unreal by the spilling of blood. His mind reeled, nothing would be the same anymore.

'That's one that'll not walk again for a while, anyway,' said Tate in a calmer voice.

'Wife wasn't bad,' observed Neeson.

'Is that all you fucking think about, you stupid cunt?'

'What did he do anyway?' Hunter asked over his shoulder.

'How the fuck should I know?' said Tate, opening a packet of throat lozenges. 'Orders is orders.'

They dumped the car on a deserted piece of wasteground up on the mountain. They opened all the doors, then Hunter wiped all the surfaces with a cloth in case of fingerprints. 'You never know,' he said. Then he took a can of petrol from the boot and sprinkled it all over the upholstery and in the engine compartment.

Eliot, Tate and Neeson stood a little distance away, watching in silence as Hunter performed the well-practised routine. Good place for a funeral pyre, thought Eliot, looking at the sprawling city laid out beneath them in the rain. A good view. Near to the gods. He glanced up anxiously at the low grey darkening sky and the far away rumble of thunder.

Hunter produced an old rag which he soaked in petrol, then took out a big yellow box of Swan Vestas. His hair was plastered to his forehead by the rain. 'Anyone want to say a few words?' he called up to them.

'Fucking hurry up,' said Neeson.

Hunter shrugged, then lit the rag and tossed it quickly into the car. The petrol caught with a quiet 'thwwump' and the blue flames spread quickly around the car.

'Another job well done,' said Tate, pulling the collar of his raincoat closer around his neck. 'Is there no end to our talents?' He grinned at the three men, then turned and began to walk down the road.

# Fruits de Mer

## RONALD FRAME

THE RESTAURANT IS ageless, which is part of its appeal. The room's proportions are high, generous, and not of this epoch. The painted seascapes on the walls have the patina of time, cigar smoke, decades of intimate conversation: the scenes themselves belong to no period, the constants of rock and sand and froth-capped waves and blue horizons are outside history. The only boundaries to the vistas and distances are the outsized gilt frames, carved with clam shells and trailing seaweed. Between the panels thin oblongs of misty mirror hold uncertain images of the room: the old glass crinkles in antediluvian folds; it's as if no one, no grouping at any of the tables, is to be taken quite on trust.

Fish and seafood, quite obviously, are the speciality here: all edible life that the brine has to offer crowds the narrow-spaced columns of the menu. The menu is another work of art, with the list of dishes flanked by exactly drawn, ornamental combinations of scallops, urchins, flat skate, pink salmon, oysters, Dublin Bay prawns, brill, whelks in their whorls, shelled and unshelled mussels, langoustes, and the waving, dark green ribbons of 'asperge de mer': tendrils, tentacles, tails, pincers, fronds entwined as if to suggest that the creatures of the deep live life as one long riotous party.

★

Which is patently not the case with the terrigenous, land-lubbing habitués of this highly esteemed restaurant, who – on the whole – behave decorously, soberly, and speak with their voices pitched discreetly low.

The businessmen, for some reason, are the least reticent. A quartet of them, seated at a round table with its pale pink cloth and gleaming cutlery, quite unashamedly discuss the losses recently inflicted on one of their clients, a shipping magnate. One of his tankers has been sabotaged and another has been holed in an accident and abandoned to sink. It looks like a double loss to the insurance concern the men represent. They discuss the tragedy quite animatedly over the entrée of smoked Tay salmon, and figures are mentioned, first single numerals and then double, which represent multiples of millions of pounds sterling. The plates are removed and others set down in their place: lobster in sherry sauce and turbot poached with sorrel are brought to the table, creatures wholly out of their element as the conversation is taken up again in full hearing of the waiters, about similar losses suffered in the Gulf over the past three or four years. More shorthand figures are aired. A few heads turn at tables close to the pin-striped group. Then, quite suddenly, as the waiters withdraw, the talk becomes blithely social and continues so for the next few minutes: Hurlingham, eventing, a hunt down in Kent. At the end of which the signal for a third bottle of Sauvignon is given and the conversation reverts, in firmer tones, to the matter of the scuppered shipping baron – while the crayfish in the illuminated tank to one side of the table continue their slow, sandy probings, quite regardless.

Next to the party on the other side, and equally oblivious, sit a couple in respectable middle-age. They are very polite, listening diligently when the other speaks and taking care not to interrupt. They act in a kind of choreographed synchronization, which must – can only be – the result of two experiences shared for many years.

They might be a husband and wife: but in that case why should there seem to be a certain degree of tension in their mutual interest for the other? Surely they're *too* animated, *too* well-behaved, for this to be a simple re-run of all the other restaurant conversations they've ever engaged in together? Perhaps today is an anniversary, a birthday, and they're celebrating: she is in a collarless Coco Chanel suit, he is in grey flannel and a white shirt with a stiff stud-collar. They've paid particular attention to the food presented on their plates – a matching choice of salmon mousse followed by Dover Sole – and their surroundings have called for comment several times.

As they pass from the second course to the third, the situation seems to become more complicated. The first mildly enquiring mentions are made: of 'her' by the woman, of 'him' by the man. (A glance at their hands shows that they don't wear rings – is it from what is now force of habit, or for discretion's sake on this one day?) The replies are hesitant, spare, and accompanied by harmless smiles. The menus go unread, the alternating nods that each gives to the other are perfectly agreeable, reasonable, understanding. The woman explains a little about how 'his' business affairs are going, he explains a little about 'her' artistic activities. More nods, just to confirm that each is enlightened enough to harbour no stirrings of jealousy for the other's new partner and spouse.

The orders for the third course are given to the waiter – they differ this time, cheese and a sorbet – and a silence follows. The man picks at a thread on his lapel; the woman takes advantage of this staged distraction (once upon a time she might have removed the thread herself) to look at him and consider, to remember what it was that persuaded them both they would be happier apart. Perhaps she doesn't have to think very hard about it; the memories may still be all too clear to her.

The man catches the thread. The woman suddenly pushes back her chair and rises to her feet. She picks up her bag, nods towards the back of the room, and starts weaving her way between the tables in the direction of the Mesdames.

The man sits watching her, his first wife, and he doesn't lower his eyes again until she reappears and begins the return journey. Her face has been repaired, she's taking steps with a new confidence and purpose.

The woman sits down. The waiter brings the couple their orders. They tackle the sorbet and cheese enthusiastically. When they've finished, coffee arrives – before they have to do more to infill an untimely little gap in the conversation than mention one of the features of the decor, the cornice frieze of sculpted plaster shells, which has been painted in a different colour from the one they remember.

Clearly they know this room. They give away the fact to anyone listening that they came on the same afternoon last year, and the year before that. Perhaps this is the anniversary of the day on which the divorce was finally settled: or – if that seems too callous a deed for a couple who appear so eminently decent-living and well-balanced, unvengeful – they've picked a date in the calendar with happier, more pleasant associations for them both, which reminds them of all the other visits in those earlier years, leading them back into the past: which is like a long tunnel to look into, a deep dark well, after all the reflections of the light and space above them in the room, overhead, in this more positive here and now they each know they wouldn't exchange in the wisdom of their quiet second marriages, which they wouldn't be tempted to give up – not at any price.

At the next table sit a quite different pairing.

The woman is fortyish and wears a youthful suede blouson. The teenage girl opposite her is rather lumpish and wears an unflattering flower-patterned dress and a matronly padded chintz jacket.

A mother and daughter: or so the situation might appear. Except that, on a second look, the two do not seem to belong wholly to each other. They have few physical similarities: neither facially, nor in the colouring of their hair, nor in their types of complexion. They even sit in their chairs in contrary ways; their attitude to the situation doesn't coincide.

The woman, tanned and as thin as a rake, does a lot of smiling, lifts her eyebrows, passes things about the table, nods her head, sympathizes, confides, suddenly makes light, laughs, calls for the waiter, reads aloud from the menu.

'Quenelles of Haddock Monte Carlo. Goodness! Would you like that, Emma?'

The words have to be pulled from the girl. Her eyes consider the crockery a good deal; she seems increasingly embarrassed to find herself where she is, having lunch with such a slimly elegant woman, being humoured by her.

'Or smoked sturgeon? Sounds a very grumpy fish, doesn't it? What about – let's see – monkfish and ginger?'

At intervals Emma's whey face fires, her fingers pull at the toggles on her rose-garden jacket. Her eyes rise dismally to the woman's, and the brave, plucky, hockey-sticks smile she manages every so often is forgotten again, stranded on a part of her face where she can have no control of it.

The situation is a sort of pastiche. Circumstances declare themselves, through what is said and what is not said. The woman isn't a mother, but a step-mother: the girl is the child of the woman's second husband, by a previous wife who is being slowly but surely and determinedly exorcized from the scenario of this current marriage. Lunch together is an attempt, by the step-mother, to turn them into one another's friend: the trim woman with the high cheek-bones and disguising, over-sized jewellery at her thin stretched throat, and the stocky girl who's still at school, with her unformed face and unruly breasts and those chubby hands that are the bane of her life, which she looks at with desperation whenever she has to wield her cutlery. These two persons have to make allies of one another and all because of a third person – the husband and father – who calmly and invisibly occupies the middle-ground between them.

They do it for *him*, and also to ensure their own survival in this arrangement that is even more complex and perilous than a marriage. They both move with the awkwardness of puppets: one hyperactively jerky and uncoordinated, the other woodenly clumsy and slow. Each is pushing the other into being a caricature of herself, and each knows the falseness and inevitability of it, that they don't understand enough about one another to think how they can admit what's happening. With time their performances have become more involuntary and the pair draw further from each other, even though – now – their hands (the chubby/the long-fingered) are almost touching on the table-top, on the carnation-pink cloth.

The woman laughs (a social, party laugh), and the gold bracelet of her watch catches the light and glints as she raises her hand to her coiffure. The girl nods but doesn't smile, her eyes look down at her breasts, burgeoning even as she sits, and maybe she mentally undresses them both and compares the rolling, fecund landscape of her own body with the arid angularities and hollows and depressions of *hers*, and for a moment a kind of justice is restored to this bleakly incomprehensible world.

While, two tables away, sit the pair of lovers.

Only the expense of the food compels them to eat. Otherwise they would be content, more than content, to feed on air, the bliss of the other's presence. The rest of the room, everything that they exclude, is of an inferior reality, and exists in (at least) one dimension less.

'I didn't know *that!*'

'You certainly do now!'

'Darling, I want to know every single thing about you –'

They may be given the benefit of the doubt: love is love, and they are natural as they've never been in their lives before nor will be again.

'You *have* to tell me. Every *single* thing, remember.'

Or . . . Or is it possible that, in their subconscious, they're each remembering scenes from films they've watched, which replay on a private mental screen for one? Are they only behaving as others in their condition have the happy obligation of behaving: with the room distanced, their eyes fixed on the other's or moving over the face's features, reading the indicators, identifying the mirror-image of joy that is inside each of them?

'Everything?'

'*Every*thing.'

'You're sure?'

'Positive.'

45

'Every weeny thing?'

'*Teeny*-weeny –'

Perhaps the pair are as much in love with love as they are with each other, and they can't tell the difference: that is their delicious confusion? But what do the pronouns – 'they', 'their' – *mean* in these extraordinary circumstances? He and she have now entered into the experience of centuries and aeons of time, of all lovers in all ages, and their identities are submerged, disowned. Almost totally so: except, of course, that this is the Modern Age, the second half of the 1980s, and in the mind's eye an imaginary, metaphorical camera lens trails us everywhere, spies over our shoulder, to possess every intimate exchange. So – that is to say, to be quite accurate – the two of them are *nearly* but never wholly alone together.

'Everyone's looking at you, you know.'

'No, they're not.'

'Yes, they are. Cross my heart. Would I tell a lie?'

'You're imagining it.'

'They're thinking, who's *he* with her? Wouldn't mind being in his shoes. Or whatever. Some chaps have *all* the luck –'

A pretty girl, a handsome boy: they might be made for each other, islanded in this room, on their own sea-bound domain. They have the confidence of their youth and their looks. People recognize in them images of themselves, only more perfect, more favoured; the couple exist as extensions of whoever see them – perhaps, it might be said, perhaps without the confirmation of those watching eyes they wouldn't be believed, they would fade into impossible abstractions?

They're laughing at something: the sight of a lobster being carried past, en route for the boiling pot in the kitchen. Such is only the way of the world, and the cruelty of its death can't offend them, it isn't conceivable in their rapturous condition.

'D'you think they'd let me eat this off your arm?'

'My *arm*?'

'Or anywhere else –'

'What?'

'I'd start on your arm –'

'You're mad!'

'I don't think so. Everything's quite clear in my head.'

'I don't care if you're mad or not, not really.'

'You'll take me as I am?'

'If you promise me you'll never change –'

They long to be everything to each other, to turn themselves inside out, to work towards the magic numeral, *ONE*, to lose themselves and also to be claimed. That, so they've read in magazine articles, is the goal. Once upon a time they might have suffered in terrible solitude, not knowing what was expected of them, how they should behave. But hearts operate nearer the surface nowadays: hearts aren't cardboard and padded velvet bibelots, Valentine-style, they are a physical function of the organism. This Romeo and Juliet eat courtesy of American Express, they already know each other intimately; gently jogging in the park they plug two sets of speakers into one Walkman set and get healthy and wise to their favourite Philadelphian blue-eyed soul music, Hall and Oates' 'Method of Modern Love'.

Failing to observe them, an elderly woman and a child sit at the next table. They're more interested in the seascapes on the walls, and the tank of fish, and the counter at the door laid with boxes of oysters in ice, garnished with wedges of lemon and loops of ribbon weed.

The location is probably a mistake. They ought not to be here: instead they should be in the din and hurly-burly of one of the superior hamburger restaurants that draw the crowds, or sitting on stools at a soda counter, if they'd known where to find one. The spectacle of fish was what had appealed, as a distraction: from the real business, the fact that they have no choice but to be lunching together, a boy of seven years old and his grandmother.

They've been dumped on each other, that is the hard truth of the matter. The knowledge shows in the woman's face: her mouth is drawn down, her expression is close to hopeless. She concentrates on the child picking at the crab leavings on his plate with the skewer. When the boy looks up from the debris of claws and broken shell she manages to smile: a tired smile, ready to proclaim defeat. The boy's eyes drop again and she loses the smile, slowly, and sits twisting the stem of her water glass as she protects the child with her gaze.

They protect one another: from total defencelessness. They construct the artifice of companionship from fifty-four years apart, from 'circumstances'.

What's to be construed of those 'circumstances'? – what would anyone sitting at another table make of them?

Let's take an inspired guess.

The boy's mother is the woman's daughter-in-law. She, the grandmother, shares their home, at her son's request, but it is presumed that the money she's saved from selling her own home will help to guarantee a fund of school fees until her grandson is eighteen. She'll manage notwithstanding, and even have enough left over for treats like this: that's what her daughter-in-law understands.

But it's not clear to the woman how much else the boy's mother understands, of her own reading of the situation for instance. She knows that all is not as it might be in the house. Now there seem to be too many business trips for the boy's father, and there are too many unexplained mysteries in the day, when the morning mail is being rapidly sifted or when the phone rings and a stranger's voice speaks (a man's voice, so it always happens) or when a taxi rolls up to collect the boy's mother and she's taken out for the evening, to 'dinner somewhere', with unspecified company.

At the age of sixty-one 'Granny' isn't meant to notice, she's supposed to have had too little experience of the world to be able to spot the give-aways for herself. Her daughter-in-law makes rather tart jokes about her forgetfulness, her old-fashioned ways, but she knows that she's a protection as well, for all of them.

Perhaps it isn't her business. But she feels it's her duty to do what she can for the child, for him at least. Eventually he'll make a discovery, push the wrong door open, pick up the telephone receiver. His life is as fraught as a novel, the kind they seem to have no end of room for on the library shelves: suburban possibilities await like tripwires, and sometimes she wishes she'd gone to live by the sea, in a modern flat with an uninterrupted view, and then she couldn't have given her son and daughter-in-law the excuse. Somehow, her presence in their home is meant to be a blind: it can't be happening with *her* there, such a worthy and thoroughly ignorant woman of the old school as she is.

That's just the cleverness of it.

A live lobster is carried past and the boy looks up.

'What's *that*?'

'It's a lobster, James.'

They both watch as a favoured customer is allowed to inspect. The man nods and grins with the relish of a character in a television cartoon, in his eager anticipation of the first taste.

They both continue to watch as the doomed creature is whisked away, to the pot of boiling water behind the kitchen doors.

James's grandmother smiles: a more forthright smile than the earlier one, which was ready to acknowledge her defeat: more forthright, but also committed to a deceit. That all is better than it is, when they are truly powerless to prevent what will happen, what must be the outcome, in spite of themselves and their wishes: even with the best and purest intentions they have become accomplices, accessories to the deed – to an event that is simultaneously taking place in another restaurant, where an overdressed woman is being entertained to lunch and champagne from an ice bucket by a man who isn't her husband.

At the very same moment – is it by some awful telepathy that bridges the years? – the boy and his grandmother shift in their chairs. *Her* eyes contract, a nervous reaction; *his* eyes blink quite matter-of-factly at the crab's fate, where the thing lies smashed to its components on his plate.

On one of the plush banquettes sits a hefty man in a business suit, squiring a woman young enough to be his daughter. But daughters are not inclined to cling limpet-like to their fathers, except emotionally, and not to link an arm through his in public *quite* so showily, or to try the finger-weaving-into-a-basket technique, which – at long last – he tells her (through a shark's smile) to stop.

They might be in a film. That is precisely her aim for herself, even if this man is not her dream of an ideal romantic lead: *she* is an actress, frizzy-haired and bony-chinned with Cleopatra eyes, and *he* catches all her references and improves on them to remind her that films are his living and his blood and that *he* calls the tune, he 'makes' her or he drops her. But that's only half the story, let's say. She's more intelligent than she appears to be, and maybe she's a little ashamed of her calling, that she's never grown out of her need to hold a room's attention by singing a pretty song in a little girl voice. She chooses to demean herself, and a gay man friend has quoted so many lines from Jean Harlow films to her that she feels as comfortable with that vocabulary as she does with her shoes off under the table, wriggling her toes inside her French silk stockings – tart supreme.

If the man on the banquette is embarrassed in turn he doesn't show it, but he tries to keep the conversation trained on her future, exploring the myth of her talent.

'I'm seeing Green on Thursday.'

'Better than seeing red!'

'I sent him your stuff, he knows all about you.'

'He does?'

'Of course he does.'

Apart from that she adds a frisson of excitement to his life, especially with her obviousness, which she has now grown into so that there is virtually no distinction to be made between what she pretends to be and what she *is*: every so often she seems (literally) to be shrugging the performance aside, to be casting that skin – only for a few seconds, though, until it's as if the line pulls tight again, she's called back into character for the occasion, which may or may not be her but in which she is by now fully implicated.

For his part, his face clouds from time to time, he seems to be elsewhere: with his wife maybe, or with his daughter, of whom his companion is a mere caricature. (His only child,

Leonie, went to a convent, and is now working in a Vigo Street art gallery.)

'I used to think I must've been made in a cinema.'

'*Made?*'

'Well . . . *you* know –'

'Oh. Conceived?'

'And that's why I was called Louise.'

'How d'you mean?'

'Louise, in "Gypsy". With Rosalind Russell. Louise was her child. You know – "Sing out, Louise!" She didn't let her grow up, but then she did, and she became Gypsy Rose Lee. The stripper. You know?'

'Oh.'

He isn't sure if this is a business lunch or not, if they really mean any of the things they're saying to each other: about his putting in a word for her when he meets Green, about how stage-talk is mother's milk to her, and she can't *not* make it big. Of late he's started to lose his delicate touch in such matters, these strictly extra-marital tête-à-têtes that may well take them off in a taxi afterwards, to an impersonal hotel behind Piccadilly where he's not a stranger. It used to be that the man always decided and set the pace, but it's not necessarily the case in these enlightened and liberated days.

She's talking about a friend of a friend of hers, called Sara Peploe – it's a crazy story – who went out to Hollywood and got 'involved' with some director who confused life and fiction and, when the movie went over-budget, he tried to kill her, for the insurance money and the publicity. Sara Peploe discovered and the man was burned to death when his house went up in flames, probably – but not positively – because his attempt to fire the building got out of hand and he hadn't time to get out. Now Sara Peploe has a different name and she's working in a Hollywood super-soap, playing an English Rose character.

'Which is the last thing he wanted for her, but too bad. Hey, what d'you think of all that?'

The man smiles, as if she's made it all up and, really, she'd better not start telling those kinds of moral tale to *him*;

51

Hollywood has its own 'modus operandi' but so does Frith Street and Wardour Street. This lunch is expenses but it's costing money all the same: everything *costs*, and no one – him or her – gets anything for free. So it always was: only now perhaps he's a little less able to anticipate all the moves in the game.

He likes the food here (he has to live with a duodenal ulcer), the ambience is discreet, there's something comforting and consoling about the decor. He's sure *she* has failed to notice, but in that respect he underestimates her. If he only knew it, she's an actress because she never feels at home anywhere, and she's very sensitive, like litmus, to her surroundings: she takes them in almost subliminally, but she has excellent recall of all the restaurants she's eaten in and the food she was 'advised' to choose from the menu. They're both conscious of the decor: he is restored by it, he's in warm womb-like waters, while she feels helpless to understand it, a geography of shore and sea and swimming things that refuses to include her. Were the lunch going less well, she might feel hostile towards the room, threatened; as it is, her host has said enough flattering things about her abilities to almost convince her they're true and she's in a frame of mind to forgive such ridiculous surroundings, knowing for the nonce that the plaster won't crack and the walls crumble and fall in and drown them with the weight of rushing flood water. She doesn't fancy the prospect of seaweed in her hair, or a silver fish slithering in the gully between her breasts, which pert appendages she's had to take an out-and-out market view on and rate as her top assets.

And then, somewhere else in the room, there's myself.

What is there to say? I can believe myself to be so sure about those who are round about me, filling a space and making an atmosphere, but what certain knowledge do I have about myself?

Principally, that I eat alone: that I choose to eat alone. There must be reasons why, but these are lost to me, they belong in the dim, nethermost recesses of personal history, where – if I were to look – I should only err and stray and never find my way back. So, it's enough to know that I prefer to eat alone, and not to feel I'm obliged to share the occasion of a meal with another person. Maybe I would only make them uncomfortable, they would imagine I wasn't concentrating on my seafood platter 'St Malo' but I was looking through them with X-ray eyes, and then they would start to fidget in their chair. I don't want the embarrassment of their reactions: I don't want the obligation of having to play through a performance with them. I prefer solitude to that.

I *can* tell you this, that I travel a lot: that the pleasure for me consists every time in the last seconds before the journey's end (wherever it is), in climbing the staircase with the key in my hand to open the door of a room I've never set eyes on before. The rooms that come closest to perfection are the barest and simplest, those with the minimum of personality and the fewest clues of prior possession. My mind expands to fill those, to furnish them and people them. To me, the view from the window is very nearly beside the point: very nearly.

I don't mean that I'm not receptive to my surroundings – most often I am – or that I only live with my recollections, or cocooned in a kind of fantasy. I mean that I'm happiest, the most free, when I give my imagination and sympathies their loosest rein.

You've read this because you've wanted to read it: so I presume that you can understand the impulse in me, as it exists in *you*, to extend the limits for yourself, to travel in experience, to see into other people's lives so that – perhaps – you can appreciate better what is worth appreciating in your own: or – perhaps, more simply – the purpose is merely to enable you to feel less lonely in yourself.

But I don't subsist by theories. The particular is always more interesting to me. On that score nothing is not important. A hand's gesture, the tic of a mouth, an eye turning, it tells an undue portion of the story. My 'story' is about being on the fringes of other people's stories. *You* are currently a character in, maybe, two dozen unfinished tales; you endure all the hazards – chance, coincidence, non-sequiturs, what isn't explained, overstatement, a trite little moral at the end. You deserve half of them ('half' at least, and let me tell you that's way above the average) to have happy endings.

In one of the mirrors between the painted panels I watch myself watching. The room is recreated in front of my eyes, then a second time in a vague pattern of words that comes into my head. The room repeats itself, just as the sea repeats and returns and re-makes a scene that never seems any different.

I am to be pitied perhaps: I'm the crazy one who always returns to the same rock, to stare out at the same unchanging stretch of breakers and foam.

The room's voices are the mesmeric song of the surf. The sea is casting up its edible offerings, the 'fruits' of a different element to our own. For this moment it seems to me that we've come here to eat – like Picasso's lolling ancients, like temporary gods – on the harvest of a very deep and lightless, maybe fathomless, place.

# Birth

SOPHIE FRANK

1

THERE'S SOMETHING WITH Nurse's smile – the lipstick's on crooked – that gives her away. Maybe last week she hurled a body out of a window. Maybe next week this business – life, death, delivery – will get too much. Today though, the job's easy. All she's got to do is hand over a bawling bundle to his mum. Nurse thinks she can manage that.

Jonathan Waters is forty-eight hours old. At least that's what he is according to the clock. Somewhere between his eyes, or in his heart, he feels old as a mountain. No one's to know that – only him. Jonathan can't talk. All he can do is cry. He howls. Nurse feels like shoving an orange in his mouth to shut him up. He's scared. Mostly he's scared of Nurse: her hands grip him tight as a nutcracker. She's treating him as if he were hardy as a walnut. But Jonathan feels vulnerable as an overripe fig. Drop him, he'd collapse and fall over the floor like the stomach of a trifle.

Nurse emits a loud hissing Ssshhh. She tries to sound comforting but, to Jonathan, she sounds insane. She rollicks him closer to her vast breasts. For a second Jonathan stops bawling. He's captivated – not by the woman's thunderous physique – but by the glint of a steel ring that clings to Nurse's rather pretty index finger. The ring is beaten into the shape of a snake. The finger with the ring on it is purply blue. It looks like it's fallen prey to the serpent that's devouring it. Nurse's other fingers are curled around Jonathan's body. But this finger, this one alone, stands erect, straight and perfect as an unlit candle.

Nurse and Jonathan slide up the corridor as easily as a ribbon of spaghetti slides over lips, into a mouth. Here, there's no natural light. Just a shiny floor, shiny walls and a repeated message that's scrawled over the walls again and again. The message reads EXIT.

Jonathan's had enough of EXITS, and journeys in the last two days. If he didn't go anywhere ever again, he wouldn't mind. But everyone's trying to make him go places. When will it ever end?

Jonathan's relieved that he's got out of another corridor alive. He stops crying. He finds himself in a room which is all air, all light. Nurse persists in singing a crazy lullaby: she sounds like a drunken bee. Why the fuck doesn't the woman shut up?

2

In the room that's all air, all light, the happy mother stands waiting. She feels so happy she could burst. Around her mouth, the tiny muscles have a will of their own. Tracey grins and grins. She dances on the spot. Whatever happened – division, multiplication – Tracey managed it. She split in two!

Tracey lights her thirty-fifth cigarette of the day in thanks to Mother Miracle. She tosses the empty packet aside: Governments have always been killjoys. She closes her eyes and sees a kitchen cupboard full of alcohol. She sees her husband pour her a gargantuan vodka. Paul. Damn him. Deliveries. Collections. Where is he?

Then a cry. A bawl.

Through the blue haze wanders Nurse – the one whose eyes look beyond, whose expressions clutch at the words just spoken, or about to be said, in a sentence. The one who's never with the moment. Tracey pummels the butt of her cigarette out with the toe of her stiletto, guiltily. Nurse sing-songs, 'All set.' Tracey nods. She reaches out to accept the howling bundle that's offered her, but she can't take hold of him. Her arms won't move.

Tracey feels nothing. She sees the child's misery: she hears his lame bleats. All she knows is, 'You are not mine.' Tracey can't speak. A giant sponge – deep in the heart of her belly – begins to clamp up. It sucks in. A hand in her stomach is tightening its grip. Tracey feels tremendous pain. She closes her legs tight. Maybe the efficient Doctor Harris left something inside. Maybe he forgot something. What is going wrong?

Finally she manages to get the words out –

'I'm sure he's not mine.'

Jonathan knows it too. The world is worse than he imagined.

## 3

Horns don't honk. They don't wail. They don't scream. No word can describe the hell of an echoing, ceaseless car horn. It gets to you.

Paul's hand presses on the horn where it's been for three minutes. Paul knows he's silly about hospitals – they are, after all, places where people go to get better, but he's never trusted the smell of disinfectant. He always wonders what's happening behind the curtains, under the bandages. So long as he stays put in his van, Paul's safe.

An ambulance draws up, a touch too close. Paul sees it and quickly turns away. But the ambulance isn't content with being ignored – it's a magnet and it sucks Paul's eyes towards it. Its rear doors crash open. Paul tries to gaze at his comforting plastic dice keyring, but again, his eyes start moving out of the window. A blue-suited man clambers up and into the ambulance's cavity. Paul checks his wrist-watch. Whilst he's doing so, out of the corner of his eyes, he can't help but see a trolley, and with it, a red blanketed lump. This time Paul is firmer than ever with himself. He will not look. He just hears the ambulance doors quietly close.

Paul fishes out his newspaper but the words and pictures

pale to insignificance beside the memory of the ambulance. When it had arrived, it hadn't been in a hurry. No flashing lights, no fuss. Paul tries not to add up the evidence. Conclusions, like the one he's just made, belong to the News at Ten.

'For every ending, there's a new beginning', 'Home is where the heart is': Paul likes sayings – they're always true and they always say the words one otherwise spends a long time looking for. 'Home is where we start from.' Who said that? Paul thinks it might have come out of his own head. He wrestles with it. As sayings go, it's a tricky one.

Very soon after, another complicated saying – this time more an arrangement of words – springs to mind. 'The start, a road, the end.' Now we're getting somewhere. Paul sees his life with Tracey as a road, and the baby's arrival a new start. Paul pinches himself. For seven days, he's been walking on air. It's a miracle – the baby, his feelings for Tracey, everything! Funny how when he'd said the word 'magic' to Tracey, she'd bitten his head off. She'd snapped something about 'blood and guts, sweat and toil'. Paul wishes she hadn't done that. She'd spoiled the intimacy. She'd brought him down to earth.

He hopes she still likes flowers. Back at home, he's put pink, yellow and white ones in every room. All he's thought of, since it happened, is of getting the three of them home. His hand presses hard down on the horn. Come on, love!

4

Nurse has checked the name tag and she's tried to be patient. The tag reads 'Jonathan Waters', and the mother is called Tracey Waters. The surnames match up. Nurse can't see the problem. She looks at her watch whose face is engraved with the maxim, 'Every one hurts and the last one kills.' Nurse has wasted ten minutes on Mrs Waters.

'But the child's not mine.' All Tracey wants is access back up to the nursery. Nurse bars her way. Once you've got a tick by your name, once you've been discharged, there's no going back. As for seeing Doctor Harris – he's on ward round.

Tracey sits back down on the numbing, orange seat. If she waits long enough, someone will see sense.

## 5

Two against one.

Since Sister joined the church down the road, St Ethelred's, four years ago, everything has made sense. She fingers her touchstone – a gold confirmation cross which hangs, day in, day out, round her scaly neck. Pity is a strange emotion. It's rooted in distance. It's an emotion which makes Sister feel warm and human inside. It's the only emotion Sister knows much about.

With Mary as a model, Sister smiles benignly on Tracey's mounting hysteria. Tears mean one thing: post natal depression. Tracey rabbits through a series of requests – asking again and again if she may see a Doctor, go back up to the ward, see anyone. Sister doesn't listen: she smiles instead. Frantically, Tracey tries another tactic. She undresses the baby.

'There. See. It isn't mine. I had a boy.'

Tracey brandishes a naked child right up close to Sister's face. It's a girl.

'Wrap her up, she'll only get cold.'

'Can't you see?'

Sister can't see. So sure of the diagnosis, she's blind to the truth which stares her naked in the face.

'Can't you see? Can't you see? Can't you see?'

Poor Mrs Waters, she's in such a state. Sister despatches Nurse off to fetch the young father.

## 6

Her nails scratch on the driver's side window. Her knuckles diffidently tap on the van's side mirror. Nurse presses her nose up to the glass of the windscreen and puffs out a steamy cloud. She opens her eyes full.

Anyone would jump a mile and Paul, who's been dozing, wakes with a start. Nurse backs away from the van, beckoning with her index finger for Paul to follow. Gingerly he clambers out.

'Your wife needs you,' 'It's all quite normal,' 'Does she get upset often?' 'Not really. Maybe a bit. Don't know really.' The sentences swirl around Paul's ears. Tracey needs him now. He's going.

## 7

I am crying. I want my mother. No one listens.

I'm in my carrycot now, looking up at the giants' faces. They've got it wrong – all but Tracey. She knows the truth but no one hears. The more she says, the more she cries, the more she proves Sister's reading of the situation to be true.

Right down to his trainers, Paul's off on the wrong track. He seems to remember having had a girl. The fact is that to him, the birth was so traumatic, that he's the one suffering hormonal hiccups.

Nurse – she's a fool.

'Boys, girls, they're all lovely.' 'You coming or not, love?' 'No I'm not. This is a girl.' 'So?' *'So?* I had a boy, Paul. Remember. Or weren't you looking?' 'Mine went up and down like a yo-yo, my hormones did.'

Finally, Tracey can't keep her feet on the ground any longer. A huge wave of aloneness and hopelessness crashes over her head. Sister seizes the moment. She winks at Paul to pick me up.

## 8

Paul's glad to be behind the wheel again. Journeys serve purposes and Paul's in control. The afternoon's been a bad dream – and it's still not over. Tracey's sobbing, the baby's crying, and the car's getting overheated in the stop-start traffic jams that congest the roads east towards the forest. Soon home.

Tracey goes over and over the facts in her mind. A few hours ago she was sure she knew the truth – she knew the child wasn't hers. But, little by little, she's losing grip of this clarity. She begins to doubt her judgement: maybe she was wrong, maybe she is neurotic. She's been through a lot – that's for certain. Tracey reminds herself of how she split in two.

Life's taught Tracey how to be a realist. She puts on her glasses. For the first time in a week walls have edges and bricks have textures.

Outside the city, in Epping, where Paul and Tracey live, the sun sets a deep blood red. Inside the city, nose-to-tailing through the estate blocks and high rises where Tracey grew up, you can't see the whole sky. Six-thirty.

'Hurry up, Paul. We'll miss it. We'll miss it.'

Sunset: Paul knows what she wants to be back in time to see. That's the old Tracey – the sobbing's stopped. Life's falling into place.

# Lingo

## PENELOPE GILLIATT

WHEN ALEX FIRST started as a barber he was told by Captain
Piggy Booter that he had begun at the top. He was apprenticed
at Stumpers, in Savile Row, where Guards officers and
millionaire stockbrokers and private-income young clubmen
who ran up long-overdue accounts liked to go. He was
interested by hairdressing and much struck by his clients' way
of interrupting themselves in a stream of the fatuous to talk
about a private concern to a stranger.

'I always think that "Stumpers" is one of those words that
describes itself, don't you?' said Piggy Booter, who was in the
Grenadiers. Where his nickname had come from was unknown but it was used incorrigibly by almost everyone who
knew him except his mother. She addressed him in full as
Percival Peregrine when she was conveying her disappointment in him. The disappointment had been without remission
in the hectoring dismay of her widowhood, starting from
when he was ten. Piggy now was tall and good-looking, with
a high forehead, and not at all like a piglet.

Alex went on shampooing the Captain, careful not to get
soap into his eyes. The suds could readily have found their
way there because of the forehead's incline.

'You know what one means,' said Captain Booter.

'Onomato thing. "Stumpers" sounds just like what it is. Only place to go. Statement of fact.'

Alex rinsed. 'Should we finish with the cold, sir?'

'One always says yes on trust but one's never known what it's for. You're the man to enlighten.'

'It leaves the hair shiny, sir.'

'You remember one's getting married.' A pause. Alex went on rinsing, making sure that the water wasn't icy, knowing that more would be said.

'The thing is,' said the Captain, 'one's not good enough for her.' He looked much troubled. 'There's something she can't say and one's not up to snuff about what's going on in her mind. What would you do?'

Alex recognized urgency in the language fog. 'If you'd like to say more, sir?'

'There's the pressure of the church being booked and the announcement in *The Times* and presents arriving by the bushel. It's not as if one could stop anything now. Let alone that one wants to. Why should she be so down?'

'Because she feels the pressure on you, sir?'

'Can't be that. She's a tower of strength. But only the other day one told her how building she was and she burst into tears.'

'Building, sir?'

'You know. Building. Sort of person who builds one up.' Pause. 'She's got a marvellous character.'

Alex towel-dried the Captain's hair. 'The auspices sound good, sir.'

'Wish *you* could meet her and talk to her,' said the Captain. Pause. 'To come back to Stumpers, sort of thing one meant was that the name's got a lot in common with Harry Piccers.'

Alex wondered if Harry Piccers was to be the best man.

'One's often thought how massively central Stumpers is. Might almost be in Harry Piccers.'

Alex wrapped the Captain's head in a fresh towel and deduced Piccadilly.

'What we all like about coming here is that one doesn't have to chat. Lot of places let one in for a fiendish amount of chat when one's trying one's level best to think.'

Of course, he is very young, thought Alex. Captain Booter was twenty-two. Alex was nineteen.

'What should one do about what's on the mind of one's wedded-wife-to-be, Alex?'

'Ask her, sir?' Alex started to razor-cut Captain Booter's hair. He had to stop for a moment after his suggestion, because the Captain was turning his head to and fro quite violently, as though a thought in his mind were a billiard ball to be bounced off several points before it fell into a pocket.

Silence. The motion ceased and Alex was able to razor again. 'I say,' said the Captain, 'how fast does one's hair grow?'

Alex detected a real wish to ask about someone else's interest. 'An average of half an inch a month, sir. In your case it seems a lot more.'

'You do like this hair business, don't you?'

'I do,' said Alex in a respondent voice, thinking to lead the Captain back to speaking of his wedding, perhaps even of his marriage.

The Captain sank his chin into his chest to give Alex an angle for working on the back of his neck. 'You've got a free run of your life, haven't you?'

Christ, thought Alex. Hasn't he? I'm enviable?

Silence.

'If you could have a go at getting rid of this wretched kink. One detests oneself with curly hair and this kink keeps rearing its ugly head. What would be the cause of it?'

'The shape of the follicles, sir.'

'Really?'

Alex went on with his work and then said, using the pronoun insisted on at Stumpers, 'Do we have the hair parted on the left as usual, sir?'

'Thanks. I say, thought follicles were round.'

'A round follicle gives us straight hair, sir. If it's oval we have wavy-to-curly hair.'

'So some of my follicles are oval. Not that one's got anything to make an opera about. But is that odd of one?'

'Round follicles are standard only in Japanese and some other Asian hair types, sir.'

Captain Booter eventually stood up, looked at his head in a back mirror, nodded a thank-you to Alex, said, 'On the account,' to the cashier (who seldom saw cash), and added softly to her, 'Put on the usual for Alex. Same appointment Monday after next, please.'

'Alex will have left us by then, sir.'

'He can't be leaving. One's supposed to be getting married, if all goes well. He's indispensable.' The Captain unnecessarily blew his nose with a linen handkerchief. 'Sustenance.'

'We can give you Gregory, sir,' said the cashier, 'though we realize the faithful connection with Alex. Gregory has been training alongside him.'

'Others do have to move on.' A heavy sigh, like a sigh of a small child trying to explain himself and thwarted by lack of language. Alex, in earshot while he waited for his next client, heard the sigh and remembered his own pent-up infancy.

Captain Booter turned to him and said, 'Where are you branching out to? When you've hit Stumpers there can't be anywhere to go. You've captured the peak, I mean.'

The cashier said, for Alex, 'He's going to another salon, sir.'

'For women,' said Alex.

'Then one must tell Virginia.'

So that was her name, at last.

'You must give one the address,' said Captain Booter. 'The hoped-for bridesmaids would come in droves. Let alone Virginia herself.'

'It's in East Croydon, sir.'

'Where is East Croydon exactly?'

'It's fifteen minutes from Victoria Station, sir.'

'That close. In one's ignorance one somehow only thinks of East Croydon as the place where one changes. Changes trains for somewhere else.'

Alex quenched the mild reply that people lived there.

'Maybe you live there,' said Captain Booter. 'Sometimes one catches oneself being horribly rude. Do you?'

'Yes.'

'You'll give me the telephone number? I know Virginia will want it.' The cashier noticed that Captain Booter could say 'I', given occasion, and wrote the number on a card for him. The Captain said, 'We really mustn't lose touch. People always say that but one does mean it, Alex.'

That evening, taking Virginia out to dinner, Piggy Booter said, 'You know Alex?'

'The Alex you call your gentle barber?'

'Well, he's branching out into women's hair and I've got his number. It's in East Croydon. Thought perhaps one should support the decision. The trains go every ten minutes. The old hag checked. I say, what has one done?'

'She's your secretary, darling. Jane. She worships you and she's beginning to feel you despise her.'

'But she must know she's irreplaceable. Has she been blubbing?'

'No, but you need to put it right. I rang you at the barracks and I could hear from her voice that there was something wrong. So I asked her and she told me. It wasn't a complaint, dove.' Virginia was from Northumberland, a county of unknotted people. Loving the Captain, she was not going to call him Piggy. 'I was surprised she was still there. Isn't she due to be on maternity leave?'

'She begged to stay on until the last minute. The baby's wildly overdue. She said she'd go nuts sitting about at home.'

'She sees things through.'

'If the infant doesn't appear by the end of the week they're going to put the ferrets up.'

'What on earth do you mean?'

'Induce it, surgeons call it, don't they? Your piece of turf.'

'Darling,' said Virginia, her small face a cry of pain, 'you've got to stop talking like this. You're a gentle soldier.'

'Did one do something wrong?'

'I'm sure you didn't do anything wrong. It's the way you speak. You're not like that.'

Captain Booter held his head and then paid the bill. His cheque signature looked fraudulent because his hand was shaking. He tore up the cheque and paid cash.

★

Virginia couldn't sleep that night. After thought, she rang the Captain. One ring only, in case he was asleep. He picked up at once.

'Couldn't you sleep either, dove?' she said.

'It's because one's used to sleeping together.'

She unravelled that sentence almost without noticing by now and said at the same time, 'Is it?'

'My fault. After one's cohabited so long I thought one should have a breather before one got spliced.' Suppose she was leaving him.

'May I come round?' she said.

'Is something hurting?'

'Something's on my mind.'

He felt not fear then, only a deep sadness. 'I'll drive over.'

'No,' she said, 'I'm already dressed. I'll be there in three minutes.' She hung up before he had time to say that he was dressed too.

Virginia sat down on his sofa, the pull-out one they had used as a bed for two years. Obviously he had made no feint at a night of sleep.

'Can I get us something?'

'Maybe some broth?'

They went together to the kitchen, waited in silence for the water to boil, used two bouillon cubes. Virginia curled her hands around the mug as she sat on the sofa again.

'You haven't taken your shoes off yet. You usually do, to put your feet up.'

'We're doing something wrong.'

'Is one being jilted?' He walked about. 'Please talk.'

'But then I'd be talking for you. I do it too much in my head as it is.' She shook her hair to get her words straight. 'That's exactly the trouble.'

'What is?'

'Oh, darling. You must hear it. "Is one being jilted." I know you're minding a very great deal but you're sounding ironclad.' She drove on, loathing it. 'I know things don't come out the way you mean them. But sometimes even I forget and start to wonder.'

'Wonder what?'

'Whether you're a boor.'

He waited.

'You do know I didn't say bore.'

'Yes.'

'And you do know you're beloved. Or else we wouldn't be here.'

'"But," you're saying. Go on.'

'This "one" instead of "I". You're disowning what you say.'

'You mean not carrying the can.'

For once she said, 'No. I mean *those* words.'

'It's because one doesn't like to make a big deal about oneself.'

She held back and he noticed that. He noticed everything about her.

'It must be something that one picked up. Hell, that I picked up.'

'I can't tell any longer. I've got so used to translating everything you say that it's humiliating between us. To you.'

'Probably to you, too.' It was when he suddenly came out with such things that she knew they must be on a firm road after all. She watched carefully and saw him now as a steadied shape. Before, even standing so stiffly that he was at military attention, he had sometimes swayed like a Druidical rocking-stone.

'What do you want to do?' he said.

'I think we should wait. And I think we shouldn't get married with red carpets and morning coats.'

'We can't send back one's presents.'

'They're from friends. Friends understand.'

'What about the Waterford jug from the great-aunt, say? The G.A. isn't a friend at all.'

'Then we shouldn't have asked her.'

'One couldn't not. I couldn't not. Hell's bells.'

'Darling, go lightly.' He got so angered by himself.

'Couldn't we just go on living together and sort things out on the way?'

'Does the G.A. get on your nerves? Things like the G.A.? If there is anything else like the G.A.'

She laughed then and things were again immediately in place, but he still made himself say, 'Go on.'

She spread her hands to batten down a word and said, 'Clutter.'

'Go on.'

'When we met, we had room. A huge amount of room to live in together. There was nothing there but the two of us. And now we're tripping over ourselves to avoid the knick-knacks.'

He gave a practically imperceptible nod and, after raising his eyebrows for accord, turned out the lights. They spent the night on the sofa, properly pulled out, the two of them sleeping not fitfully. Next morning, after coffee, Virginia rang East Croydon and asked if she could have an appointment with Alex when he had started.

'The hair looks good,' said the Captain. 'What did you make of him?'

'There's a lot to him, isn't there,' she said. They were in her bed-sitter, which had a small kitchen.

'Always thought so. How did you get on?'

'He thinks a lot of you, too.' She smiled and added, 'He said you talked more.'

'Did he think you were still-waters-running-deep department?'

'Darling!'

'What's he up to?'

'I don't know him much yet. While he was combing me out he told me a bit about his wedding-photographer job. And a lot about his brother. Not the one who's just moved his vet surgery but the younger one at the Indian laundry who's practising to be an accompanist. Alex asked us both to his wedding.'

'*Alex's?* It can't be the same man.'

'Of course it is. He knew loads about us.'

'But one's been going to him for ages and he never said any of this.'

'Perhaps he's more at home in East Croydon.'

'Alex a wedding photographer and getting married? He can't take photographs as well as getting married and doing women's hair.'

'Truly. He can and is and does. He showed me a portfolio. Also a pic he took of his girlfriend. She's Pakistani.'

Captain Booter thought, then said 'Ooh-ah' at his own expense with an assumed look of vacuity.

'He does the wedding photographs in his spare time because of the mortgage. Also he obviously enjoys doing them. He's good. He's booked every Saturday and Sunday and he says it's much less tiring now that he doesn't have to travel up to Stumpers. He spends the whole day on each wedding. Mornings getting to know the families for the candid shots, which he says he likes the best, then the groups, which he's not keen on, then the church or synagogue or registry office, then the cake-cutting and the going-away if the wedding's formal. Then he picks up his younger brother from the laundry and takes him to night school. The brother hasn't got a driving licence yet, but Alex has a moped that seats two. He's working on the engine of a secondhand car to get it ready for his own wedding.'

'You did get a lot out of him. Not the man he was at Stumpers.' There was a long pause. 'Did he ask about one?' He checked back. 'In this case, us? About the wedding and all that, in fact?'

'Best wishes, twice.' That 'one' was hesitancy, she thought, getting the signal at once because she had been talking too fast herself. She fell into a more usual silence and got dinner for the two of them. The room filled with the smell of pasta basilica and garlic. The first time she had ever cooked for him she had given him pasta basilica and he had hated it. And of course, he thought, I've gone and left it too late to tell her.

'Has one left everything too late?' he said, speaking out loud without meaning to. She heard the intent and thought it best not to trample by pursuing. There were always other ways.

★

In this fashion, they lived in unuttered happy suspension for two months. The church was cancelled, the wedding presents kept and thanked for. The 'one's came and went, voice of irresolution. Then, just before Alex's wedding, Virginia said after work, 'I'm going down to Alex's tomorrow. Why don't you come?'

'Is one's hair looking long? Gregory's not the same as Alex.' Pause. 'Well, he wouldn't be, would he?'

Virginia said, 'You do miss him, darling, don't you?'

'I was going to ask if one wouldn't get into your hair.' Pause. 'Lordy me, I've done it again. But anyway, isn't Alex only doing women's hair now?'

'He's gone back to doing men's, too, to put some extra money by for the mortgage.'

Alex isn't dithering about between two places and held up by roadblocks of presents, he thought. 'Alex is way ahead of us,' he said. She looked at his alert face with love of his elation.

In East Croydon, Alex shampooed Virginia's hair first and then the Captain's. While the Captain watched the professional Alex blow-drying her hair, he was struck afresh by the way she listened.

A man beside him, small and quailshaped, with a fussed expression, wearing a tennis-club blazer with a carefully drooped handkerchief in the chest pocket, leaned over and said heftily, 'I suppose I should introduce myself.'

The Captain nodded cordially and looked back at Virginia and Alex.

'I'm Campbell. Not the soup. I'm in instrument hiring. Uprights and Wurlitzers for the most part. And I'm thinking of getting into a synthesizer or two.'

Captain Booter had a vision of this portly man squeezing into a Moog or two.

'Name of the firm is Fine-Eared Music-Makers. This is my lady wife, Mrs Campbell.'

Captain Booter shook hands with Mrs Campbell. 'She trotted along in my wake to oversee my moustache.' The Captain jumped slightly and then went back to watching Alex at work. Alex's Pakistani fiancée came into the shop and, after

71

putting a towel over her sari, started shampooing her long hair.

'Immense row of heads in the mirror. Like a display of beheadings on spikes at the Tower of London, except that we're not beheaded, of course,' said Mr Campbell, putting his index fingers to his moustache to shape it in his mind as he intended it to be clipped. 'Who's the beauteous oriental, one asks oneself.'

Captain Booter suddenly caught a reflection of his own voice coming back at him as if they were all in a fun-fair hall of distorting mirrors. Virginia had been watching and made a gesture brushing away his thought.

'Alex's fiancée,' said the Captain.

'Indian or Siamese or what?'

'Pakistani.'

'Going to have a Buddhist wedding, then, are they? Only connection I've had with Buddhism was with a caterer from Wales unemployment. Sudden convert. I engaged her all unknowing to cope with the ponies and my letters. Offered her a shorthand course, even. Would she take it? Said she had too much to do. Praying every twenty minutes some days, one found, so no wonder.'

The Captain looked at Alex's fiancée for fear she would have heard, but her ears were under water.

'Too busy meditating to clean the boiler. We had to get rid of her. Tell him what I said about my victory, dear.'

'You say,' said Mrs Campbell.

He fingered the gold embroidery on his tennis-blazer badge. 'Last serve, double fault by the unemployable, match to Fine-Eared Music-Makers.'

'How vile,' said Captain Booter.

Fine-Eared Music-Makers heard 'dire' and said, 'Yes, dire straits indeed. Good riddance, one said.'

'Both of you?' said Captain Booter dryly, getting up and taking Virginia away after leaving their wedding present of a red leather photograph album for Alex and his fiancée to find at the till desk.

★

Back at his place in London, Captain Booter looked out of the window for a few minutes and then said, 'One was lucky you didn't get rid of me.'

'A "one" and a "me",' she said. 'We're more than halfway there.'

'Am I like that man?'

'Not remotely. You told him exactly what you thought.'

She looked at him with simplicity. 'I'm daft. We're totally there.'

# Spoils

## NADINE GORDIMER

IN THE WARMTH of the bed your own fart brings to your
nostrils the smell of rotting flesh: the lamb chops you
devoured last night. Seasoned with rosemary and with an
undertaker's paper-frill on the severed rib-bones. Another
corpse digested.

'Become a vegetarian, then.' She's heard it all too many
times before; sick of it, sick of my being sick of it. Sick of the
things I say, that surface now and then.

'I want no part of it.'

We are listening to the news.

'What? What are you going on about? *What?*'

What indeed? No: which. Which is it I choose to be no part
of? The boy who threw a stone at the police, had both his arms
broken by them, was sodomized by prisoners into whose cell
he was thrown; the kidnapped diplomat and the group (men,
as I am a man, women, as she is a woman) who sent his fourth
finger by mail to his family; the girl doused with petrol and
burned alive as a traitor; those starved by drought or those
drowned by flood, far away; the nineteen-year-old son of Mr
and Mrs killed by the tremendous elemental thrill of 220 volts
while using an electric spray gun on his motorbike. The
planned, the devised, executed by people like myself, or the

74

haphazard, the indifferent, executed senselessly by elemental forces. *Senselessly.* Why is there more sense in the conscious acts that make corpses? Consciousness is self-deception. Intelligence is a liar.

'You're not having great thoughts. That's life.'

Her beauty-salon philosophy. Stale, animal, passive. Whether I choose or not; can't choose, can't want *no part.*

The daily necrophilia.

'Become a vegetarian, then!'

Among other people no one would ever think there was anything wrong. He is aware of that; she is aware of his being aware, taking some kind of pride in appearing exactly as they have him in their minds, contributing to their gathering exactly what his place in it expects of him. The weekend party – invited to a lodge on a private game reserve – will include the practical, improvising man; the clown who burns his fingers at the camp fire and gets a laugh out of it; the woman who spends her time preparing to feed everyone; the pretty girl who perks up the company sexually; the good-timer who keeps everyone drinking until late; the quiet one who sits apart contemplating the bush; one or two newcomers, for ballast, who may or may not provide a measure of serious conversation. Why not accept? No? *Well.* What else has he in mind that will please him better? Just say.

Nothing.

There you are!

He, in contrast to the clown, is the charmer, the wit. He knows almost everyone's foibles, he sets the anecdotes flowing, he provides the gentle jibes that make people feel themselves to be characters.

Whatever their temperaments, all are nature lovers. That is nothing to be ashamed of – surely, even for him. Their love of the wild brings them together – the wealthy couple who own the reserve and lodge rather than race horses or a yacht, the pretty girl who models or works in public relations, the good-timer director of a mining house, the adventurous stockbroker, the young doctor who works for a clerk's salary in a hospital for blacks, the clowning antique dealer . . . And he has no right to feel himself superior – in seriousness, morality (he knows that) – in this company, for it includes a young man who has been in political detention. That one is not censorious of the playground indulgences of his fellow whites, so long as the regime he has risked his freedom to destroy, will kill to destroy, lasts. That's life.

Behaving – undetectably – as one is expected is also a protection against fear of what one really is, now. Perhaps what is seen to be, is himself, the witty charmer. How can he know? He does it so well. His wife sees him barefoot, his arms round his knees on the viewing deck from which the company watches buffalo trampling the reeds down at the river, hears the amusing asides he makes while gazing through field-glasses, notices the way he has left his shirt unbuttoned in healthy confidence of the sun-flushed manliness of his breast: is the silence, the incomprehensible statements that come from it, alone with her, a way of tormenting her? Does he do it only to annoy, to punish? And what has she done to deserve what he doesn't mete out to others? Let him keep it to himself. Take a valium. Anything. Become a vegetarian. In the heat of the afternoon everyone goes to their rooms or their makeshift beds on the shaded part of the deck to sleep off the lunch-time wine. Even in the room allotted to them, he keeps up, out of sight of the company (but they are only a wall away, he knows they are there) what is expected. It is so hot he and she have stripped to their briefs. He passes a hand over her damp breasts, gives a lazy sigh and is asleep on his back. Would he have wanted to take her nipples in his mouth, commit himself to love-making, if he hadn't fallen asleep, or was his a gesture from the wings just in case the audience might catch a glimpse of a slump to an offstage presence?

The house party is like the fire the servant lights at dusk within the reed stockade beside the lodge. One never knows when a fire outdoors will smoke or take flame cleanly and make a grand blaze, as this one does. One never knows when a small gathering will remain disparate, unresponsive, or when, as this time, men and women will ignite and make a bright company. The ceremony of the evening meal was a bit ridiculous, but perhaps intended as such, and fun. A parody of old colonial times: the stockade against the wild beasts, the black man beating a drum to announce the meal, the chairs placed carefully by him in a missionary prayer-meeting circle well away from the fire, the whisky and wine set out, the smell of charred flesh from the cooking grids. Look up: the first star in the haze is the mast-light of a ship moving out, slipping moorings, breaking with this world. Look down: the blue flames are nothing but burning fat; there are gnawed bones on the swept earth.

He's been drinking a lot – she noticed: so that he could stomach it all, no doubt he tells himself.

The fire twitches under ash and the dinner orchestra of insects whose string instruments are their own bodies, legs scraping against legs, wings scraping against carapace, has been silenced by the rising of the moon. But laughter continues. In the huge night, not reduced to scale by buildings, tangled by no pylons and wires, hollowed out by no street- and window-lights into habitable enclosures, the laughter, the voices are vagrant sound that one moment flies right up boldly into space, the next makes a wave so faint it dies out almost as it leaves the lips. Everyone interrupts everyone else, argues, teases. There are moments of acerbity; the grapes they are eating pop into sharp juice as they are bitten. One of the quiet guests has become communicative as will the kind who never risk ideas or opinions of their own but can reproduce, when a subject brings the opportunity, information they have read and stored. Bats, the twirling rags darker against the dark: someone suggested, as a woman cowered, that fear of them comes from the fact that they can't be heard approaching.

'If your eyes are closed, and a bird flies overhead, you'll hear the resistance of air to its wings.'

'And also, you can't make out what a bat's like, where its head is – just a *thing*, ugh!'

The quiet guest was already explaining, no, bats will not bump into you, but not, as this is popularly believed, because they have an inbuilt radar system; their system is sonar, or echo-location –

'I wear a leopard-skin coat.'

The defiant soprano statement from a sub-conversation breaks through his monologue and loses him attention.

It is the pretty girl; she has greased her face against the day's exposure to the sun and her bone-structure elegantly reflects the frail light coming from the half-moon, the occasional waver of flame roused in the fire or the halo of a cigarette lighter. She is almost beautiful.

'– D'you hear that!'

'Glynis, where did you find this girl?'

'Shall we put her out to be eaten by her prey, expose her on a rock?'

'No leopards here, unfortunately.'

'No, because people kill them to make fur coats.'

The wit did not live up to his reputation, merely repeated in sharper, more personal paraphrase what had been well said, no one remembered by whom. He spoke directly to the girl, whereas the others were playfully half-indignant around her presence. 'The coat would look much better on the leopard than on you.' But the inference, neither entirely conservationist nor aesthetic, seemed to excite the girl's interest in this man. She was aware of him, in the real sense, for the first time.

'Wait till you see me in it.' Just the right touch of independence, hostility.

'That could be arranged.'

This was a sub-exchange, now, under the talk of the others; he was doing the right thing, responding with the innuendo by which men and women acknowledge chemical correspondence stirring between them. And then she said it, was guided to it like a bat, by echo-location or whatever it is, something vibrating from the disgusts in him. 'Would you prefer me to wear a sheepskin one? You eat lamb, I suppose?'

It is easy to lose her in the criss-cross of talk and laughter, to enter it at some other level and let fall the one on which she took him up. He is drawn elsewhere – there is refuge, maybe, rock to touch in the ex-political prisoner. The prisoner holds the hand of his pale girl with her big nervously-exposed teeth; no beauty, all love. The last place to look for love is in beauty; beauty is only a skin, the creature's own or that of another animal, over what decays. Love is found in prison; this no-beauty has loved him while his body was not present. And he has loved his brothers – he's talking about them, not using the word, but the sense is there so strongly – although they live shut in with their own pails of dirt; he loves even the murderers whose night-long death songs he heard before they were taken to be hanged in the morning. 'Common criminals? In this country? Under laws like ours? Oh yes, we politicals were kept apart, but with time (I was there ten months) we managed to communicate. (There are so many ways you don't think of, outside, when you don't need to.) One of them – young, my age – he was already declared an habitual criminal, inside for an indeterminate sentence. Detention's also an indeterminate sentence, in a way, so I could have some idea . . .'

'You hadn't killed, robbed – he must have done that over and over.'

'Oh, he had. But I hadn't been born the bastard of a kitchen maid who had no home but her room in a white woman's backyard. I hadn't been sent to a "homeland" where the woman who was supposed to take care of me was starving and followed her man to a squatter camp in Cape Town to look for work. I hadn't begged in the streets, stolen what I needed to eat, sniffed glue for comfort. He had his first new clothes, his first real bed when he joined a gang of car thieves. Common lot; common criminal.'

Common sob story.

'If he had met you outside prison he would have knifed you for your watch.'

'Possibly! Can you say "That's mine" to people whose land was taken from them by conquest, a gigantic hold-up at the point of imperial guns?'

And the bombs, in the streets, in the cars, in the super-markets, that kill with a moral, necessary end, not criminal intent (yes, to be criminal is to kill for self-gain) – these don't

79

confuse *him*, make carrion of brotherhood. He's brave enough
to swallow it. No gagging.

Voices and laughter are cut off. You don't come to the bush
to talk politics. It is one of the alert silences called for now and
then by someone who's heard, beyond human voices, a cry.
*Shhhhh . . .* Once it was the mean complaining of jackals, and
– nearer – hawking from a hyena, that creature of big nostrils
made to scent spilt blood. Then a squeal no one could identify:
a hare pounced on by a wheeling owl? A wart-hog attacked by
– whom? What's going on, among them, that other order of
the beasts in their night?

'They live twenty-four hours; we waste the dark.'

'Norbert, you used to be such a night-club bird!'

And the young doctor offers: 'They hunt for their living in
shifts, just like us. Some sleep during the day.'

'Oh, but they're *designed* as different species, in order to use
actively all twenty-four hours. We are one species, designed
for daylight only. It's not so many generations since –
pre-industrial times, that's all – we went to bed at nightfall. If
the world's energy supplies should run out, we'd be back to
that. No electricity. No night shifts. There isn't a variety in
our species that has night vision.'

The bat expert takes up this new cue. 'There are experi-
ments with devices that may provide night vision. They're
based on –'

'*Shhhhh . . .*'

Laughter like the small explosion of a glass dropped.

'Shut up, Claire!'

All listen, with a glisten on eye movements alone, dead still.

It is difficult for them to decide on what it is they are
eavesdropping. A straining that barely becomes a grunt. A
belching stir; scuffling, scuffling. But it could be a breeze in
dead leaves. It is not the straw crepitation of the reeds at the
river; it comes from the other direction, behind the lodge.
There is a gathering, another gathering somewhere there.
There is communication their ears are not tuned to, their
comprehension cannot decode; some event outside theirs.
Even the ex-political prisoner does not know what he hears; he

who has heard through prison walls, he who has compre-
hended and decoded so much the others have not. His is only
human knowledge, after all; he is not a twenty-four hour
creature, either.

Into this subdued hush breaks the black man jangling a tray
of glasses he has washed. The host signals: be quiet, go away,
stop fussing among dirty plates. He comes over with the smile
of one who knows he has something to offer. 'Lions. They kill
one, two maybe. Zebras.'

Everyone bursts the silence like schoolchildren let out of
class.

'Where?'

'How does he know?'

'What's he say?'

He keeps them waiting a moment; his hand is raised, palm
up, pink from immersion in the washing-up. He is wiping it
on his apron. 'My wives hear it, there in my house. Zebra, and
now they eating. That side, there, behind.'

The black man's name is too unfamiliar to pronounce. But he
is no longer nameless; he is the organizer of an expedition; they
pick up a shortened version of the name from their host. Siza
has brought the old truck, four-wheel drive, adapted as a large
station wagon, from out of its shed next to his house.
Everybody is game. This is part of the entertainment the host
hoped but certainly could not promise to be lucky enough to
provide; all troop by torch light the hundred yards from the
lodge, under the mopane trees, past the bed of cannas outlined
with whitewashed stones (the host never has had the heart to
tell Siza this kind of white man's house does not need a white
man's kind of garden) to Siza's wives' pumpkin and tomato
patch. Siza is repairing a door-handle of the vehicle with a
piece of wire, commanding, in his own language, this and that
from his family standing by. A little boy gets underfoot and he
lifts and dumps him out of the way. Two women wear
traditional turbans but one has a T-shirt with an advertising
logo; girl children hang on their arms, jabbering. Boys are
quietly jumping with excitement.

Siza's status in this situation is clear when the two wives and children do not see the white party off, but climb into the vehicle among them, the dry-soled hard little feet of the children nimbly finding places among the guests' shoes, their knobbly heads with knitted capping of hair unfamiliar to the touch into which all in the vehicle are crowded. Beside the girl with her oiled face and hard slender body perfumed to smell like a lily, there is the soft bulk of one of the wives, smelling of wood smoke. 'Everybody in? Everybody OK?' No, no, wait – someone has gone back for a forgotten flash-bulb. Siza has started up the engine; the whole vehicle jerks and shakes.

Wit is not called for, nor flirtation. He does what is expected: runs to the lodge to fetch a sweater, in case she gets chilly. There is barely room for him to squeeze by; she attempts to take a black child on her lap, but the child is too shy. He lowers himself somehow into what space there is. The vehicle moves, all bodies, familiar and unfamiliar, are pressed together, swaying, congealed, breathing in contact. She smiles at him, dipping her head sideways, commenting lightly on the human press, as if he were someone else: 'In for the kill.'

It is not possible to get out.

Everyone will be quite safe if they stay in the car and please roll up the windows, says the host. The headlights of the old vehicle have shown Siza trees like other trees, bushes like other bushes that are to him his signposts. The blundering of the vehicle through bush and over tree-stumps, anthills and dongas has been along his highway: he has stopped suddenly, and there they are, shadow-shapes and sudden phosphorescent slits in the dim arch of trees that the limit of the headlights' reach only just creates, as a candle, held up, feebly makes a cave of its own aura. Siza drives with slow-motion rocking and heaving of the human load, steadily nearer. Four shapes come forward along the beams and stop. He stops. Motes of dust, scraps of leaf and bark knocked off the vegetation float, blurring the beams surrounding four lionesses who stand not ten yards away. Their eyes are wide, now, gem-yellow, expanded by the glare they face, and never blink.

Their jaws hang open and their heads shake with panting, their bodies are bellows expanding and contracting between stiff-hipped haunches and heavy, narrow shoulders that support the heads. Their tongues lie like red cloth, the edges rucked up on either side by long white incisors.

They are dirtied with blood and, to human eyes, de-sexed, their kind of femaleness without femininity, their kind of threat and strength out of place, associated with the male. They have no beauty except in the almighty purpose of their stance. There is nothing else in their gaunt faces: nothing but the fact, behind them, of half-grown and younger cubs in the rib-cage of a zebra, pulling and sucking at bloody scraps.

The legs and head are intact in dandyish dress of black and white. The beast has been, is being eaten out. Its innards are missing; half-digested grasses that were in its stomach have been emptied on the ground; they can be seen – someone points this out in a whisper. But even the undertone is a transgression. The lionesses don't give forth the roar that would make their menace recognizable, something to deal with. Utterances are not the medium for this confrontation. Watching. That is all. The breathing mass, the beating hearts in the vehicle – watching the cubs jostling for places within the cadaver; the breathing mass, the beating hearts in the vehicle, being watched by the lionesses. The beasts have no time; it will be measured by their fill. For the others, time suddenly begins again when the young doctor's girlfriend begins to cry soundlessly and the black children look away from the scene and see the tears shining on her cheeks and stare at her fear. The young doctor asks to be taken back to the lodge; the compact is broken; people protest: Why, oh no, they want to stay and see what happens. One of the lionesses breaks ranks and turns on a greedy cub, cuffing it out of the gouged prey. Quite safe; the car is perfectly safe, don't open a window to photograph. But the doctor is insistent: 'This old truck's chassis is cracked right through, we're overloaded, we could be stuck here all night.'

'Unreal.' Back in the room, the wife comes out with one of the catch-alls that have been emptied of dictionary meaning so that they may fit any experience the speaker won't take the trouble to define. When he doesn't respond she stands a moment, in the doorway, her bedclothes in her arms, smiling, gives her head a little shake to show how overwhelming her impression has been.

Oh well. What can she expect? Why come, anyway? Should have stayed at home. So he doesn't want to sleep in the open, on the deck. Under the stars. All right. No stars, then.

He lies alone and the mosquitoes are waiting for his blood, upside-down on the white board ceiling.

No. Real. *Real.* Alone, he can keep it intact, exactly that: the stasis, the existence without time, and without time there is no connection, the state in which he really need have, has no part, could have no part, there in the eyes of the lionesses. Between the beasts and the human load, the void. It is more desired and awful than could ever be conceived; he does not know whether he is sleeping or dead.

There is still Sunday. The entertainment is not over. Someone has heard lions round the lodge in the middle of the night. The scepticism with which this claim is greeted is quickly disproved when distinct pugs are found in the dust that surrounds the small swimming-pool which, like amniotic fluid, steeps the guests at their own body temperature. The host is not surprised; it has happened before: the lionesses must have come down to quench the thirst their feasting had given them. And the scent of humans, sleeping so near, up on the deck, the sweat of humans in the humid night, their sighs and sleep-noises? Their pleasure- and anxiety-emanating dreams?

'As far as the lions are concerned, we didn't exist.' From the pretty girl, the remark is a half-question that trails off.

'When your stomach is full you don't smell blood.'

The ex-prisoner is perhaps extrapolating into the class war? – the wit puts in, and the ex-prisoner himself is the one who is most appreciatively amused.

After the mosquitoes had had their fill, sleep came as indifferently as those other bodily states, hunger and thirst. A good appetite for fresh pawpaw and bacon, boerewors and eggs. Hungry, like everybody else. His wife offers him second helpings; perhaps he needs feeding up; there is a theory that all morbid symptoms are in fact of physical origin. Obsession with injustice – what's wrong with the world is a disease you, an individual, can't cure; that's life. The one who went to prison may be suffering from a lack of something – amino acids, vitamins – or an excess of something, over-feeding when a child or a hyperactive thyroid gland. Research is being done.

Siza confirms that the lionesses came to drink. They passed his house; he heard them. He tells this with the dry, knowing smile of one who is aware of a secret to-and-fro between bedrooms. After breakfast he is going to take the party to see in daylight where the kill took place last night.

'But is there anything to see?'

Siza is patient. 'They not eat all. Is too much. So they leave some, tonight they come back for eat finish.'

'No thanks! I don't think we should disturb them again.'

But nobody wants the young doctor and his girlfriend to come anyway and spoil the outing.

'The lions they sleeping now. They gone away. Come back tonight. Is not there now.'

The wife is watching to see if she and her husband are going along. Yes, he's climbing, limber, into the old vehicle with the cracked chassis; he's giving a hand up to the hostess, he's said something that makes her laugh and purse her mouth.

The black women are thumping washing at an outdoor tub. Neither they nor their children come on this expedition. There is room to breathe without contact, this time. Everything is different in daylight. It is true that the lionesses are absent; the state that he achieved last night is absent in the same way, like them, drugged down by daylight.

Not a lion to be seen. Siza has stopped the vehicle, got out, but waved the passengers to stay put. The scrub forest is quiet; fragile pods that burst and sow their seed by wind-dispersion spiral slowly. Everybody chatters. The stockbroker leaves the vehicle and they shout at him. All right. All right. Taking his time, to show his lack of fear, he climbs aboard. 'Lions are not bulls and bears, Fred.' They laugh at this mild jeer which is the kind expected to sustain the wit's image – all are amused except the stockbroker himself, who knows the remark, in turn, refers to his image of himself as one whom no one would guess to be a stockbroker.

Siza comes back and beckons. The vehicle is quickly quit. And now the emptiness of the scrub forest is untrustworthy; all around, you can't see what's behind dead brush, fallen logs and the screens of layered branches that confine vision to ten feet. They talk only softly, in the sense of being stalked. The black man is leading them along what looks almost like a swept path, but it has been swept by a large body being dragged through dust and dead leaves: there is the carcase of the zebra, half-hidden in a thicket.

'No tyre-tracks, we didn't drive right into here! This can't be the place.'

'They pull him here for when they come back tonight.'

'What! To keep the meat fresh?'

'For the birds mustn't see.' Siza gives a name in his language.

'He means vultures. Vultures, eh, Siza?' A mime of the vultures' hunched posture.

'Yes, those big birds. Come look here –' The tour continues, he takes them a few paces from the carcase and stands beside a mound over which earth has been scratched or kicked. Flies whose backs spark tinny green and gold are settled on it. The black man has his audience: taking up a stick, he prods the mound and it stirs under dust like flour-coated meat moved by a fork.

'Christ, the intestines! Look at the size of that liver or spleen!'

'You mean lions can do that? Store things covered? How do they do it, just with their paws?'

'It's exactly the way my cat covers its business in the garden, scratches up earth. They're cats, too.'

The young jailbird and his girl and the antique dealer have made a discovery for themselves, having, in the confidence of excitement, retraced for a short distance the way along which the kill was approached. They have found the very pile of the contents of the zebra's stomach that someone noticed last night. It is another mound. He has come over from the mound of guts they are marvelling at. There is nothing to watch in dead flesh; it is prodded and it falls back and is still. But this mound of steaming grass that smells sweetly of cud (it has been heated by the sun as it was once heated by the body that contained it) is not dead to human perception. What's going on here is a visible transformation of an inert mass. It is literally being carried away by distinctly different species of beetle who know how to live by decay, the waste of the digestive tract. The scarabs with their armoured heads burrow right into the base of the mound and come out backwards, rolling their ball of dung between their strong, tined legs. The tunnels they have mined collapse and spread the mound more thinly on its periphery; smaller beetles are flying in steadily to settle there, where their lighter equipment can function. They fly away carrying their appropriate load in a sac – or between their front legs, he can't quite make out. A third species, middle-sized but with a noisy buzz, function like helicopters, hovering and scooping off the top of the mound. They are flattening it perfectly evenly, who can say how, or why they bother with form? That's life. If every beetle has its place, how is refusal possible. And if refusal is possible, what place is there. No question mark. These are statements. That is why there is no point in making them to anyone. There is no possible response.

The mound is slowly going to disappear; maybe the vehicle is about to take the party back to the lodge, the weekend is going to be over. He is walking back to the rest of the party, still gathered round the carcase and the black man. For the space of a few yards he is alone; for a few seconds he is equidistant between those at the dung mound and those up ahead, part of neither one nor the other. A sensation that can't be held long; now he is with the group at the kill, again. There is some special stir of attentiveness in them, they crowd round and then herd back a step, where Siza, the black man, is crouched on his hunkers. He is business-like, concentrated, not taking any notice of them. He has given them all he could; now he has the air of being for himself. He has a knife in his hand and the white man who has just joined the group recognizes it; it is the knife that is everywhere, nowhere without the knife, on the news, at the dark street-corners, under the light that the warders never turn out. The black man has thrust, made his incision, sliced back the black-and-white smooth pelt on the dead beast's uppermost hind leg and now is cutting a piece of the plump rump. It is not a chunk or hunk, but neatly butchered, prime – a portion.

They laugh, wondering at the skill, curious. As if they can't guess, as if they've never sunk their teeth into a steak in their lives. 'What're you going to do with that, Siza?' Ah yes, put it in a doggy bag, take it home when you've already stuffed your own guts, taken the land (as the jailbird would say).

The black man is trimming it. Along with the knife, he has brought a sheet of newspaper. 'For me. Eat it at my house. For my house.'

'Is it good meat?'

'Yes, it's good.'

One of the men chides, man to man. 'But why not take the whole haunch – the whole leg, Siza? Why such a small piece?'

The black man is wrapping the portion in newspaper, he knows he mustn't let it drip blood on the white people.

He does it to his satisfaction in his own time and looks up at them. 'The lions, they know I must take a piece for me because I find where their meat is. They know it. It's all right. But if I take too much, they know it also. Then they will take one of my children.'

# High Teas

## GEORGINA HAMMICK

IT WAS OVER tea that Mrs Peverill had her weekly skirmishes
with the vicar. Unsatisfactory skirmishes, where no ground,
it seemed to her, was ever gained. The teas, the skirmishes,
had come about this way: a year before, at her daughter
Imogen's insistence, Mrs Peverill, in her late seventies, long
widowed but only recently infirm, had moved from a big old
house in the North-East to a little new house in the South-
West. The village, five miles from the market town where
Imogen and her family lived, had been chosen because it was
large enough to support a Church of England church and a
high street of shops that between them purveyed meat,
groceries, wine and tapestry wools. There was even a
miniature Lloyds Bank.

More than anything else, it was the shortness of the walk to
church that appealed to Mrs Peverill. She had been uprooted.
She had left behind in Yorkshire all that survived of a lifetime's
friends and acquaintances. She was in need of spiritual solace.

What she could not know was that the church notice-board
by the lych-gate, whose comforting promises, in black and
gold letters, of Matins, Holy Communion and Evensong,
were – if she leaned out a little way into the cherry tree – visible
from her bedroom window, was a relic merely. By the time

89

Mrs Peverill arrived in Upton Solmore, the service that prevailed at St Werburgh's was one entitled Family Eucharist.

That first Sunday when, in good faith and in good time and carrying her father's prayer book and *Hymns Ancient and Modern*, Mrs Peverill stepped into the porch, she was handed ('they were forced upon me,' she told Imogen later) a small, red, laminated notebook and a revised *New English Hymnal*.

Mrs Peverill had known, of course, of the existence of the new services, but they had never been a threat to her. At home in Yorkshire, the rector had said he was to old to learn new tricks, and his Parochial Church Council was determined not to. The trial offers of Series 2 and 3, and later, of Rites A and B, had been speeded back whence they came. (A few years earlier, the New English Bible had met with a different fate – relegated, within six months of its introduction, to a shelf in the vestry broom-cupboard, where Mrs Peverill had encountered it each time her name came up on the cleaning rota.)

In her pew at the back of the church, Mrs Peverill opened the red notebook and turned its pages in dismay and disbelief. They were printed in alternate blue and black type. The service was to be conducted by someone called a President. The prayers and responses, when not new and unfamiliar, had been chopped and changed almost beyond recognition and seemed to be in the wrong order. God was addressed throughout as *you*. The Nicene Creed began '*We* believe . . .'

When the service was over, Mrs Peverill stumbled out of the porch close to tears, and did not hear the vicar's words of welcome or notice his proffered hand; but later in the week, on Friday, at teatime, he came to call. He followed her into the kitchen and stood while the kettle boiled, and then he carried the tea tray into the sitting-room.

'You've managed to make this room most attractive already, I must say!' the vicar said. 'It was rather sombre when old Jerry Cartwright lived here.'

'Thank you,' Mrs Peverill said. She didn't like the idea of the vicar having an earlier knowledge of her house and her sitting-room.

'This cake is really something!' the vicar beamed. 'Did you make it yourself?'

'In Yorkshire,' Mrs Peverill said, 'I was used to making a fruit cake on Fridays, in case I had visitors at the weekend.'

'Old habits die hard,' the vicar said. He munched his cake with enthusiasm. Mrs Peverill sipped her tea.

'Er, forgive me if I'm intruding,' the vicar put his plate on the tray and brushed crumbs from his trousers, 'but you seemed very distressed after the Eucharist last Sunday. And then you rushed away before . . .' He abandoned this sentence and tried out another: 'Have you some troubles you feel you might like to tell me about? A bereavement? A loss of some kind?'

'Yes,' Mrs Peverill said. 'Yes, I have.'

The vicar leant forward, his hands on his knees. They were square hands. He was a stocky young man, whose upper arms bulged through the sleeves of his blouson jacket. A muscular Christian, Mrs Peverill supposed. He peered at her expectantly. His eyes were very blue, and round.

'I have suffered a loss,' she said, 'the loss of the Book of Common Prayer, the King James Bible and *Hymns Ancient and Modern*. This happened to me in church, in your church, last Sunday.'

'Oh dear, oh dear,' the vicar said. He seemed amused. 'Oh dear.'

'I had never been to a service of Rite A before,' Mrs Peverill spoke very slowly, 'and I could not follow it. I did not understand it. Nothing, very little, was familiar. They have even altered the Creed, you know, and mucked about with the Lord's Prayer.'

The vicar smiled. He began to say something, but Mrs Peverill continued: 'I felt, I feel – I'm not sure if I can explain this – robbed and cheated. Robbed of comfort. Cheated of drama and mystery. Of poetry.'

'Poetry?' the vicar said – as though, Mrs Peverill thought afterwards, she'd said something blasphemous ('as though I'd said something blasphemous,' she told Imogen on the telephone).

'Poetry,' Mrs Peverill said, and after that she was silent. For the vicar was laughing. Not in a scornful way, but in a hearty and appreciative one, as at a good joke. From now on, Mrs Peverill vowed, she would keep her emotions to herself, and fight him on the facts.

'You left out the Comfortable Words on Sunday,' she said, 'though there was some sort of version of them in the notebooks.'

'Optional,' the vicar said. 'Optional.' He tried to drain his cup, but it was already empty. 'I do say them sometimes.'

Mrs Peverill felt obliged to offer him more tea, and more cake. He accepted both.

'I think I understand how you feel,' he said presently. 'Some people, usually senior citizens like yourself, tend to have a bit of difficulty at first. But they get used to it, and when they do, they prefer it. Hopefully, you'll come to see Rite A in terms of a refresher course to your faith, one that adds a new dimension of participation and corporate worship. The laity have far more to do nowadays. No chance of falling asleep while the minister does all the work for you!' He laughed. His teeth were very white, his gums very red. 'Anyway, the 1662 Prayer Book, that you set such store by, is a distortion, a *travesty*, of the 1549 original. The spirit of the new liturgy – one of celebration rather than sacrifice – is far closer, you know, to what Cranmer had in mind.'

Mrs Peverill did not know, and she didn't believe it.

'In what way, Vicar?'

'Tony, please,' the vicar said. 'We won't go into it now,' he continued heartily, rising to his feet, 'but I'll call again, if I may, so that we can go on with our chat and, hopefully, iron out some of your problems. By the way,' he said at the door, 'we won't have to make do with those rather naff little pamphlets much longer. Our ASBs – Alternative Service Books – should be here any day now.'

At home in Yorkshire, Mrs Peverill remembered, watching the vicar jog down the path, the rector had once, over a post-PCC meeting glass of sherry, asked the members for their interpretation of the initials ASB. '*A Serious Blunder*, I imagine,' Miss Hawkley, the secretary, had drained her glass and reached for her coat, 'unless *A Synod Botch*.'

★

Mrs Peverill did not grow to like Rite A, let alone prefer it. A year later, she had, however – and this frightened her – become used to it, in the same way that she'd grown used to, while not approving them, frozen vegetables and decimal coinage. She kept her grief and anger alive by repeating, in church, the true, the only, Lord's Prayer and the Creed; and by responding 'And with Thy spirit' when the rest of the congregation chanted 'And also with you'. She kept her grief and anger alive by thinking up, during arthritically wakeful nights, questions of doctrine and liturgy to tax the vicar with, and by planning traps for him to fall into. He had got into the habit of calling in, on his way home from weekly visits to the hospice, on Friday afternoons, at teatime.

'Tell me, Vicar,' she said on one occasion, having waited till his mouth was full of cake, 'do you believe in the responsibility of the individual?' The vicar nodded; he could not speak.

'The new Rite does not seem to,' Mrs Peverill said. 'I refer to the Creed, and this "we believe" business –'

' "We believe" is compatible with the new spirit of unity and sharing,' the vicar said, ' "though we are many, we are one body" – you see.'

'No, not really.' Mrs Peverill sipped her tea. 'How can I know what anyone else believes? I can only speak for myself. In any case, Creed comes from *Credo*, not *Credimus*.' In the night, when she'd planned the assault, the vicar had turned pale at this point, and run his fingers distractedly through his hair. In her sitting-room, he remained rosy and unruffled and finished his cake without hurry. Afterwards he beamed at her.

'You're a tease, Mrs Peverill. But I don't think this sort of – how shall I put it? – nitpicking, pedantry, over one small word, is really helpful, do you?' It was not pedantry, Mrs Peverill knew, it was passion, and the following Friday she renewed her attack.

'This Gradual nonsense,' she began as, having finished tea, they walked down the garden to inspect the herbaceous border she had recently planted. 'Every Sunday you announce: "The hymn for the Gradual is . . ." You can't have a hymn *for* the Gradual, you know. A Gradual is. What it is is an antiphon,

sung between the Epistle and the Gospel, from the altar steps.
You don't, we don't, sing it from the altar steps. Last week
you stuck it in between the Gospel and the sermon. Moreover,
there's no mention of it in Rite A or the Prayer Book. It
belongs, properly, in the Roman Catholic mass.'

I have got him now, she thought, I've got him now.
Confronted with this evidence, he will faint quietly away into
my new delphiniums.

The vicar continued his progress along the path. 'The new
rite,' he said in equable tones, 'has been designed with a wider
and deeper ecumenism in view, and it allows, at certain stages
in the service, for the personal discretion and preferences of the
president. There's no room any more for a separatist
approach. We live in a secular age. The Church is under siege.
We must appeal, we must be seen to appeal, to all our brethren
of no matter what denomination, to all who fight under
Christ's banner. You are very brave,' he said, as they reached
the end of the garden, 'to plant perennials – all that splitting
and staking. We go for annuals at the vicarage. The minimum
of work, I always say, for the maximum of colour.'

Mrs Peverill could not always wait for Fridays to bombard
the enemy. Sometimes she accosted him in God's house, or
rather in His porch.

'No prayer of Humble Access today, I notice,' she said,
shaking out her umbrella, opening it. 'Your version of it, that
is. Or is that optional too?'

'We were running a bit late.' The vicar smiled kindly. 'But
yes, since you ask, it is up to me whether or not I include it. If
you look at your service book, you'll see that the words "all
may say" precede it. *May*, not *must*. On the credit side, I trust
you noticed that the Epistle this morning was read from the
Authorized Version – especially for you! You didn't receive
the Eucharist today. I hope your leg isn't playing you up?'

'I was not in a state of grace.' Mrs Peverill gave him a sharp
look from under her umbrella, before braving the rain. 'I did
not feel in love and charity with my neighbour.'

'I can never make out whether he's High or Low,' she said on the telephone to Imogen, 'he says minister, not priest, but the bell rings before Communion and his vestments are all colours of the rainbow. High, I suppose. And Low. A bit of both.'

'I don't know why you go on with all this, Ma,' Imogen said. 'It isn't getting you anywhere. You won't get the Prayer Book back, or King James. You won't change anything.'

Mrs Peverill said nothing.

'If I were a believer,' Imogen said, 'and if it were me, I'd be quizzing your Tony on the issues of the day – his stand on women priests, for example, and the homosexual clergy. Things that matter. There isn't a *Mrs* Vicar, by the way, is there?' she added darkly.

'History matters.' Mrs Peverill was getting cross. 'And language. A prayer book is a book of prayer. A service book, on the other hand, is the maintenance bumph one keeps in one's glove compartment –'

'Kept, in your case,' Imogen said. 'You haven't got a car any more,' she reminded her mother.

'I bet you didn't know they've mucked about with the hymns as well,' Mrs Peverill said.

'Did they have to change the hymns too?' she asked the vicar over tea.

'Have they?' The vicar put his hands to his head, as though to ward off blows. 'Not substantial alterations, surely?'

'Last week we had "Lead Us Heavenly Father", and while I was singing "Lone and dreary, faint and weary, Through the desert Thou didst go", you were all singing about Jesus being self-denying and death defying and going to Calvary. Odd, isn't it, that we continue to address God as 'Thou' in hymns? He must be rather confused, I imagine.'

'Perhaps "dreary" is not the adverb we'd ideally choose to describe Our Lord?' the vicar suggested, stretching a hand for a third piece of cake.

Mrs Peverill took the last silver-paper angel from the box at her feet and hung it on the lowest branch of the St Werburgh's Christmas tree.

'Angels from the realms of glory,' the vicar sang tunelessly in her ear, 'wing your-ur flight o'er all the earth . . .' He was hovering at her elbow, waiting for her to finish her decorating so that he could test the fairy lights. These, a collection of alternate red and yellow bulbs strung along a chewed flex, were more giant than fairy, and too clumsy for the branches. They quite ruined, Mrs Peverill opined, the effect she was wanting to create. She sighed.

'In Yorkshire,' she remarked, even to her own ears sounding like a children's nanny extolling the virtues of a past employer to a present, unsatisfactory one, 'we had real wax candles on the tree. Candle-flame sheds a holy light.'

'So you mentioned last year,' the vicar said, 'and I can only repeat: the fire risk is too dodgy.'

'Is it too dodgy to ask, Vicar, if we could have 1662 for Midnight Communion this Christmas? I am, after all, seventy-nine. It could well be my last . . .'

The vicar laughed. 'I doubt that, Mrs P,' he said. 'But it will certainly be my last Christmas – in Upton Solmore. I couldn't tell you before, because I hadn't informed the churchwardens, but the fact is, I'm off to fresh fields and pastures new. I've seen the bishop. Merseyside will present a very different sort of challenge, of course, but hopefully one . . .'

Mrs Peverill didn't hear the vicar's next words. She was in a state of shock. It was not his misquoting Milton – hardly a surprise – that upset her, but the implication of his news. What would she do with herself on Friday afternoons? How would she spend her wakeful, painful nights? How would she fill her life at all?

'I shall miss your teas,' the vicar was saying when she'd found herself a pillar and enlisted its support, 'and our chats. But who knows? If the PCC deems fit, the new minister may reinstate a form of service that's more up your aisle.'

Mrs Peverill said nothing. The next incumbent would not restore the Prayer Book: the ASBs were already in the pews. Far more likely he'd be a rock guitarist manqué, and invite the congregation to sing 'Lord of the Dance' for the Gradual. The devil she knew was, at least, unmusical.

The devil she knew moved the step-ladder away from the Christmas tree.

'That looks great, Mrs P. Now for our Regent Street happening! If you'd like to turn off the overhead lights, I'll switch on the tree.'

She reached up for her switch; he bent to his. And in the second before the ancient bakelite plug burst (setting fire to the flex, and dispatching the vicar to pastures newer, and more challenging, even, than Merseyside), the dark tree bloomed with a thousand candles, while on every branch – Mrs Peverill would later swear – angels from the realms of glory stood poised to wing their flight.

# The Buddha of Suburbia

## HANIF KUREISHI

ONE DAY, WHEN my father came home from work, he put his briefcase away behind the door and stripped to his vest and pants in the front room. He spread the pink towel with the rip in it on the floor. He got onto his knees – and he was by no means a flexible man – placed his arms beside his head, and kicked himself into the air.

'I must practise,' he said.

'Practise for what, Dad?'

Now he was standing on his head on the pink towel. His stomach sagged. His balls and prick fell forward. The muscles on his arms swelled and he breathed energetically. My grandmother, who was not unkind but no physical radical, came into the room with a cup of tea. She looked at Dad and looked at me.

'Practise, practise, practise,' Dad said.

Grandma raised her grey head and called out immediately. 'Margaret, Margaret, he's doing it again!'

'Leave it, Grandma,' I said. 'Please.'

'What are you, a policeman?' she said. She called out once more. 'Margaret! Just when we're having our tea!'

Soon my mother hurried into the room to see the spectacle. She wore an apron and wiped her hands again and again on a tea towel.

'Oh God, Haroon,' she said to my father. 'Oh God, oh God, oh God. All the front of you's sticking out like that so everyone can see!'

She looked at me violently.

'You encourage him to be like this!'

'No I don't.'

'Why don't you stop him then?'

She sat down and held her head. 'Why can't he be a normal husband?'

My grandmother blew on her tea. 'Don't upset yourself,' she said. 'That's why he's doing it.'

'That's not true,' I said.

My mother's voice rose. 'Pull the curtains someone!'

'It's not necessary, Mum.'

'Do it now!'

I quickly pulled the curtains. We sat there for a while and looked at oblivious upside-down Father. Neither my mother nor my grandmother smiled or said anything. When my father spoke his voice came out squashed and thin. His insides must have got pretty bent up when he did his positions.

'Karim, Karim, read to me from the book.'

I fetched the book from among all his other books on Buddhism, Hinduism, Confucianism and Sufism which he bought at the Oriental bookship in Cecil Court off Charing Cross Road. I squatted down beside him with it open. Now he was breathing in, holding his breath, breathing out and holding his breath. I read – and I was a good reader, fancying myself at sixteen as a potential actor: 'Suryanamaskar revives and maintains a spirit of youthfulness, an asset beyond price. It is wonderful to know that you are ready to face up to life and extract from it all the real joy it has to offer.'

He grunted his approval at each sentence and then opened his eyes, seeking out my mother. But she had her hand over her face. I read on: 'This position also prevents loss of hair and reduces any tendency to greyness.'

That was the coup. Satisfied, my father stood up and put his clothes on. 'I feel better.'

'Have you finished then?' Mother said.

'For today. But I see it as a very regular thing.'

'Oh no,' she groaned.

He softened. 'By the way, Margaret, coming to Mrs Cooper's tonight?'

'No,' she said.

'Oh come on, sweetie. Please. Let's just go out together for once.'

'But it isn't me that Cheryl wants to see,' my mother said. 'It's you. She ignores me. She treats me like muck. I'm not Indian enough for her.'

'You could wear a sari,' he said.

This was my opportunity. 'I'll come with you then, to Cheryl's, if you want me to. I'd planned to go to the chess club but I'll make the effort.'

I said this as innocently as a vicar, not wanting to stymie things by seeming too eager. I find that in life if you're too eager others tend to get less eager. And if you're less eager it tends to make others more eager. So the more eager I am the less eager I seem.

Dad slapped his bare stomach rapidly with both hands. The noise was loud and unattractive. It filled our small house; it drove my grandmother out of the room like bad news.

'Okay,' Dad said to me. 'You get changed, Karim.' He turned to my mother. 'Margaret, Margaret. If only you'd come.'

'I'm not wanted.'

'You're pathetic,' I said hotly.

'Yes, I'm pathetic.'

And I added, having been reading Nietzsche recently: 'You don't matter.'

She sighed, having been reading the Gospel: 'No, I don't matter.'

I charged upstairs to get changed. I could hear my parents talking downstairs. Would he persuade her to come? I hoped not. My father was more cheerful when my mother wasn't around.

It took me a long time to get ready. But at seven o'clock I

came down dressed for Cheryl's. I had on turquoise flared trousers; a blue and white flower-patterned see-through shirt; blue suede boots with Cuban heels, and a scarlet Indian waistcoat with gold stitching around the edges. On my head I had a brown headband. On top of all this I put on my grandmother's fur coat, strapping a belt around my stomach. I was right up to date.

My father waited at the door for me, his hands in his pockets. He had on a black polo-neck sweater, black leather jacket, and grey cords. He looked very handsome. When he saw me he looked agitated.

'You haven't shaved,' he said.

'No. And now there isn't time. I forgot.'

'Well. Next time.'

He could be kind like that. Unlike Mum, he was no big conformist. In the living-room my mother was watching TV and eating a big bag of sweets. Without turning round she said: 'Karim, don't show yourself up. Get changed! You can't go out like that!'

'What about Grandma?' I said.

'What about her?'

'Well . . . she's got blue hair,' I said.

'But she's a woman. And you're not a woman!'

My father and I got out of the house as quickly as we could. At the top of the street we caught a bus. It wasn't far – about four miles to the Coopers'. But my father wouldn't have been able to get there without me. I knew the streets and every bus route and short-cut perfectly. I spent as much time as I could outside the house.

My father had been in Britain since 1947 – twenty-two years – and for eighteen of those years we'd lived in the South London suburbs. But he still stumbled around the place like a new immigrant. He asked people incredible questions like: 'Is Dover in Kent?' I would have thought, as an employee of the British Government, as a Civil Service clerk, he'd just have to know these things. But he didn't. I'd crawl under the table with embarrassment when he halted strangers in the street to ask directions to places that were a hundred yards away in an area he'd lived in for almost two decades. But people weren't repelled by his naivety and women seemed drawn by his innocence; they wanted to wrap their arms around him or something, so lost and boyish he looked at times. Not that he was a complete innocent. When I was small and we'd sit in Lyon's Corner House he'd send me like a message pigeon to an attractive woman at another table and have me announce: 'My daddy wants to give you a kiss.' Looking at him, they were never offended; they were inevitably amused.

So he taught me how to flirt with everyone; but I don't think he'd slept with anyone but my mother while married. I suspected that Mrs Cheryl Cooper – who Dad met at a 'writing for pleasure' class – wanted to chuck her arms around him.

On the way to Mrs Cooper's we stopped off at a pub and had a pint of bitter each. I wasn't used to alcohol and became drunk immediately.

'Your mother upsets me,' Dad said. 'She doesn't join in things. It's only my damn effort keeping this whole family together! No wonder I need to make my mind blank!'

I suggested: 'Why don't you get divorced?'

'Because you wouldn't like it,' he said. 'Otherwise – who knows.'

'I see. It's all up to me then.'

But I knew they wouldn't divorce, even though they fought all the time. It wasn't something that could possibly occur to them. In the suburbs I knew, people rarely dreamed of striking out for happiness. It was all familiarity and endurance. Nothing would change.

The Coopers were better off than us and had a bigger house, with a drive and a garage. Their place stood on its own in the tree-lined road off Beckenham High Street. It had an attic, a garage, a greenhouse, three bedrooms and central heating.

I didn't recognize Mrs Cooper when she greeted us at the door. I thought we'd come to the wrong place. The only thing she had on was a full-length multi-coloured kaftan. Her hair was down, and out, and up, and wild-looking. She could have benefited from my headband. Her eyes she'd darkened with kohl. Her feet were bare, the toes painted green. My mother never painted her fingers or toes.

When the front door was safely shut, Cheryl hugged my father and kissed him all over his face. This was the first time I'd seen him kissed with interest. There was no sign of Mr Cooper. When Cheryl moved, when she turned to me, she was like a kind of human crop-sprayer, puffing out clouds of Eastern-smelling perfume, like some of the hippy girls I went to concerts with at the Round House in Chalk Farm. I was trying to think if Cheryl was the most sophisticated person I'd ever met, or the most pretentious, when she kissed me on the lips. She looked me all over and kept saying: 'Karim, Karim, you look so exotic, so original! It's so you!'

'Thank you, Mrs Cooper. If I'd had more notice I'd have dressed up.'

'With your father's wonderful wit too, I see!' she said.

I looked up and saw that Paul, her son, who was at my school but a year older, was sitting at the top of the stairs, behind the banisters. He was smiling at me. On the way to Cheryl's I'd deliberately excluded him from my mind. I hadn't believed that he would be in, that he would have waited in to see me, that he wouldn't have had something terrifically important to do that evening, like doing a psychedelic painting, playing a noisy gig with his band or making love to his girlfriend at a party.

'Hallo baby,' he said to me, coming downstairs. 'Glad to see you.'

He embraced my father and called him by his first name. What confidence and style Paul had! He followed us into the living-room.

What the fuck was going on?

Cheryl had pushed back the furniture. The Liberty patterned armchairs and Habitat glass-topped tables were up against the bookshelves. The curtains were pulled. Four middle-aged men and four middle-aged women, all white (terribly white), all suburban, sat cross-legged on the floor, eating peanuts and drinking wine. There was some terrible old-fashioned chanting music playing that reminded me of funerals.

'Don't you just love Bach,' Paul said.

'It's not really my bag.'

'Okay. Fair enough. It's not everyone's. I think I've got something that's more your bag upstairs.'

'Where's your dad?'

'He's having a nervous breakdown.'

'Oh.'

'He's gone back to his mother.'

'I see.'

I realized then that in a lot of ways we were just a plain family. Divorces and nervous breakdowns weren't really within our ambit; nervous breakdowns were as exotic to me as New Orleans. I thought of Paul's father in a strait-jacket, perhaps in a padded cell.

Now my father was sitting on the floor talking to some of the people in the room. The talk was of music and books, of people like Dvorak, Krishnamurti and Jung. Looking at them closely I reckoned the men were in advertising or design or something almost artistic like that. I remembered that Paul's father designed advertisements. Whoever these people were, there was a terrific amount of showing-off going on – more in this room than in the whole of the rest of Southern England put together.

At home my father would have roared with laughter at all this hot air, telling my mother how much he hated jumped-up people. But now, in the thick of it, he looked as if he was having the highest time of his whole life. He was leading the discussion, talking quickly and loudly. He talked over other people and kept interrupting them and he wasn't afraid of touching whoever was nearest. I could see the men and women slowly gathering in a circle around him on the floor. I wondered why he saved all the sullenness and resentful grunting for us. Did these people know he'd sit with his back to us, his supper on his knees, staring out at the back garden while we ate unhappily at the table? Did they know he would go a fortnight without speaking to any of us? *typical*

I noticed that a man who was sitting near me turned to the man next to him and indicated my father. Dad was now in full flow about the oneness of the cosmos with a woman who was wearing nothing but a man's shirt and a pair of black tights. The woman kept nodding enthusiastically at Dad.

The man said to his friend: 'Why has Cheryl brought this brown Indian here?'

'To give us a demonstration of the mystic arts.'

'And has he got his camel parked outside?'

'No, he came on a magic carpet!'

I gave the man a mean little kick in the back. Sharply he looked up.

'Sorry,' I said, and touched the palms of my hands together and bowed my head. I could hardly believe it myself, but he did the same back to me.

Paul turned to me. 'Pretentious,' he said.

'What?' I moved closer to him, holding his arm. 'Yes, the sound of one buttock farting.'

'Come to my pad, Karim.'

'Okay, let's go.'

Before we could leave the room, Cheryl came back in and turned off the lights. Over the one remaining lamp she draped a large diaphanous neckscarf. I noticed that her movements had become rather balletic. One by one people fell silent. Cheryl looked down and around at everyone, smiling like mad.

'So why don't we relax?' she said. Three or four of them nodded their agreement. Someone said: 'So why don't we?'

'Yes, yes,' someone else said. This person then flapped his hands like loose gloves; he opened his mouth as wide as he could and thrust his tongue out.

Cheryl turned to my father and waved her arm at him.

'My good and deep friend Haroon here, he will show us the way. The Path.'

'Oh Christ,' I whispered to Paul, thinking how my father couldn't even find his way to Beckenham. 'Christ Almighty.'

'Watch, watch,' Paul said.

My father stood up and Cheryl sat down. Now Dad moved easily amongst the sitting people. They looked keenly and expectantly at Dad, though two men glanced at each other as if they wanted to laugh. Dad spoke slowly and with confidence, as if he knew for sure he had all their attention and they'd do everything he asked. I was sure he had never done anything like this before. He was going to wing it.

'The things that are going to happen to you this evening are going to do you a lot of good. They may even change you a little. But there is one thing you must not do. You must not resist. If you resist it will be hopeless. If you resist it will be like trying to drive a car with the brakes on.'

He paused. They didn't take their eyes off him.

'We'll do some floor work. Please sit with your legs apart.'

They parted their legs.

'Raise your arms.'

They raised their arms.

'Now, breathing out, stretch down to your right foot.'

They all stretched out for their right foot, the women being more flexible and graceful than the men. They came up, looking a little flushed and distracted.

'Down to your left foot! And hold it!'

After five or six basic positions which I recognized from the yoga book Dad had got out of the library, he had them lying on their backs. Obviously unused to exercise, they were glad to be resting. To his soft commands they were relaxing their fingers one by one, then their wrists, their toes, their ankles, their foreheads, their scalps. They were making the low 'Om' sound, their stomachs vibrating. They were imagining beaches, gardens and palm trees. They were taking a psychic holiday. Even I felt weak.

Meanwhile Dad had removed his shirt and vest, shoes and socks. He padded around the circle of dreamers, lifting an arm here, a leg there, testing them for tension. Cheryl, lying there on her back, was watching my father with one eye open. When he walked past she lightly touched his foot with her hand. She pinched his big toe. My mother was eating sweets in front of the TV.

I hissed to Paul: 'Let's get out of here before we're hypnotized like these fucking idiots.'

'Okay. But isn't it fascinating?'

'Absolutely unique.'

Paul and I climbed the ladder to the attic where he had the whole huge space to himself. It stretched out across the top of the house. He'd painted Zen scripts, mandalas and hippy heads on the sloping walls and low ceiling. His drum-kit stood in the centre of the floor. Big cushions were flung about.

'Heard anything good lately?'

'Yeah,' I said. After the calm silence of the living-room our voices sounded absurdly loud and strained. 'The new Stones' album. *Get yer yas ya's out* it's called. I played it at the school music society today and people threw off their jackets and ties and danced. I was on top of my desk! You should have been there.'

I knew immediately that I'd been crude. Paul threw his hair back.

'On top of your desk? I think I'd better play you something really good, Karim.'

So he put on a record by the Pink Floyd called *Ummagumma*. While I forced myself to listen he sat opposite me cross-legged and rolled a joint.

'Your father. He's the best. He's wise. D'you do that stuff every morning?'

I looked at him. I nodded. A nod can't be a lie.

'And chanting too?' he asked.

'Chanting? No, not chanting every day. At least not in the morning.'

I thought of the morning in our place: the toast on fire; me frantically conjugating French verbs for my first class; my father running around the house, his face covered in shaving-cream, looking for his train pass; my sister and I wrestling over the newspaper; my mother complaining about having to go to work in the shoe shop.

Paul handed me the joint. I pulled on it and handed it back. I'd never taken drugs before. I was so excited and dizzy I stood up immediately.

'What are you doing?'

'I have to go to the bathroom.'

'Now?'

'Yes, yes!'

I flew down the attic ladder. In the Coopers' bathroom there were framed theatre posters for Genet plays. There were bamboo and parchment Zen scrolls with flamboyant ink writing on them. There was a bidet. As I sat taking it all in, I realized suddenly and with excitement I wanted all my life to be lived this intensely: mysticism, alcohol, sexual promise, clever people and drugs. I hadn't come upon it all like this before, but now I wanted nothing else.

And Paul? Paul had the longest hair in the school. Parted in the centre, it curtained his face and fell straight down his back. He was a painter, a poet, a musician, as well as the school rebel. He had a motorbike and a girlfriend with Pre-Raphaelite hair. To me Paul was a god. But my love for him was unusual: it was not generous. I admired him more than anyone but I didn't wish him well. It was that I preferred him to me: I wanted to be him. I wanted his talents, his skills, his face, his taste. I wanted to wake up with them all transferred to me.

When I'd finished in the bathroom I stood in the hall. The whole house seemed to be silent, though from the attic came the distant sound of 'A Saucerful of Secrets'. Someone in the house was burning incense. I crept down the stairs to the ground floor. The living-room door was open. I peered round it into the dim room. The advertising men and their wives were sitting up, cross-legged, straight-backed, their faces open. They breathed deeply and regularly. Neither Cheryl nor my father was in the room.

I left the hypnotized Buddhas and went through the house and into the kitchen. The back door was wide open. I stepped outside into the darkness. It was a warm evening; the moon was full. I might have guessed.

I got down on my knees. I knew it was the thing to do – I'd gone intuitive since my dad's display. I crawled across the patio. They must have recently had a barbecue since razor-sharp lumps of charcoal stuck into my knees, but people have suffered worse. I reached the edge of the lawn. I could see vaguely that in the centre of the lawn there was a garden bench. As I moved closer there was enough light from the moon and kitchen window for me to see that Cheryl was on the bench with her kaftan up around her neck. If I strained I could see her chest. And I did strain. I strained until my eyeballs went dry in their sockets. Eventually I knew I was right. Cheryl had only one breast. Where the other usually was, there was nothing. She was flat, one-sided.

Beneath all this and virtually hidden from me was my father. I knew it was Dad because he was crying out, 'Oh my God, oh my God, oh my God,' across the Beckenham gardens with little concern for the neighbours. Was I conceived like this, I wondered, in the suburban night air, to the wailing of Christian curses from the mouth of a Muslim masquerading as a Buddhist?

Suddenly Cheryl slapped her hand over my father's mouth. This was a little peremptory, I thought, though I refrained from objecting. But my God, Cheryl could bounce! Head back, eyes to stars, kicking up from the grass like a footballer, her hair flew. But what of the crushing weight on my father's backside? Surely the impress of the thrusting bench would remain for days burnt into his poor buttocks, like grill marks on a steak? Shouldn't I rescue him? This could not be pleasure.

Then Cheryl released her hand from his mouth and he started to laugh and laugh. It was the laugh of someone I didn't know. It was pleasure all right.

I rapidly crawled away, wondering if Cheryl was watching my wriggling rear. In her kitchen I poured myself a glass of whisky and threw it down my throat.

Paul was lying on his back on the attic floor. I took off my boots and lay down beside him. He passed me the joint he was smoking.

'So Paul. Everything all right?'

'You're all right, Karim. You're terrific.'

'Am I?'

I was encouraged and uplifted by his words.

'But listen,' he said. 'You're not to take this badly.'

'No, never.'

'You've got to wear less.'

'Wear less, Paul?'

'Dress less. Yes.' He got up onto one elbow and concentrated on me. I loved his beautiful mouth being this close. 'Levi's, I suggest, with an open-necked shirt, maybe in pink or purple, and a thick brown belt. Forget the headband.'

'Forget the headband?'

'Yeah.'

I ripped my headband off and tossed it across the floor.

'For your mum,' I said.

He laughed. 'You see, Karim, you tend to look a little like a pearly queen in that gear.'

'A pearly queen? I see.'

I, who only wanted to be like him, as clever, as artistic, as attractive in every way, tattooed his words on my brain. Levi's, with an open-necked shirt, maybe in purple or pink. I would never go out in anything else for the rest of my life.

While I contemplated myself and my entire wardrobe with absolute loathing and wished to urinate on the lot, Paul lay there massively calm with his eyes closed. Everyone in the damn house but me was practically in heaven. And the dope was refusing to fly me anywhere.

When I put my hand on Paul's thigh he made no response. I rested it there for a few minutes until sweat broke out on the ends of my fingers. Then I moved my hand up a couple of inches. His eyes remained closed. But in his jeans he was growing, the dirty bastard. I grew confident. I became insane. I dashed for his belt, for his fly, for his cock, and I took him out to air. I held him without moving my hand for several hours, thinking of nothing but whether I should go on, go back or remain. But then he twitched himself. A sign! He was alive too! Whenever I stopped moving he twitched himself. Through such human electricity we understood each other.

'Where are you, Paul?' I said, moving to kiss him. He avoided my lips. He turned his head to one side.

'Do you dig this?' I asked.

'Me?' he said. 'But you know me, Karim. Try anything once.'

'Can't you . . . won't you try to kiss me then?'

He evaded my lips.

When he came, it was, I swear, one of the great moments of my earlyish life. There was dancing in my streets. My flags flew, my trumpets blew!

I was licking my fingers and thinking of where I could possibly buy a pink shirt when I heard a sound that was not the Pink Floyd. I turned sharply and looked across the attic to see Dad's flaming eyes, nose, neck, shoulders, chest and fat stomach hiking itself up through the square hole in the floor. Paul quickly put himself away. I wiped my mouth with my waistcoat and leapt up, sticking my hands behind my back like Prince Philip. My father rushed over, followed, I was pleased to see, by smiling Cheryl. Dad looked from Paul to me and back again. Cheryl sniffed the air.

'You naughty boys,' she said.

Paul said lazily: 'What, Mum?'

'Smoking drugs,' she said.

Cheryl said it was time for her to drive us home. In the car she tried to talk about the evening and how brilliant Dad had been, but he was in a gloomy mood by now, he'd lost all his mystical qualities and said nothing except: 'In my opinion, children are just a big pain in the arse.'

When we arrived outside the house we got out of the car and I said goodnight to Cheryl and went in. From the porch I could see Cheryl trying to kiss Dad while he was trying to shake her hand. She lunged her pursed lips at him two or three times. Eventually she got the message and swaggered off back to her car.

The house was dark and quiet when we crept in, exhausted. Dad had to get up at six-thirty to go to work and I had my paper round. When we were in the hall he raised his fist to punch me out. I grabbed him. He was much drunker than I was.

'Shhh . . . Dad!'

'What the hell were you doing?'

'What?'

'I saw you, Karim! Oh my God, you're a bloody shitter! A shitter! A bum-banger! A dirt-boxer! My own son! How can it be?'

He jumped up and down as if he'd just heard the whole house had been burnt to the ground. I didn't know what to do. So I started to imitate the voice he'd used earlier with the advertisers and with Cheryl.

'Relax, Dad. Relax your whole body from your fingers to your toes and send your mind to a quiet garden somewhere, where there are roses and sandcastles –'

'I'll send *you* to a fucking garden! I'll send you to a fucking doctor, you fucking bum-banger!'

He really was mad and he was at full volume. I had to stop him before we had the neighbours round.

'But I saw you, Dad,' I whispered.

'You saw nothing!'

'I saw you.' Then I added significantly: 'I saw everything.'

'Don't be so stupid.'

But he looked at me with a shadow of worry on his face.

'At least . . .' I said.

'At least what? What?'

'At least. At least our mother has both breasts.'

'What? Oh yes. All right. I understand. I get you.'

He went into the toilet without shutting the door and started to vomit. I went in behind him and rubbed his back as he threw up.

'It's all right, it's all right,' I said as kindly as I could whilst he cried and heaved, heaved and cried, splattering his shoes and turn-ups, the floor and walls, with his turmoil.

'I'll never mention tonight again,' I said. 'And nor will you.'

He nodded his head and pressed it against the cool rim of the toilet.

'Why did you bring him home like this?' said my mother, who stood behind us in her dressing gown. It was so long it almost touched the floor. It made her look square.

'Couldn't you have looked after him?' She kept plucking at my arm. 'I was looking out of the window and waiting for you for hours.'

My father eventually stood up straight and pushed past us.

'Make up a bed for me in the front room,' Mum said. 'I can't sleep next to that man.'

When I'd made up the bed for her and she'd got into it – and it was far too narrow and short for her – I told her something. I told her that whatever happened she was to understand one thing, one thing that I'd decided.

'What?' she said.

'I'll never be getting married. Okay?'

'I don't blame you,' she said, turning over. 'I don't blame you at all.'

# Vigil

## JIM MANGNALL

I WAS SHOWN, for a moment, into a room in deep shadow and vaguely realized that two children were asleep there. Their faces were serene but beneath the long white coverlet a small foot twitched in a dream. Outside, a bird came to the window sill, its wings swishing suddenly out of the grey sky, and the new year began as I tip-toed out, leaving them under their quilt of snow, smiling at their dreams.

I forget the number of the year that began with the bird and the children. I even forget which proud father it was that softly opened the door for me to see. It must have been a close friend – an old friend, even older now, with children grown and gone.

Happy New Year! The words said so many times in the houses of the past. Houses where a big fire crackled in the grate, all the old faces illuminated and memories queuing up outside in the hall. Houses where the edges of the tables and the arms of the chairs were flecked with flame and great bookcases stood with their keys still in their locks, and the books sleeping mysteriously on their wooden shelves, dusty in spite of the glass.

Those rooms are empty now. The memories have slipped out of the door and there seems little point to old friends, hallways or book-case keys. Yet I remembered the closed eyes of those children and the flutter of the bird's wings. You would think it would be easy to trace an old friend with two children. To identify him and his house, to pin down the year and the moment, but it is impossible. Yet I still try.

The children are sleeping. Their breathing is so soft that you hear nothing. On the bedside table there is a Christmas angel and a roundabout. The curtains are not drawn at the window and just before the bird comes, a white snowflake drifts against the pane and is instantly transformed into a crown of glass.

Could it have been the beginning of 1955? In the blue evenings of the previous summer I still had feelings. I felt a freshness in my step. I let the wind buffet my head. I spoke little and thought less and I wandered alone with a kind of love inside me. Yes, it could have been 1955.

One day, hiding my amorous heart under a severe suit, I passed a yellow shop, a shop that today would be called a boutique, and saw for the first time, her mouth. I went inside and actually spoke to her, my dark sleeve next to the pale skin of her arm and all around us a fence of peach-coloured skirts and long, unbuttoned dresses.

Some men have an urge to travel great distances. That summer my whole life was lived within walking distance of that small shop. Sometimes we sat in a little square of trees and flowers and watched strangers pass, sweating in the heat, carrying their morning papers and their shopping bags. Sometimes, as August arrived, we would walk between café tables, hand in hand, listening to the clink of coffee cups and when autumn came, and with it those beautiful, serious evenings, we did everything but dream of winter.

But no, it couldn't have been the dawn of 1955. Otherwise she would have been with me when I was permitted to look into that room, and she was noticeably absent.

That year began badly. For eight days I uncorked bottles, fell down in the street, found myself with table legs towering over me. I saw a girl in an enormous feathered head-dress open her big green mouth and suck the sunlight from the room. I heard a clock and smelled cooking. My hands trembled. The plates were very close to me – too close. I wanted to lie down again. No, that was not the year.

My friend quietly opened the door and indicated with his head that I should step inside. There were the children sleeping. The angel and the roundabout. The snowflake. The bird was about to fly to the window sill and I can see my friend's hand on the door knob but not his face.

Perhaps I am approaching this from the wrong angle. Perhaps I should try to remember the wife of my elusive friend, the mother of the two children. She had strong brown hands, tanned by the summer. She took her coffee black. She had charming knees and rolled her own cigarettes. I watched those hands arrange nectarines in a blue bowl and pour whisky into heavy glasses. I watched her in the forest as well as in the kitchen. Her hands were always precise, even when she shifted gear, yet for all I observed her, I'm afraid that sometimes I didn't see the ring on her finger. Could those sleeping children have been her children? It seems unreasonable.

It was New Year's Eve. The bedroom door was white. Earlier I had been in town, in streets full of strangers, but I had made it back to my friend's house for the party. I remember that it was cold and I wore no overcoat. It was the third room along the landing and I had in my hand a long drink which felt awkward and out of place as I stood at the foot of the bed.

At four in the morning the party was over. Guests were putting on their overcoats. As they left in twos, always in twos, and the front door was opened, I could see that the snow had fallen heavily. Everyone was tired but happy and a little drunk. I remained after the last guest had gone and was given the second bedroom along the landing. I first made sure that no bird was about to fly to my window sill and then I drew the curtains and lay down but did not sleep. I lay, as it were, in the bosom of a family. My friend and his wife on the other side of the bright wallpaper on my right; their children through the wall where the big octagonal mirror hung on my left. The snow was deep. A soft music seemed to fill the house and I lay, still as a corpse, while the colours of my life danced about the isolated bedroom. The music was distant and behind me and I moved on a great avenue lined on either side with old friends. I saw things in the past which I had forgotten. I saw things that were to come. For a moment I made sense out of the chaos and then, as the whole house waited expectantly, I fell stupidly asleep.

I remember all this so clearly but for some reason the incident has been extracted from the flow of time. I have a disturbing feeling that if I was finally to conjure up the face of my friend, his features would not fit the circumstances. His would not be the face that should have lain next to the woman in the room beyond the wallpaper. And the children through the mirror would not be his children but two sleeping strangers.

When it comes, that is, when a man's autumn comes, he remembers forgotten things. Small sadnesses, brief pleasures and with the remembering comes the desire to make alterations, corrections. A futile desire.

I must sit down for a moment and reconstruct the vision from the viewpoint of the children. It was New Year's Eve. There was the town, the road, the garden, their house in the garden, their room in the house, and before they fell asleep and their lives stopped, they had known the comfortable presence of a man and a woman. Father and mother. More secure than old friends. More permanent than Christmas. They would not have been aware of the party, which began late, or of my arrival which was even later. They closed their eyes on the black wooden ball of the world and stepped out onto a sandy beach inside a musical house and they counted to a hundred before coming to find me. But they never found me. Not until I was old and they were no longer children.

It is a morning in some October and there is a taste of ashes in the air. Brown dogs scamper in the park and I am old. It is impossible to express the dullness of days surrounded by grey furniture but at night I have discovered a special window, one window and a string of stars. And here I sit trying to see faces and calculate years. It is a game I play to avoid admitting to myself that there never was an old friend; that the doors that opened and closed were my responsibility alone.

When the stars are obscured and the window becomes a mirror, the face I see is not the one I remember, the one that I have searched for. That one has been lost along with the woman and the children. Frozen in an unnameable year behind a bedroom door.

# Remission

## ADAM MARS-JONES

*Yoghurt.* YOGHURT TAUGHT me something yesterday. I was eating a yoghurt, not one I'd bought, something one of the lovers picked up for me, a really creamy one with a crust of fat, not at all my usual style of yoghurt. Maybe it was the creaminess, or maybe it was the absurd clashing of the fruits (apricot and mango, of all combinations), but I could really taste it; first thing I've really tasted in months. The fruit was only there in shreds, but there was enough juice in those shreds, juice or sugar or something, electricity for all I know, to give my mouth the feel of something vivid. And I thought – first thinking I've done in months, too, I dare say – I thought, illness is a failure, that's obvious. You don't have to be well to know that. But what is it a failure of? And at that moment, the answer seemed to be: imagination. It seemed to me then, reeling as I was from the impact of the fruit in the yoghurt, that with a little effort, with a little imagination, I could taste anything, take pleasure in anything.

The yoghurt didn't stay down, of course; it wasn't such a new beginning as all that. But what it had to teach me it taught me on the way down; on the way up it had nothing to say. And even that was a lesson of sorts. It was no more unpleasant to vomit that yoghurt than it was to throw up my usual watery

119

potlet. Its curds were no viler as they rose in my throat. I suppose I've been following a policy of appeasement with my stomach, and that's always a mistake. I've been behaving as if my insides were just being temperamental, and if I could find some perfectly inoffensive food for them, they would do the decent thing and hang on to it. And it just isn't so. I might as well eat what has a chance of giving me pleasure. My stomach will lob it up indifferently.

At the end of all that, after I had vomited, I was – I imagine – just fractionally weaker than when I had started. I had used some energy (vomiting is hard physical work) and I hadn't managed to get any nourishment. Trying to break down the yoghurt had been, as it turned out, a costly waste of gastric juice. But in spite of that, I had had three distinct phases of pleasure – one, the taste of the yoghurt itself; two, the long, incredulous moment when it seemed that it would stay down; three, the euphoria, after it came up, of having expelled poison, of knowing it wouldn't be fizzing in my guts for the rest of the day – and only one phase of unpleasantness when it was actually coming up. In some strange way it seemed that I was ahead on the day's transactions. That's when I thought of making this tape.

It's only a cheap little secretarial Sony, this machine, but it's got everything I need. The controls are very simple; you don't even have to look at them. When things get bad, I can curl up with it under the bedclothes, a muttering foetus that can't get comfortable. [    ] If I get a coughing fit, I can edit it out, like that, by using the pause button. I've just got the two tapes, so I can change them over very easily, with the minimum of fumbling around.

There's the shits-and-vomits tape, which I'll use when I'm making the same old complaints, when I'm sicking up the same old record of bodily disasters. I'm never going to play it back. I'll just record on top of it, same old rant anyway. It's not for listening to, just for getting out of my system.

This tape is different. I've written the word *remission* on the spine of the cassette, and that's what I mean to concentrate on, every little quantum of forgiveness I can find in my body or my circumstances. I'll play it back eventually, but I'll wait as long as I can, so that I have a real hoard of positive moments to refresh myself with.

It's a bit odd, using the same channel to get rid of some experiences and intensify others. But I don't have to look further than my underpants to remember a similar arrangement.

And if there's a medical breakthrough soon, very soon – in the next twenty minutes, say – then I may not have to go back to the shits-and-vomits tape at all, just steam on with my remission. But I'll still go on thinking *remission*, however long it lasts: I'll never say *cure*. I can't be doing with that word. It makes everything impossible. It's a real obstacle to getting on with things.

What else fits the requirements for the remission tape? *The video*. Sleep is sweeter than it ever was, and I resent time wasted on anything else. But my video has taken all the angst out of insomnia. I sleep quite a lot in the day, so I'm likely to wake up in the middle of the night, quite suddenly, as if there was someone flashing a torch an inch from my eyes. Television will have packed up hours before, the sleepy-head announcer yawning after the late film (it's past midnight, imagine!), wishing all the other sleepy-heads out there good-night. There's a programme on before close-down that has the nerve to call itself *Night Thoughts*. It's on at different times depending on the schedule, but always before one. *Night Thoughts* indeed! Can you beat it? The tube trains are hardly tucked up in their sheds for the night, and there's a lot of thinking to be done before morning, unless you have a video.

I bought the video quite a while ago, and it was one of those bits of self-indulgence that turn out to be good resolutions in disguise (having said that, I can't think of any others). I thought I'd turn into an addict, and I certainly taped a lot of programmes, but I never got round to watching them. I'd just buy more tapes as they got filled up. I never got into the habit of labelling the cassettes, so now I never know what I'm watching. I watch episodes of *Hill Street Blues* from two different series, and the only way I can tell them apart is by seeing whether Henry Goldbloom has a moustache or not. Promotions and romances don't help me much with the chronology, but with Henry's moustache I know where I am. I always did like moustaches. On top of that, Henry Goldbloom is always talking suicides down from their high places, reasoning with them through his megaphone of good intentions, and I suppose that's bound to strike some sort of chord.

The great thing about the video, of course, is that I can play things as fast or as slowly as I want. The other night I watched an old episode of *The Avengers*, in which John Steed was meant to dispose of a bomb by lobbing it into the bell of a euphonium. The detonation made the euphonium uncoil, like one of those irritating party-blowers. Except that the actor was too clumsy, or too drunk, to throw the bomb properly, and it rolled under a chair. The euphonium blew up all the same, of course, but if you rewind the video and play the sequence again you can see that it had no reason to. I found the whole thing extravagantly amusing, the other night, and I played it again and again, perhaps because it was one of the few things I'd come across in some time that was in no way a metaphor of my present condition.

That can't be right. Surely I can do better than that. With the explosion, all the instrument's brass knitting unravels. What remains on the carpet is revealed as an intestine, tarnished and smoking. Good. Do better. What *The Avengers* was telling me, in an episode made around the time of my puberty, is that euphoniums end up unrolled and in ruins, even if they don't take a bomb in the bell. That's just what happens, with euphoniums. Good thought. Hang on to that.

Change the subject. *The lovers.* I have two lovers at the moment. *Lovers* is the wrong word, but then it always is. All I can say is, these two do everything for me a lover could do, and that's pretty amazing. We treat each other as if we had a history of sex, but that isn't the intimacy that binds us. I've had half-lovers before, even three-quarters lovers, once or twice, but these two are somehow fully loving towards me, and that's worth putting down on this privileged spool of tape (chrome dioxide for a longer life).[

]*Dead parents.* Anyone whose doctors are not cheerful should try as a first step not to have parents alive. I'm not being unduly oriental here; it's not that I think it's disrespectful in some way to turn in while your parents are still around and about. But I'm sure it confuses things. There's a touch of the bailiff about parents, I've always thought, as if they were waiting for you to fall behind with the payments on your life, so they could repossess it. What a terrible thing to say.

I'm not always so cynical, but I try. Anyway, I'm sure it makes it worse, having your parents around. Not my problem. Having your parents die is unpleasant in its own right of course, and not only in the expected ways. Example: my father had this terrible rightness about him. From his hospital bed he corrected the doctors' pronunciation and finished their sentences for them. I always hated that. It makes me think, now, how robust he was in his dying, how reliable his vitality was right up to the moment that it fell away from him. But the point is that while he was alive, I didn't realize that I have a scarcely less terrible rightness myself, though everyone I've known must have noticed it. I finish people's sentences for them too – I just interrupt them later on in their flow – so I've always fooled myself I'm a good listener. And compared to my Dad, I *am* a good listener, but the people I've shut up over the years didn't know that.

The lovers are going to get a bit of a shock, when I get some strength back and start bossing them about. I think they deserve an entry of their own, while their patience has yet to be tested, while my character is still blurred by my powerlessness.

*The lovers.* I had a lover, of a sort, when I was diagnosed, but I soon got rid of him. I'd already placed a small ad which defined me as a Lonely Heart, which was my way of serving notice to myself that I was going to serve notice on him, and then I was diagnosed. I thought at once, that settles it (that was my first thought), I've got to get rid of him, and I did. He thought his health made him necessary to me, and I had hell's own job convincing him it made him even more of a nuisance than he was before, more of a menace, more of a pest. I couldn't carry him and illness too.

So when the magazine forwarded the replies to my ad, everything had changed, and they were replying to someone who didn't exist any more. There were only two replies, perhaps because I was never the world's most beautiful man, and my advert wasn't exactly raging with self-esteem. But I thought they deserved an explanation, and I arranged to meet them, both of them together so I didn't need to repeat myself.

By treating these strangers well after behaving so badly to someone who thought he was close to me, I think I was exercising in some final way the prerogatives of vigour. That's how I've worked it out since then. It was a choosing spree, and now my choices are made.

All the same: it wasn't as easy as I thought. I felt a terrible lurch when I started talking, and I had something like an anxiety attack. Perhaps it was simply grief for the person who had placed the ad and wasn't around any more. It's hard to be sure what it is you're having when you know your body is scheduled to fail you piecemeal – and your mind doesn't have a lot to look forward to, come to that – and you experience a sensation of intense heat and horror. Whether it was only an anxiety attack or what, I wasn't able to stay as long as I'd meant to, and I stumbled out while their drinks were still half finished. And a couple of hours later they phoned, the two of them, to ask how I was, and to say they'd like to help me in any way they could, if I'd let them.

If I try, knowing them as well as I do now, I can probably reconstruct the conversation that led up to their phone call. But I don't care to analyse something that has become so necessary to me. I answered. They offered. I accepted. We've developed some useful routines.

Diagnosis broke me up, the way a plough breaks earth, and all the recent growth, rooted so lightly, was pulled right up. But I was left all ready for seeding. When they phoned – it was Rory actually holding the phone and doing the talking – I remember I said, 'Let's get one thing straight. I have never depended on the kindness of strangers.' Then I had to break it to them that what I was saying was Yes.

*The lovers.* Leo and Rory, my lovers, my lions. They pay

their visits separately; I know they meet up at least once a week to arrange their timetables. They used to visit in the day, but now they know that day isn't really the time they're most useful. They used to be great soup-merchants, the pair of them, but they soon got sick of eating their own soups. Now Rory helps me with housing benefit, which is much more important. Leo has a car, and Rory doesn't, so it's Leo who stays the night, assuming he's free, when I have a clinic appointment in the morning. If it's Rory keeping me company, we take a taxi.

The taxi costs money, of course, but I prefer Rory's company at the clinic. Leo gets very tense, and I more or less have to look after him. Rory is different. I've been particularly unwell for a few weeks, and the hospital wanted a stool sample. That's not easy when your stools move at a hundred miles an hour, like mine do at the moment. With a straight face they gave me a little pot with a screw top, as if what they wanted collecting was a butterfly and not a bowel movement. Rory wasn't with me that day. Anyway, I tried. Day after day I'd go to the lavatory with my little pot, but I was never quick enough. It was as frustrating as my train-spotting days as a boy, when I would stand by the main line in the early morning mist as the express thundered by, trying to read the number on the engine. Anyway, I got my sample at last, and took it along. After a week, I went back for the results, and they told me the sample had leaked and couldn't be used for analysis. They hadn't phoned me, of course, to say so. Didn't want to depress me, I dare say. So they gave me another pot and sent me back home again, to wait for the express.

These grumbles shouldn't be on this tape at all – they're classic shits-and-vomits stuff – but it all leads to Rory and why he's good to have around. When I'd got my second sample to the hospital and they'd analysed it at last, the doctor prescribed Dioralyte, which she said I have to take every time I have a loose bowel motion. She added, 'It comes in three flavours, avoid the pineapple,' and I could catch Rory's eye and know that he was feeling the same tickle of amusement at her phrasing. The doctor pinched the skin of my arm to see how

125

dehydrated I was, and we both watched the little swag of raised flesh she left, which took a good long time to fade. If they'd told me about Dioralyte earlier on, of course, I wouldn't be dehydrated in the first place, but you can get it from the chemist even without a prescription, so it's not the sort of thing that holds a highly trained person's attention.

Or she can be explaining about *cryptospiridion*, the guest in my gut, and be saying, 'It produces nausea in the upper tract and diarrhoea in the lower, you see, because the whole intestine is implicated.' I can look at Rory and know he's thinking what I'm thinking: *Implicated? It's up to its bloody neck.* Leo would just sit there squirming, willing her to change the subject and talk about something nice.

I wish I'd had Rory with me when the doctor – the first doctor – asked me his three little questions. Did I receive anal intercourse? On occasion I did. He made a note. Had I visited Central Africa? On occasion I had. He made another note. Had I received blood there, by any chance? I seemed to remember something of the sort, when I was weak and confused from hepatitis. As I came out with the last of my answers, I could see the doctor's lips framing a word that looked like 'Bingo', and it would have been handy having Rory's eyes there for mine to meet.

Not that Rory's perfect. When we first heard about *crypto*, he and I, when she first mentioned the name, he blurted out, 'Oh dear, that's a stubborn one, isn't it?' I couldn't resist saying, 'Thanks a bunch, that's all I need,' just to see him flinch, though it really doesn't make any difference to me. In fact I'm glad he knows what he's about, if he does, so I don't have to worry about him the way I worry about Leo.

It's at night that Leo comes into his own, and not because he sleeps in the buff. He has a beguiling little body and all that, hairless and pale-skinned, but it's really only memory that tells me so. I let him sleep on the side of the bed away from the window, otherwise he thinks he won't sleep. It doesn't bother me which side of the bed I'm on, but with Rory I pretend I have a preference for lying away from the window. That way I know who it is that's staying over, even when I'm half asleep, just by our positions, just by feeling which side the warmth's coming from.

I couldn't really be in any doubt, anyway. Leo may wear no night-clothes, but he keeps to his side of the bed, and he turns his back on me – slowly, quietly, as if I'll be offended – when he's going to sleep. Rory sleeps in a night-shirt, but all the same he hugs me and holds me to him, which is all very nice. Just as he's dropping off to sleep, he's been known to stroke my nipple absent-mindedly with his thumb, but my nipple, quite unlike itself, inverts instead of stiffening.

There can't be much doubt in their minds about who they're sleeping with, that's for sure. The guest in my gut, the gatecrasher in my gut, sends out smells beneath the duvet. And when I have my sweats, I can't think it's pleasant for them. The sheets spread my wetness pretty widely.

I cheat them both, I suppose, by sleeping so much in the day. But it makes such a difference having a lover installed and snoring if I'm not doing much sleeping at night. And Leo is perfect, regularly breathing, just the minimal presence I need. Leo's snoring is my night-light. Sleep works on him like a humane killer, stunning him before it bleeds the consciousness out of him. If he stays up too late, he slurs his words, and then starts to doze with his eyes open, and I expect he's replying to my conversation in his head, and doesn't realize he's making no sound.

In the morning it works the other way round. He opens his eyes when I bring him a cup of tea, but it's a minute or two before he can properly hold the cup. Till then he blinks, yawns, changes position, groans and scrabbles at his hair. I know he's embarrassed that I bring him tea in the morning, but I'm solidly grateful that he sleeps so soundly, and I'll reward him in any way I can, even if it involves effort.

Rory is a much more partial sleeper, and when I get up he often joins me in front of the video. Or he'll go to the kitchen and mix up some Complan, with bananas and honey, the way I 'like' it, the way I can sometimes even tolerate it.

As he pads in, Rory asks me which series we're in, that is are we escaping to 1982 or 1984? Does Henry Goldbloom have a moustache?

I tell him what year it is in the violently reassuring world of *Hill Street Blues*. Sometimes Rory seems to be doing a Henry Goldbloom himself, but all it means is that he's skipping shaving for a day or two. He gets rid of the growth before it has a real prospect of changing the balance of his face. It's a shame, he's got a great thick growth of hair right up his neck – what we used to call a poor man's cravat – so he actually looks a little odd clean-shaven.

It's wonderful of him to keep me company, I know, but I wish he'd go back to bed. Sometimes I put on a yawning routine, and we both go back to bed again, then I sneak out and go back to the video. It's not him I mind, it's the company he brings with him. If I can slide out of bed without waking him, I can get half an hour uninterrupted in front of the video. But when he gets up, and especially when he starts moving with a sort of muffled purposefulness round the kitchen, a gnawing and a churning wake up too. The gnawing is hunger and the churning is nausea, and wouldn't you know it, the gnawing is exactly in the middle of the churning, so there's no way I can get to it. So what with Rory and the Complan and the gnawing and the churning, it gets to be too much of a huddle round the video, and my view of the screen gets blocked off.

*Lower levels of illness.* I'm supposed to have mellowed: that seems to be the general verdict. I don't believe a word of it, myself. What really happens is different. There's an awkward interval, when you're ill but not yet conditioned by illness. You're far enough down to be spending all your time below ground, but every now and then you come across shafts of something very like daylight. That makes you impatient and hard to deal with. Things get easier, for other people at least, when you don't have moments of real vitality to show up the false. By now it's second nature for me to follow the cues I get from Leo and from Rory, and not to hang around waiting for my own spontaneity. Only if that draining away of impulse is mellowing can I take credit for it.

The new, eroded me – but for form's sake we'll say *mellow* – the new mellow me has learned to put up with a lot of goodness from people lately. I had to get Rory to pay for this tape recorder, for one thing, and for everything I needed for quite a while. I could have given him cheques, of course; all it would have cost was a little embarrassment if I'd needed help writing them. But he didn't mind waiting for his money. I have this memory thing, you see. I have trouble remembering how to spell, particularly the last part of words for some reason. The words are all there, but I can't seem to spell them. That's what makes this recorder such a good idea. But it also means I can't remember the code number for my cashcard. I hadn't written it down, so I couldn't tell it to Rory. If I'd been up to it, I would have gone to the cashpoint myself, just to see if there was still some memory in my fingertips when I stood in front of the machine. As it was, Rory went for me. I told him he could take his revenge for every time the machine has been out of money on a Saturday night, or swallowed his card without provocation. I told him to mash the keys just as hard as he liked, all three times the machine gave him a chance of getting the number right. Then the card was swallowed up, and my bank sent me a replacement, and by the next post the new number for it. This time I gave the number to Rory to look after.

He's earned my patience. He tries to get me to lie down when I eat, as if that was going to help me hang on to my food, when all it means is more trouble being tidy when I throw up, but I forgive him for that. I know he means well even when he mixes me up some Dioralyte the moment I've had my *loose motion*, though I'm quite capable of throwing up the Dioralyte on the spot, before it's even properly gone down, just to make it clear that my system discriminates against digestion impartially, from both ends of the process.

These days I keep my mouth shut when Rory talks about diabetes. His dad is diabetic, but so what? When Rory talks about it I get rather too clearly the feeling he's trying to teach me something. He tells me diabetes used to be a fatal illness, and that insulin is the crudest sort of treatment you could imagine: just a matter of smashing up bits of animals and injecting them into you, but that's enough to change everything. I want to say, wasn't there a film about the heartbreak of diabetes in that season they had on the box, just recently, of socially concerned American dramas (made for TV, naturally)? I'm sure I taped some of those. Instead I listen to what Rory has to say about his father. Before too long I'll ask Rory if he thinks there might be something of the same sort coming my way, some sort of vinegar-and-brown-paper job, some way of jury-rigging the body, just to show him I've been listening.

Eroded as I am into mellowness, I've even learned to have mercy on Leo. We were in bed the other night, but for once he wasn't sleeping, for the very good reason that every time I lay down in bed I was having an attack of coughing. I tried sitting up in bed for a while, and then gradually sliding down to horizontal, but you can't fool a cough that way. I was trying it one more time just the same, when there was a knock on the door. It was very late, and we were both surprised. Leo put on a shirt and went to answer it. When he came back, he took off the shirt and got back into bed without explaining. I asked him who it was, and he said it was someone delivering pizza who'd got the wrong address.

'At this time of night?' I asked him.

'Yes.'

I didn't even know you could have pizza delivered around here.

'What address was he looking for?'

'Don't know.'

'Did he find where it was?'

'Don't know.' We lay there for a moment, and Leo turned slowly over in bed, away from me.

Suddenly I had the idea that what I wanted most in the world was pizza. A sudden flow of saliva even soothed my cough for a moment. I suppose it was partly because it was so late, my nausea was deeply asleep, and for a moment I had a clear view of my hunger. And then the pizza seemed so near, so ready on the other side of a door. So I said, 'Leo, this may sound silly, but could you go out and see if that pizza man is still around? If he is, tell him I'll take it off his hands. I'm not fussy about toppings. I'll even pay full whack.'

Leo dragged himself slowly out of bed, put on the shirt again, some trousers and some shoes, and stumbled across the room towards the door. Then he came back and sat on the bed. He told me then that he'd made it up about the pizza. When he'd opened the front door there was a man there in dressing-gown and slippers, holding out a bottle of Benylin, that heavy-duty cough stuff, and saying, without a lot of warmth, 'Try this.' Leo hadn't wanted to tell me. He put the Benylin somewhere where he was going to pick it up the next morning and take it away with him. He hadn't known what else to do.

Nor did I for a moment, and then I asked him to fetch me the bottle, I'd have a swig anyway, just to be friendly. The nausea was wide awake by then, so it didn't cost me a lot to be generous, just a little. Leo undressed again and fell asleep soon after that, and so did I, I think, though I woke up towards morning for a little practice hacking, which Leo slept through, and I hope everybody in the street did too.[

]*Salmon sperm!* What's the word? Milt. It's unbelievable! They just told me today. It turns out that milt is clever stuff. It has a Suppressing Effect. What it Suppresses is Replication. It's such clever stuff. And what that means is, salmon sperm is on my side. Milt loves me! And I love milt.

They're very dour about it. They say, don't build up your hopes too high. They never said that about fears. They never said don't build up your fears too high. And I'm not getting carried away. All I say is, milt loves me and I love milt! I don't even need to fellate the fish to get at it, though God knows I'd do it if I had to. They've synthesized it for me. They say, warning me, that it'll taste like metal. I say, you're wrong, it'll taste like Life. And they say, warning me, that I'll have to take it every four hours at first, day and night. And I say, nursing mothers have to put up with a lot more than that. I'll set the alarm for the middle of the night, and when it goes off I'll know what makes it worth while waking, there's no sleep so deep that I won't know. I'll know it's my Life waking me for its four o'clock feed.

They tell me it isn't a cure, as if I didn't know that. I tell them I know it could only be a poison, that's all doctors can ever give you, poison; you just have to hope that it hates you less than it hates what you've got. They tell me salmon sperm can attack your red cells, and your white cells come to that, so it might help to take some iron and vitamin B. I tell them I've always liked spinach. Oh, I've got all the answers. I just want to be able to put off the questions a bit.

*Remission.* Maybe I'll be able to move over to this tape for good. Shut away the shits-and-vomits tape in its little case and never need to pull it out again.[

]Remission. I had my remission.[

]I had my remission, and I didn't record it. I didn't even write anything down.[

]When I listen back to this tape, I hear myself explaining what I'm going to use it for, but I never do. I never do.[

]Some things I don't need help remembering. I remember getting the first prescription for my salmon sperm, and going along with it to the hospital pharmacy. Rory was with me that day, but he was shutting up for once. The new twist my case was taking seemed to have robbed him of his small talk. The Aussie I've always hated was on duty in the pharmacy, with his usual tan, only more so, and the stupid bleach-streaked hair, only more so. And of course the awful voice! When you're waiting your turn, eyes down or looking at the warnings on the walls for innocent things like whooping-cough, and he's bellowing instructions to the customers before you in the line, you can think he must have picked up an old copy of *Punch* from the table, and rolled it up to make his voice so deafening. Then when it's your turn you find it's even worse. He *roars* at me as he passes over the box of Dioralyte, 'Make up a sachet after every loose bowel movement,' and then tells me how many times a day I need to take my antibiotics, as if it wasn't written on the container. He seems to have a heroic notion of his job, as if he was still a life-guard back in Australia – though I think you need broad shoulders for that – striding across toasted sand and warning red-heads not to sun-bathe. Then he pushes across the salmon sperm. I'd expected it to be a liquid, somehow, a heavy metallic liquid, what with its being so new and precious and rationed. I must have been thinking, too, of cod-liver oil. So I was dis-appointed for a moment when it was just ordinary capsules, like the timed-release symptom-suppressors you take for a cold, except with a different paint-job, white with a thin blue belt at the middle. Then I was impressed all over again by the size of the bottle, it wasn't really big, but bigger than I'm used to, so it looked like a sweetie-jar in an old-fashioned corner shop. For a moment I thought, almost tearful with gratitude, *All that, for me?* £250 for a fortnight's treatment isn't peanuts, but why should I have been so surprised to be worth it? Then the Aussie booms out, 'You have to take these every four hours, day and night, do you understand? The best thing is to take 'em at four, and eight, and twelve. That way you only need to get up once in the night.'

And I thought, this idiot knows *nothing*; if I was sleeping eight hours a stretch I wouldn't be needing the salmon sperm, would I? I'd be holding down a job, wouldn't I, the way a paper-weight holds down a pile of prescription forms, the way you hold down yours. The week before, I'd just have let it wash over me, but this time it was as if the salmon sperm was giving me strength already, just by sitting there on the counter, so I said, 'Oh, I think I'll miss the four o'clock dose, get a full night's sleep.' I tried to make my voice campy. 'I'm not really an early morning person.' I could see Rory out of the corner of my eye, trying not to giggle.

But of course the Pharmacist From Bondi Beach looked really concerned, and he even lowered his voice, and he said, 'You really should, sir, it's important.'

If I'd had more than just the sight of the salmon sperm to give me strength, perhaps I'd have said something really crushing. But I couldn't think of anything anyway, so I just lowered my voice, all the way down to a whisper, and said, 'Just to please you, then.'

There was no holding me. I nipped into the waiting room on my way out, flashed the nurse a big smile and asked, 'Would it be possible, do you think, to trace the kind person who brings along all those back numbers of opera magazines?' Then, just as she got launched on the sort of smile that says you've made someone's day, I said, 'Because I'd really like to push him off a small cliff. That would make my day.'

I remember that day because I had only had a premonition of health. I was still outside the world of the well, that world which I understand so little of now.

I have to reconstruct those weeks, those (admit it) months, from what they left behind, like a pathologist reconstructing a dead person's last meal. I remember looking at my first capsule, with a tiny animal printed on it in blue, like the little lions that used to be stamped on eggs, and what I took to be the word WELCOME in tiny letters. I remember thinking with real fervour, *Welcome yourself*, before I saw that the L in the word was double.

I know I became impatient with Leo and Rory almost instantly. They seemed so petty and nannyish, so ignorant of the real business of life. They nagged me to take my salmon sperm, as if it was something I'd forget just to be annoying. In fact I became very good at waking up seconds before the alarm went off for the three o'clock and seven o'clock feeds – I just had to be different, didn't I? – as if there really was a baby in the room, screaming. It should have struck me as funny when Leo struggled out of sleep at ten past seven one morning and started shaking me, convinced that I'd missed the seven o'clock feed and probably the three o'clock too, which of course he'd also snored through. It should have seemed funny, but it didn't. I suppose it was hard for them. They had suited themselves to me by an effort of will: it must have seemed ungrateful on my part to discharge myself – and so suddenly – from the intensive care I had demanded from them. But that didn't stop me from thinking what my mother used to say, poor bitch, of a piece of furniture that no longer pleased her: I'd rather have your space than your company.

Something peculiar must have happened. I stopped being feverish all the time, in that low-level way that becomes your new normal after a few months. But I entered another kind of fever; I was in a fever of health. That must be the explanation. I know I took a lot of trouble to repeat, in my new health, experiences that I'd had in sickness. That must be a very sophisticated pleasure.

I know, for instance, that in my sickness I had made a trip to Highgate Ponds. I needed to be driven, by Leo of course, and I needed to take a little rest at the unofficial gay sun-bathing area before I tottered down to the nudists' compound.

Leo and I laid out our towels on the concrete. I'd brought along a blanket and a pillow (which Leo was carrying, of course) for a little extra padding, but at least I laid the towel on top. I wasn't ashamed to strip off, though of course I was worried in case I had to run for the dingy lavatory, under the eyes of the ghastly crew by the weight-bench. But shame didn't get a look in. As far as I was concerned, this was strictly between me and the sun. I wasn't going to be done out of our date just because I could hardly walk.

I was surprised to see that Leo was shy, and kept a pair of swimming trunks on. I wanted to tempt him out of them, so I could at least look at the label and see whether they were bought from C&A or the British Home Stores.

After a while I struggled into a swimsuit myself, and walked weakly through to the pond. I was hoping that I would feel strong enough for a dip at least, which was a pretty bizarre hope. Perhaps I thought that, all other sources of energy having failed, I would turn out to be solar-powered. I lay down on the diving-board. I had been there about ten seconds, feeling the wind on me almost warm, and watching the people sprawled on the raft in the middle of the pond, when a man came out of a hut and shouted at me that sun-bathing was not allowed in the swimming area.

The trip I made in my health, I seem to think, was very different. I took bus after bus to get there, by myself. I strode past the sun-bathing area, and straight into the compound, though this time I was reluctant to take off my underwear. By then I had a little roll of tummy fat which I was very proud of, and which showed to best effect above the waistline of a pair of underpants, and I wasn't in any hurry to have it vanish the moment I took my briefs off and lay down. I expect I was waiting for someone to call out, 'Wonderful! I can't see your ribs. Well done!'

Before the sun had properly got to work I was standing up

again and pulling my swimming trunks up. I went out into the swimming area, but I wasn't quite brave enough for the diving-board. The water looked cloudy, but I knew it was supposed to be pure and clean, equally free of pollution and disinfectant. I let myself down an iron ladder that had a lot of weed attached to it. The ladder wasn't full-length, as I had assumed, it stopped only a little below the surface, so I slipped into the coldest water I have ever touched. My body gasped and went on gasping. The water was unexpectedly deep, too, considering it was so near the edge of the pond. I set out to swim to the raft, which supported what looked like the same group of sun-worshippers, but I found myself swimming instead in a tight circle back to where I started. I wanted to strike out for that floating island of health, but my body wasn't having it. My feet had no memory of the ladder, and scrabbled for purchase where the rungs were imaginary. Then I remembered, and felt for the actual bottom of the actual ladder, and managed to pull myself out.

I slumped on the jetty to recover. Not even the most officious attendant, seeing me there flat out and wheezing, could imagine I was having a sun-bathe on the sly, but the men on the raft set up a round of ironic applause that I could hear even through the numbness of my ears.

I wasn't going to give up. I didn't hang around until my skin had dried off and my trunks felt cold and clammy. I went back down the ladder and swam out through the cold. The water got warmer after a while, or else it stayed cold and I got used to it. The raft was only fifty feet or so away, but that was quite far enough. I could feel the special uneasiness of swimming in water of unknown depth. As I got near the raft, all I could see above the edge of it was the soles of someone's feet, those odd sort of feet with the second toe longer than the big one.

The ladder by the raft was even shorter than the one on the jetty. In my memory, it has only two rungs. I know I had to pull myself up with what felt like the last of my strength. But when I looked round at the raft, which rocked under my weight and wasn't as securely tethered as I'd expected, it was covered with shit. I don't mean that the men there were lying in it: they were too fastidious for that, with their uniform tans, as if they'd all chosen the same shade from a paint card. But there were substantial little turds scattered all over the raft. They were bigger than anything I've known a bird do, but I couldn't imagine what beast could have got there to lay them. I was tired out from my swim, but lying in shit was too recent a memory – from nights when I improvised a pair of incontinence pants out of an old Marks and Sparks bag – for me to be able to stay on the raft. I climbed down the rusty ladder, losing my footing one more time, and swam back to the jetty. It may be that my strength was failing towards the end, but I think the water near the jetty was the coldest of all.

I know I did all that. I even remember it all, in the sense that I still bear traces of those thoughts and sensations. I remember what my body felt in its health, what it touched, how it reacted. But I have no sense of how my body felt to itself. Health was just one more thing that happened to me, and I have kept nothing from it. The tape is blank for all those weeks and months.

And now I am back in my siege of fevers. What it feels like, as always, is shame, as if this raised temperature was nothing more than a hideous extended blush, which I could get rid of if I just did the right thing. I find myself wondering what it was I did wrong, what crime my body remembers with this heat of shame. They didn't lie to me about the salmon sperm. I knew it could nibble away at my cells. I knew there was a price to be paid for the job it did. I knew it wasn't a medicine so much as a protection racket; I just hoped we could get along. I took vitamins, I took iron, I took supplements. Was there one night when I passed up a dish of green vegetables, in my feverish health, snubbing all those B vitamins, and went out instead? There must have been. I know there were times when I was too bound up in the play I was watching to remember my feed. I'd glared in the dark at people whose watch alarms went off in the theatre for too many years to commit that crime myself. And there was the terrible day I lost my bottle of capsules. I had to dash across London, whimpering, for replacements. I'd lost six expensive days' worth. To make myself feel better I asked if anyone had lost their salmon sperm before me. But I was the first.

How can I put it, to make myself feel I have made heroic choices? Health for me is more than being not-yet-dead. It's not something you patrol; it's something you must forget to patrol or it's not any sort of health at all. That should do it. That sounds right. That must be why I didn't use this tape to hoard up bits of my health, so I could live off them at a later date.

And here I am with a body that's ashamed of itself, that's burning with remorse for something it did or didn't do, and with the word *surge* beating at my ears. They warned me what would happen when I came off the salmon sperm. A surge of virus. Virus replicating uninhibited. *Surge* is a word that sounds overwhelming even on the smallest scale, down on the cellular level. What chance do I have, against a *surge*?

Every time I went to hospital for some more salmon sperm, and they took blood, I must have known they were monitoring my levels. Fourteen. Twelve and a half. Eleven. Nine. It was more than a pit stop. And when I went below nine, and they started to give me transfusions, I knew what they were about. But I tried to think, closing my eyes when the prick came in my arm, and then the slowly growing ache in it, that I was giving blood rather than getting it, that from my overflowing health I was giving freely of my surplus. Nine and a half. Nine. Eight. I tried to think I was paying my taxes, when all the time my bloodstream was being heavily subsidized. On long car journeys as a child, I remember, to stop from feeling sick – from motion, from too many boiled sweets, from my father's Senior Service and my mother's Piccadilly – I would close my eyes and try to interpret the sensations in terms of movement backward, though I don't quite know why that was comforting. I could produce a surprisingly strong and consistent illusion until I opened my eyes at a bump in the road, or when my mother asked if I was asleep, and the world came crashing back at me.[

]The lovers are back. They can deal with me again. And I suppose that really means that I can deal with them. Rory has

that handsome look in the face that means he's certain to shave
in the morning, and Leo smells so strongly of soap he must
wear a bar around his neck.[

]They've done something very tactful with the key. I'm not
very steady on my feet just at the moment, and my neighbour
has a spare set of keys. She's always been a hypochondriac,
can't bear to be in the room with anyone who has a cold, so I
suppose it's something of a miracle that she's not returned
them, or that they don't reek of disinfectant. This I noticed
today, and it qualifies for inclusion on this tape. That's what
this tape is supposed to be for, isn't it? Sometimes my
neighbour even leaves groceries outside the door. Anyway,
when Rory last came by he let himself in, and explained that he
had happened to run into my neighbour outside the house.
Then *Leo* let himself in next time he paid a visit, and he looked
all tense and startled, as if at any moment he might be called
upon to lie. So my guess is they've made a policy decision not
to make me walk any more than I have to. They must knock
on my neighbour's door every time they come round. For all I
know, they get her to leave the key under the mat when she
goes out. I think they're waiting for me to twig and get angry,
but they'll have to wait a little while longer. I'll either keep it to
myself or let it hitch a ride on a real grievance. 'And another
thing,' I'll say, 'about the keys . . .'[

]We've started taking baths together, the lovers and I. Rory
lifts me into the tub very competently, which is so reassuring
it's sinister, but at least he climbs right in with me, like no
nurse in the world who wants to remain in employment.
Suddenly I wonder if he answered my ad – poor idiot – to get
his life moving again after grief, and has to keep his teeth
clenched on his knowledge. So I'm more than usually grateful
that he gets into the bath with me. He sits behind me with his
knees bent, so I can rest my head on his chest, and he strokes
me a little awkwardly with a sponge. It's a posture I like
anyway, and now in particular I'm glad of it because it's not a
position that encourages talking. We can't really see each
other's faces. I think he closes his eyes in the steam, and from
time to time he seems to drift off. He doesn't seem to mind

that the water gets cold; perhaps he doesn't even feel it. If there was just a little more water in the bath I'd be floating. As it is my head bumps softly against Rory's chest. Here and only here, in this limbo inside another, I remember my lover, the lover I disposed of so efficiently, dumping his body in an acid bath of resentment. What I remember isn't the friendship, which I resisted, or even the sex, which I wanted only when I wanted it, but the game we used to play when we were out together, the game he taught me and that he may even have invented, the sweetly innocent game he called *compelled*-to-fuck. One or other of us would say, 'If you were *compelled* to fuck a set number of people – under pain of death, mind . . .' (or later just, 'If you were *compelled* . . .'). Then the other would say, 'How many?' And the answer would be, 'One on this bus,' or 'Two before we leave the Food Hall,' or 'Three before the next traffic light.' Then he would say, 'Three? You'll be lucky. That one, at a pinch. Another one? No chance. All right, the thinner of these two bobbies, the less fat I mean. That's the lot. That's my last offer. One more? Do I really have to? Let it be the one with the tie, then. Cancel that. The other bobby. If I have to.' What I remember best is the grudging lust in all its variety that he could call up on his face, as he made his protesting selections.

Sooner or later I have to tell Rory that it's time for me to get out. I start shivering, even in the water, even against his skin. He doesn't risk trying to lift me out while he's wet and slippery, so he dries himself as quickly as he can and comes back for me with a hot towel. By now I'm really shivering. He helps me stand up and pulls the plug out. He wraps the towel round me and rubs away until at last a tingle passes to me from the towel. By then I'm likely to be exhausted, and once he even had a shot at carrying me to the bed. He was staggering by the time we got there, and he didn't so much lay me down as fall with me down on to the mattress.

Leo is different, of course. He has a hard time lifting me into the bath, so I hang on to the towel rail just in case – though I'm not sure I could support my weight for more than a second or two, if he lost his grip. He puts stuff in the bath so that it's full of nutty-smelling bubbles by the time I arrive in it, which relaxes me and relaxes him too, because he doesn't have to see me naked for more than a few moments. I'd rather he joined me in the bath – the edge of the tub is hard against my shoulders – but he likes to stay where he is. Still, he's become something of a pro as a back-scrubber, and that's something. At first he used a nail-brush, but one day he couldn't find it so he used my toothbrush instead, and we've never gone back to the nail-brush. He's even brought along a toothbrush which is specifically for scrubbing my back.

He starts on my left shoulder, pressing hard with the bristles, moving his wrist in tiny circles. It's extraordinary how – even the first time he did it, and much more so now – my skin anticipates the sideways progress of the brush as he moves it across my back, so that I develop a roving itch that is always just a fraction ahead of the scrubbing. When he has reached the outside edge of my right shoulderblade, he drops his hand an inch or so and scrubs steadily back to the left again. I try to concentrate all my attention on the itch, which moves ahead of the toothbrush all the way. It's as if there was a poem written on my back that I learnt by heart in childhood. I have wholly forgotten it, but each word that I am prompted to remember sparks the memory of the next. I close my eyes. The travelling itch holds still, for once, at the extremity of my back, until the brush comes to scrub it out.[

]I lose the ability to talk. My voice unravels, and speech drops away from me like the mouthpiece of an instrument I am suddenly unable to play, a medieval instrument that I don't even recognize as a possible source of music.

When I open my eyes again, they are both there, both the lovers. Leo and Rory. Imagination is the last thing to fail me. I see them lying side by side on their fronts, their arms around each other, their faces pushed into the pillows. They turn slowly to each other, and I see Rory trace a line with his finger down Leo's cheek. I can see a tear on Leo's skin by the tip of Rory's finger, but from my point of view I can't make out whether Rory is following its progress as it trickles, or drawing it out of Leo's eye with the gesture he makes. Rory leans over and kisses the tear where it has come to rest, and I flinch in spite of myself. Leo turns away from the kiss, so they are both on their sides now, facing the same way.

Rory sets up a gentle motion of the hips, which Leo's hips take up. A terrible rattle of protest and warning bursts from me, behind clenched teeth. Their hips are in rhythm now, and Rory's face is pressed against Leo's neck, just as it was against the pillow a few moments ago.

I turn my head away, and see the cardboard box that contains all my medicines in their varied containers. I see also the little piles of Leo's and Rory's clothes. Their two pairs of trousers have fallen in an oddly symmetrical pattern, forming a sort of star, and I can see among the keys attached to one belt-loop a new pale-silver copy of a familiar shape. I glance at the keys on the other trousers, to locate the twin of it. But I forgive my lovers their ability to comfort themselves and each other, and I forgive myself for bringing them together, as I cross the room as quietly as I can and open the door, as quietly as I can. Then I close the door after all, walk back across the room, not worrying any more about whether I make any noise, and sit back down on the edge of the bed.

# Horse Sense

## DEBORAH MOGGACH

WHEN I FIRST moved to the estate my only companions were Terry Wogan and a horse. Terry was just on the radio, but the horse was real enough. It was a big brown thing that lived in a field at the end of my garden. I'm not used to horses but soon it was hanging its heavy head over my fence and I was feeding it chappatis. At first it alarmed me, baring its slimy yellow teeth, stained like a smoker's.

I come from London. So does my husband. But we moved to this place near Swindon because it's Silicone Valley and he was making his way in the world. I was proud of him then.

The estate was full of children. They passed fast on their skateboards; their laughter made my chest hurt. Sometimes, waiting for the bus, there would be a little girl standing in front of me and I felt weak, from wanting to touch her hair.

The neighbours weren't unfriendly. We just didn't have that much in common, me having no kids. I don't think it was to do with prejudice – after all, I didn't go around in a sari or anything. I was born and bred in England, the same as them. We didn't perform weird rites. The only thing Ranjit worshipped was the silicone chip.

I talked to the horse when I was hanging out my washing. It might have looked funny otherwise. I had these one-way conversations behind the flapping sheets. I told it what I was cooking for dinner, and what was going on in *EastEnders*. One day I said to it, quite distinctly: 'I think I'm going mad.'

That was the day I had been to the shoe shop in Swindon and made such a fool of myself. The horse went on eating, of course, and flicked away a fly.

I should have told my husband but he didn't like disturbance. He's older than me – he had been a bachelor for years and his family had started to despair. The grey flecks in his hair gave him a weighty look, as if he had deeper thoughts than me. So I cooked and cleaned the house – when he saw a smeary surface he cleared his throat – and, before the panics got too bad, I took the bus into Swindon and went to Marks and Spencer's. I had been married two years.

I'm probably making him sound unattractive. I knew I would. But he was kind. He was always buying me gadgets for the kitchen. Have you tried a microwave? I only used it once, and after that I pretended. He would spear a baked potato and pronounce: 'Ten minutes. A miracle.' I would lower my eyes; in marriage you learn to be silent.

He liked things with digital numbers; our house bleeped like a space-ship. He fiddled with the video recorder and indexed all our tapes. From the back I could see the small boy he once was. I wanted to touch him then, but he only handled me in the dark. And then, according to the statistics in my *Woman's Own* survey, infrequently.

But I didn't mention that, even to myself. I told myself I was lucky. He didn't drink like other men, coming home to a burnt dinner and a snorting wife. He kept himself in trim. He never lost his temper. He gave me generous amounts of housekeeping each week. I tell myself these things, and I tell them to you. I don't like to talk of them.

I'll tell you about the horse. It meant a lot to me. Silly, wasn't it? But I stroked its neck and it blew into my hair. We were two lonely creatures together. My husband worked late; he was one of the marketing managers of a computer firm. Under my hand, the horse breathed.

I'll tell you what happened in Lilley and Skinner's. I went

into Swindon to buy a pair of shoes. A woman was there, with her child. He was a small boy, aged about six, and he wanted blue trainers. But she wanted him to have the red ones, and then he started crying and she slapped him. That was all. And I burst into tears.

I felt such a fool. I had to leave the shop. It was such a small thing, wasn't it? I felt a fool.

Soon after that, it was a cold day in spring, the field was empty. The horse was gone. For a silly moment I thought I had told it too many secrets. The field was bare, with just the dents where its hooves had stood; pitted mud around my back fence. And a week later the bulldozers arrived and they ploughed up the field and started building a service station.

So there was only Terry Wogan left but he was on the telly now; he had his own chat show and instead of talking to me there he was, making film stars simper. It wasn't the same.

I should have got out more. With the warm weather starting, other women went off to garden centres and MFI. People talked about a local beauty spot – a hill with the shape of a white horse cut out in it. Standing there, they said, you could see three counties. But now, just thinking about the bus made my heart thump. I was getting worse.

I had these panics when I got to Swindon. It happened in supermarkets; in Sainsbury's I'd break out in sweat. I couldn't think what to choose. Little tins suddenly made me sad. I'd fumble in my bag for my wallet – it wasn't there, I'd forgotten it, I'd forgotten my keys. What could I possibly choose to buy? How could I want all that stuff? And why? Wasn't everybody looking at me?

I kept glancing at my watch and worrying I'd miss the bus. I'd hurry to the bus station; there were so many buses, so many numbers. Sometimes they would roll the numbers around on the departure boards, losing me. It was the central depot, and though I knew my queue I pictured the wrong bus being there, or my own bus just leaving. However early I turned up, my stomach churned.

I didn't tell Ranjit. He always seemed to be doing something else. Besides, I didn't want to worry him when he was working so hard. They were about to launch a new product, he said, and he was often away overnight – he had to give pep talks, he said, to his countrywide network of sales executives. He spent more and more time, too, working late.

It was best not to speak. If I spoke I would alarm myself; once I made it real, into words, I would start panicking, in earnest.

Then one day I lost my nerve and missed the bus altogether. For a week I had been putting off going into Swindon; just outside the estate, next to the newly built filling station, there was a parade of shops and I'd been going there. I could do that quite easily – no timetables, no countdowns; just a short walk, whenever I felt like it, quite calmly. No problem with that.

But I needed some upholstery fabric. Days went by and I made excuses to myself, delaying things until the last bus had gone and it was too late. Finally, on the Friday, I did make it to the bus stop. But when the bus arrived, I flunked it and went back home.

The next Monday I did something that was out of character. We all do that on occasion, don't we? That morning I picked up the phone book, found a number and ordered myself a minicab.

And look where it led me. My advice: don't do anything that surprises yourself. There's a good reason why you've never done it before.

Eric was the name of the driver and we got to know each other well. He was more responsive than either the horse or Terry. I could talk to the back of his neck, which was red.

The first journey he talked all the way about his late wife. I think he was lonely.

'There was fields here then,' he said, nodding at the passing discount centres. 'She grew up on a farm, all the fields they were yellow with cowslips.' A lorry, hooting, passed us. 'It's an ancient bit of country, this. Those chalk hills, see, far over there? The oldest bit of land for miles.'

I agreed politely, though I couldn't see how one bit of country could be older than another. I was wondering if I dared tell Ranjit about the minicab. He would think me so odd. I would take the money out of the housekeeping and he might never notice.

'Money, money,' Eric went on. 'Nobody doesn't have any respect for the land. Plough it up, concrete it over, bung all those little boxes on it. There was a song once, little boxes, and they all look just the same.'

'They're not,' I said. 'Ours has a through-lounge – some of them have separate dining rooms.' I liked my house.

'One huge suburb,' he went on, 'full of foreigners.' He looked in the driving mirror. 'Begging your pardon.'

'I know,' I said. 'Most of us come from London.'

He must have been about sixty. He talked about the days when he was courting as if it was yesterday. He said it felt like that. He said there was a big harvest supper and his wife-to-be was there, and how they had horses then to pull the carts. Being a town boy, he said, he was alarmed by their huge feet.

While he talked I thought how in a minicab I didn't feel so panic-stricken, though I still felt twinges: should I tip him? Would he pick me up outside Marks and Spencer's at the right time? He did.

The weeks went by and I realized I was looking forward to our trips. His neck got browner in the sun. He said he subscribed to *Psychic News* and that he still talked to his wife. She wasn't really gone. To him, she wasn't. He said his house was on a steep hillside and in the evening, when the place was in shadow and he came through the front door, he heard her voice. She always seemed to be in the next room, but when he got there, the house was silent.

'Do you have any children?' I asked him.

He shook his head.

Outside the window the suburbs of Swindon passed. As I looked out at the industrial warehouses I thought of Ranjit, pyjama'd in the dark. Did he dream?

I said to Eric: 'Last night I dreamed I was in a plane but it wouldn't take off. It just bumped through the streets, faster and faster. Its wings battered at the houses, it made such a mess. I was scared to death. I was sitting inside it, all the passengers were rolling about but it wouldn't go up in the air. There was somebody next to me and he was telling me to open a parcel. The plane was lurching around, he forced me to open it. I didn't want to. Inside the parcel – it was made of old newspapers – inside it there was something moving.'

I didn't tell him there was a baby inside. To tell the honest truth, I don't think he was listening.

I do blush, though, when I think of the things I told Eric. The stuffy car made me careless and I just spoke to the back of his neck. I told him about my funny turns, and how I would speak to the furniture. It didn't seem so odd when there he was conversing with his dead wife. At least the washing machine was solid. 'Can you cope with all these sheets?' I would ask it. 'I've never fancied this pink shirt of Ranny's. It makes him look like a disc jockey.' At first it surprised me, hearing, in my empty home, my own high voice. But once you've been doing it for a while it seems quite normal. And at least I wasn't speaking into thin air.

I told him how I'd stand in the middle of a shop and suddenly feel so empty – a sort of scraped-out, hurting hollow – and I'd go up the escalators and buy three belts. I knew I would never wear them, they didn't go with any of my clothes. But I would bundle them into the back of my cupboard and keep them safe.

Ranjit wouldn't have minded the expense – I told you he was generous – but he would have been worried. Eric was restful because nothing surprised him.

I said: 'Yesterday I burst into tears, thinking of all the chickens that must have died to make me live.'

Eric just replied: 'Once chickens tasted like chickens. Now they're pumped full of hormones.' No wonder I could talk.

It was the hottest summer for years. At night I slept badly, dreaming of horses and slippery slopes. I was helpless; often the plane or carriage in which I was travelling was out of control. I heard trees creak as we knocked against them;

banging along the streets, I heard the breaking masonry. Sometimes Ranjit appeared – an altered, panting Ranjit. His hands were rude, and he pulled my skirt up over my head and did such things to me, front and rear, that at breakfast I couldn't meet his eye.

Inside the house was stifling. The garden was both too stuffy and too exposed – have you ever felt that? While Ranjit slept I stood on the lawn listening to the hum of the motorway. The filling station blared at me close; its Texaco sign hurt my eyes, it reminded me of my childhood when I had dared myself to look at the sun. I hid behind the shed, where none of the houses could see me, and I gazed at the orange sky above Swindon. I pictured cows and wives buried under concrete and wondered if I would ever have a child. I thought suddenly: am I having a nervous breakdown? Is this the beginning of it? Perhaps I'm one of those housewives I read about in the newspaper. Inside, beside the bed, emerald numbers flipped on our digital clock, telling me that at least something was in order.

The weather grew stifling, as if somebody had closed the doors on England. Towns, cities, old and new hills – they were all one room. I found it more and more difficult to sleep. At first I thought it was the thunder; each evening it rumbled, way beyond the hills I had never visited. But then I realized why I felt uneasy. Ranjit was looking at me.

I would see him out of the corner of my eye; I could catch sight of him reflected in the glass-fronted cabinet. His eyes were on me. I behaved as normal but I started to sweat. I thought: he knows something's wrong.

The next Thursday Eric took me to Sainsbury's. The sky was grey, and weighed down on the car. I felt so faint I nearly asked him to stop, but that would have alarmed me so I just leaned near the open window and tried to concentrate on the passing buildings . . . Everest Double Glazing . . . Little Chef . . . Elite Used Cars. When we arrived at Sainsbury's it was busy and I felt the familiar fluttering. So I sat still for a moment and held the door handle.

Then I spoke. I said: 'Does it frighten you?'

'Pardon?'

I didn't reply. I meant: does it frighten you, that it seems normal to talk to your wife? But then I realized, as he settled himself in the driver's seat and lit his pipe, that he considered himself the sane one in a world that was mad.

Later, when I unpacked my shopping, I found all sorts of packets that were new to me – frozen scampi, assorted Elastoplast. I couldn't remember buying them. My face heated up and my mouth went dry. I thought: yes, I am mad. I'm mad and I'll have to tell Ranjit. What will he do with me?

And then, as I lifted out a jar of pickled onions, I realized I had simply got someone else's shopping by mistake. Someone, somewhere, was looking at alien chicken quarters and feeling just the same way as me.

For a moment I didn't feel lonely. Standing there beside the fridge I laughed out loud, until the noise I made frightened me.

Some nights later I was lying on my side looking at the street light glowing through the curtains. Beside me Ranjit slept. It was four o'clock; I felt damp and restless. My dreams had been disturbing and I was trying to calm myself by measuring the distance between the tulips on the curtains. Far away, a dog barked. I could hear my own heart thumping; these stupid panics were worse at night.

Then I turned my head and froze. Ranjit was lying there with his eyes open.

I don't know why it gave me such a shock. Straight away he closed his eyes; this made it worse. After a moment I touched his shoulder, but he started breathing deeply, as if he were asleep. He couldn't be – he knew that; I knew that.

Suddenly I felt cold. I turned away and pretended to sleep. That dog went on barking; it sounded like somebody sawing through bones, on and on. I thought, for the first time: perhaps it's not just me who's mad.

A place gets to you. Even in our ultra-modern estate it got to me. I had never really listened to Eric and he'd never listened to me, but what he said seeped through, or maybe it was that unsettling midsummer air. All those digital bleeps couldn't reason away the uneasiness I felt in this foreign countryside. Because it was a strange place. Despite its motorways and its Happy Eaters it was pulling at me. Or perhaps the pulling came from inside.

Whatever the reason, the next time I had to take a trip into Swindon – I was going to change my library books, though I hadn't read them all – the next time I said to Eric, as we drove away past Elite Used Cars: 'It's too hot. Let's go somewhere else.'

To tell the truth I didn't mind where we went. My hands stuck to the carrier bag of books; my torpor made me bold. I just wanted some air. I remember exactly what I was wearing – my yellow C & A dress – and I remember Eric, who was never surprised, taking a right turn at the roundabout, with a car hooting behind him, and saying that if I'd never gone there before I ought to see the famous beauty spot. He started going on about local superstitions, and how ancient it all was and how you could see three counties from up there. But my eyes were closed and my mouth tasted last night's dreams – they caught me off my guard each day, they rose in my throat.

The drive took ages. I started to worry about the money and then I must have dozed off. Blurred, my horse was leaning over my garden fence and talking to me, its jaw working like a horse in a pantomime. It was blurred because I was jolting in the car, just like my dreams when I was jolted along in planes, and I started to feel queasy. And then I opened my eyes and we were driving up a narrow, bumpy lane and above me there was a hill, bleached in the sunlight. The sky was a block of blue above it. Somebody was talking but it was Eric, and he was asking me if I could see the horse carved out of the chalk but we were close up now, and all I could see, between the bushes, was a large dingy-white gap in the grass, too wide to recognize. He was saying they had once worshipped that horse, in pagan times. I felt sick; I wanted to go home. I didn't know how long I had slept or whether it should strike me as odd, to take a minicab on a joy-ride, except it didn't feel joyful. I was too far from home; I would never find my way back. I wanted my kitchen, and my front door closed behind me. I wanted to be busy unpacking carrier bags. My heart fluttered. I wanted it to be a safe weekday, or as safe as I could make it.

I don't know if I thought all this then, but I do know that I was already feeling tight and headachy, the panic swelling, long before I saw the glint of Ranjit's car.

In front of me was a chalky car park, with litter bins. I remember it exactly – that swift moment when I glanced around – even though all this happened a year ago. A few empty cars were parked there, not many, it was a Wednesday lunchtime. But there was another car parked in the far corner, apart from them, and for a moment I thought idly: a white Escort, just like his.

Eric was asking me something but I didn't hear. We bumped across the car park, closer now. I told myself it was only one head in there, not two. The sunlight flashed against the rear window; I told myself I must be mistaken. I wanted to go home.

But Eric was driving nearer, and I was telling myself: they're just looking at the view. That's why their heads are so close together. And then we were close up and I saw what they were doing. And then my head was down between my knees and I was saying to Eric *take me home.*

The sunlight blinded me. As we bumped down the track I squeezed my eyes shut. Eric never knew anything was wrong.

I might have understood, if it was a woman. In fact, in some way deep down I had expected it. But not a man. I hadn't expected a man.

When we got home I told Eric to wait outside. I hurried in.

It's surprising, once you look around a place for the last time, how little you want to take. I packed two suitcases and that was it. The whole process took about ten minutes. Oddly enough, my head was clear. It hurt, but it was clear. For the first time in years everything seemed quite simple. That panicky feeling had gone.

I climbed into the cab and told Eric to drive to London. It was half past two. I leant against the back seat.

We got quite merry in the car, and stopped in Hungerford for a cream tea. Apparently people get like this – a bit hysterical – at funerals. God knows what Eric thought as I stuffed myself with fruit cake. I was suddenly hungry. I thought of the cupboards at home, full of food; they waited for my husband. I thought how little I had known him, and wondered if other wives ever felt the same. Not the circumstances – the feelings. No wonder I had found myself talking to horses.

I'm living with my sister now. I never told her the real reason I left Ranjit. I just said I couldn't stand it, living in the sticks.

'I don't blame you,' she said. 'All those cows for company.'

'And a horse,' I replied.

'It would drive me round the bend,' she went on.

'It did.'

# Good Advice is Rarer than Rubies

## SALMAN RUSHDIE

ON THE LAST Tuesday of the month, the dawn bus brought Miss Rehana to the gates of the British Embassy. It arrived pushing a cloud of dust, veiling her beauty from the eyes of strangers until she descended. The bus was brightly painted in multicoloured arabesques, and on the front it said 'MOVE OVER DARLING' in green and gold letters; on the back it added 'TATA-BATA' and also 'OK. GOOD-LIFE.' Miss Rehana told the driver it was a beautiful bus, and he jumped down and held the door open for her.

Miss Rehana's eyes were large and black and shiny enough not to need the help of antimony, and when the advice expert Muhammad Ali saw them he felt himself becoming young again. He watched her approach the embassy gates and heard her ask the lala who guarded them when they would open. The lala usually enjoyed insulting the embassy's Tuesday-women, but he spoke to Miss Rehana with something approaching courtesy. 'Half an hour,' he said gruffly. 'Maybe two hours. Who knows? The sahibs are eating their breakfast.'

The dusty compound between the bus stop and the embassy was already full of Tuesday-women, some veiled, a few barefaced like Miss Rehana. They all looked frightened, and leaned heavily on the arms of uncles or brothers, who were trying to look confident. But Miss Rehana had come on her own, and did not seem at all alarmed. Muhammad Ali, who specialized in advising the most vulnerable-looking of these weekly supplicants, found his feet leading him towards the strange, big-eyed, independent girl.

'Miss,' he began. 'You have come for permit to London, I think so?' She was standing at a hot-snack stall in the little shantytown by the edge of the compound munching chili-pakoras contentedly. She turned to look at him, and at close range those eyes did bad things to his digestive tract.

'Yes, I have.'

'Then please, you allow me to give some advice? Small cost only.'

Miss Rehana smiled. 'Good advice is rarer than rubies,' she said. 'But I cannot pay. I am an orphan, not one of your wealthy ladies.'

'Trust my grey hairs,' Muhammad Ali told her. 'My advice is well tempered by experience. You will certainly find it good.'

She shook her head. 'I tell you I am poor. There are women here with male relatives, all earning good wages. Go to them. Good advice should find good money.'

I am going crazy, Muhammad Ali thought, because he heard his voice telling her of its own volition, 'Miss, I have been drawn to you. This is fated. I too am a poor man only, but for you my advice comes free.'

She smiled again. 'Then I must surely listen. When fate sends a gift, one receives good fortune.'

He led her to the low wooden desk in his own special corner of the shantytown. She followed, still smiling, eating pakoras from a little newspaper packet. She did not offer him any. He put a cushion on the dusty ground. 'Please to sit.' She did as he asked. He sat cross-legged across the desk from her, conscious that two or three dozen male eyes were watching him enviously, that all the other shantytown men were ogling the latest young lovely to be charmed by the old greyhair Muhammad Ali. He took a deep breath to settle himself.

'Name, please.'

155

'Miss Rehana,' she told him. 'Fiancée of Mustafa Dar of Bradford, London.'

'Bradford, England,' he corrected her gently. 'London is a city only, like Multan or Bahawalpur. England is a great nation full of the coldest fish in the world.'

'I see,' she responded gravely, so that he was unsure if she was making fun of him.

'You have filled application form? Then let me see, please.'

She passed him a neatly folded document in a brown envelope.

'Is it OK?' For the first time there was a note of anxiety in her voice.

He patted the desk quite near the place where her hand rested. 'I am certain,' he said. 'Wait on and I will check.'

She finished her pakoras while he scanned her papers.

'Tip-top,' he pronounced finally. 'All in order.'

'Thank you for your advice,' she said. 'I'll go now and wait by the gate.'

'What are you thinking?' he cried loudly, smiting his forehead. 'You consider this is easy business? Just give the form and poof, with a big smile they hand over the permit? Miss Rehana, I tell you you are entering a worse place than any police station.'

'Is it so, truly?' His oratory had done the trick. She was a captive audience now, and he would be able to look at her for a few moments longer. Drawing another calming breath, he launched into his speech. He told her that the sahibs thought all the women who came on Tuesdays, claiming to be dependants of bus drivers in Luton or chartered accountants in Manchester, were crooks and liars and thieves.

She protested, 'But then I will simply tell them that I, for one, am no such thing!'

Her innocence made him shiver with fear for her. She was a sparrow, he told her, and they were men with hooded eyes, like eagles. He explained that they would ask her questions, personal questions, questions such as a lady's own brother would be shy to ask. They would ask if she was a virgin, and, if not, what her fiancé's lovemaking habits were, and what secret nicknames they had invented for one another. Muhammad Ali spoke brutally, on purpose, to lessen the shock she would feel when it actually happened. Her eyes remained steady, but her hands began to flutter at the edges of the desk.

He went on. 'They will ask you how many rooms in your family home, and what colour are the walls, and what days do you empty the rubbish; they will ask your man's mother's third cousin's aunt's stepdaughter's middle name. And all these things they have already asked your Mustafa Dar in his Bradford. And if you make one mistake, you are finished.'

'Yes,' she said, and he could hear her disciplining her voice. 'And what is your advice, wise old man?'

It was at this point that Muhammad Ali usually began to whisper, to mention that he knew a man, a very good type, who worked in the embassy, and for a fee all the necessary papers could be delivered, with all the proper authentic seals. It was a good business, because the women would often pay him five hundred rupees or give him a gold bracelet for his pains and go away happy. They came from hundreds of miles away – he always checked this before he tricked them – so even when they discovered how they had been swindled they were very unlikely to return. They went away to Sargodha or Lalu Khet and began to pack, and who knows at what point they found out they had been gulled, but it was at a too late point anyway. Life is hard, and an old man must live by his wits. It was not up to Muhammad Ali to have compassion for these Tuesday-women.

But once again his voice betrayed him, and instead of starting his customary speech it began to reveal to her his greatest secret. 'Miss Rehana,' his voice said, and he listened to it in amazement, 'you are a rare person, a jewel, and for you I will do what I would not do for my own daughter, perhaps. One document has come into my possession that can solve your worries at a stroke.'

'And what is this sorcerer's paper?' she asked, her eyes unquestionably laughing at him now.

His voice fell low-as-low. 'Miss Rehana, it is a British passport. Completely genuine and pukka goods. I have a good friend who will put your name into it and then, hey-presto, England there you come!'

He had said it! Anything was possible now, on this day of his insanity. Probably he would give her the thing free-gratis, and then kick himself for a year afterwards. Old fool, he told himself, the oldest fools are bewitched by the youngest girls.

'Let me understand you,' she was saying. 'You are proposing I should commit a crime, and go to Bradford, London, illegally, and so justify the low opinion the embassy sahibs have of us all. Old babuji, this is not good advice.'

'Bradford, *England*,' he corrected her mournfully. 'You should not take my gift in such a spirit. I am a poor fellow and I have offered this prize because you are so beautiful. Do not spit on my generosity. Take the thing. Or else don't take, go home, forget England, only do not go in that building and lose your dignity.'

But she was on her feet, turning, walking away toward the gates, where the women had begun to cluster and the lala was swearing at them to be patient or none of them would be admitted.

'Be a fool,' Muhammad Ali shouted after her. 'It is the curse of our people. We are poor, we are ignorant, and we refuse completely to learn.'

'Hey, Muhammad Ali,' the woman at the betel-nut stall shouted to him. 'Too bad, she likes them young.'

That day Muhammad Ali did nothing but stand around the embassy gates. Many times he told himself, Go from here, fool, the lady does not wish to speak with you any further. But when she came out she found him waiting.

She seemed calm, and at peace with him again, and he thought, My God, she has pulled it off. The British sahibs have also been drowning in her eyes, and she has got her passage to England. He smiled at her; she smiled back with no trouble at all.

'Miss Rehana Begum,' he said, 'felicitations, daughter, on what is obviously your hour of triumph.'

Impulsively, she took his forearm in her hand. 'Come,' she

said. 'Let me buy you a pakora to thank you for your advice and to apologize for my rudeness, too.'

They stood in the dust of the afternoon compound near the bus, which was getting ready to leave. Coolies were tying bedding rolls to the roof. A hawker shouted at the passengers, trying to sell them love stories and green medicines. Miss Rehana and happy Muhammad Ali ate their pakoras sitting on the front bumper.

'It was an arranged engagement,' Miss Rehana said suddenly. 'I was nine years old when my parents fixed it. Mustafa Dar was already thirty then, but my parents knew they were dying and wanted someone who could look after me. Then two months after they died he went to England and said he would send for me. That was many years ago. I have his photo, but I do not know what his voice sounds like. He is like a stranger to me.'

The confession took Muhammad Ali by surprise, but he nodded with what he hoped looked like wisdom. 'Still and all,' he said, 'one's parents act in one's best interests. They found you a good honest man who has kept his word and sent for you. And now you have a lifetime to get to know him, and to love.'

He was puzzled, now, by the bitterness that had infected her smile.

'But, old man,' she asked him, 'why have you already packed me and posted me off to England?'

He stood up, shocked. 'You looked happy, so I just assumed . . . They turned you down?'

'I got all their questions wrong,' she replied. 'Distinguishing marks, bathroom décor, all. Now I will go back to Lahore and my job. I work in a great house, as ayah to three good boys. They would be sad to see me leave.'

'But this is tragedy!' Muhammad Ali lamented. 'Oh, how I pray that you had taken up my offer! Now it is not possible. They have your form on file, cross-check can be made, even the passport will not suffice. It is spoilt, all spoilt, and it could have been so easy.'

'I do not think,' she told him as she climbed aboard the bus and gave a wave to the driver, 'I truly do not think you should be sad.'

Her last smile, which he watched from the compound until the bus concealed it in a dust cloud, was the happiest thing he had ever seen in his long, hot, hard, unloving life.

# Stopover

## GRAHAM SEAL

JOE SPEIRS TOLD his wife he would take the train to Vancouver.

'What's wrong with the plane?'

'I've been feeling a bit tired lately. The rest might do me good.'

This was true, but there were other reasons. The return of an old childhood fear of flying, for instance. He thought of telling her this, but she would call it a phobia. She pooh-poohed phobias. And anyway the fatigue and the fear of flying stemmed from a huger, deeper fear he could not explain to her, even if he had wished to: he could not even explain it to himself.

It took the form of moments of inexplicable terror, brought on by the simplest things. Familiar objects would take on a strangeness: he would find himself skirting tables and chairs at home and office with a sudden loathing; or, on the point of reaching out for his telephone, draw back his hand as though from a living, evil thing. Lately, too, he had felt increasingly estranged from friends and colleagues. He sensed behind their smiles dislike or even hatred: there was something threatening simply in the way they stood. At such moments he was strongly aware of their physical presence: body smells, grossness of gesture and feature. Worst of all were the moments of vertigo when people and objects seemed literally to be falling away from him, like figures vanishing into a nightmare's void; he would find himself reaching out to clutch, to hold back, to hang on. A premonition of disaster hovered always at the fringe of his consciousness, so much so that he had put away his car and had taken to walking to work in downtown Montreal.

On the morning he was to leave for Vancouver, he went round the house and hugged each member of his family. This was not customary. He was frequently away on business and usually was content to leave to a chorus of offhand shouts from distant rooms.

'Hey,' said his wife, 'easy!' She was massaging cream into her skin before the bathroom mirror. He stepped back but reached out a hand to touch her in some light way that would correspond to the fear he felt. He saw a reflected flicker of annoyance in her eyes – these bathroom rituals were sacrosanct – and his hand fell away. He stood very still, watching her with the intensity of his whole being.

'What's the matter?' she said.

'Why don't you all come with me?'

She turned on a tap abruptly. 'You know we can't do that. Children's schools. Things.' Frowning, she picked up her toothbrush, squeezed paste on it, began to brush her teeth. All her movements were swift, vigorous, sure. Between brushings, she said: 'We'll open up the cottage when you get back. I'll maybe go up there while you're away, clear the place up, okay?'

He watched her in silence.

She rinsed out her mouth, patted her lips with a tissue, and stepped back from the mirror, preoccupied, rapt. He could see that she was parcelling up the days ahead, the weeks that followed. She reached out a hand to pat him on the cheek, and he stepped back.

'What's wrong?' she said.

'Nothing.'

'Maybe you're right about the train, after all. You do look a bit peaky.'

He watched her as she arranged tendrils of hair about her ears. Her skin was perfectly smooth; even without the cream there was not the suggestion of a wrinkle in it. He studied her child's blue eyes, the softly rounded chin, the smooth bland forehead. Ten years, two children.

*He was looking at a stranger.*

Before he left he went into his small conservatory. He had spent a lot of time there, lately. He liked the awareness of things growing around him, the soft green light, the feel of soil between his fingers. Often, just fingering leaf and stem, an old peace would return. He did this now, but the fear stayed in him. His hands were sweating. He rubbed them dry on his pants and called for his family to see him off.

He could hear groans from the children, a sigh from Harry: 'Do we *have* to?' But they came out and stood on the patio with him. There was a chill in the air. The spring sky was a cold powder blue. He put his arms round his children and hugged them hard. They squirmed self-consciously, puzzled and embarrassed by this display of affection.

He turned before he reached the sidewalk. They stood as he had left them: Ella with the gold band round her teeth, Harry with his freckles, Clare cool and pretty in her white shirtwaist and slacks; all still wearing the faintly puzzled smiles, arms stiffly raised. For a moment he was one of them: a father, a comfortable family man, then some trick of the light seemed to distance him; the shutter clicked, the light moved on; his family stood like cardboard figures in a photograph. Behind him the taxi thrummed. He climbed in, turning once more before they drove away. But already the patio was deserted: all that was left was a pale sheen of light glazing the brown mosaic.

He was going to a convention. His firm made lightweight alloys, widely used in the electronic and aeronautic industries. These made for greater precision, higher speeds, and so were in huge demand, even though their life span was brief. The past year had seen record sales and as sales director Joe was to receive a special award.

He sat in the rear parlour car of the train as it burrowed its way through the north Ontario bush, a successful forty-five-year-old businessman. His briefcase was tucked behind his legs, a glass of whisky stood on the table before him, stars floating on the pale amber liquid. His hands were comfortably folded; a gold ring blinked in the green light thrown back from the tunnel of trees. He wore a modest dark tie with a club pin and his suit was grey, expensively tailored. Beneath the sandy hair, carefully brushed to cover a bald patch, his face had just the right weight of executive gravity. A casual onlooker might say 'bland', but behind the horn-rimmed glasses his eyes held that faint trace of fear and bewilderment one sometimes sees in the eyes of a child who has been sent away to amuse himself in a strange room with unfamiliar toys.

Nevertheless some inner ease and order had returned. He had felt its onset even as the train slid out of Montreal. He simply needed to be alone, to rest a while; he had been overworking: it was as simple as that.

The incessant motion, the continual flow of green past the windows, induced drowsiness. His eyes closed, he smiled comfortably. His fears were shadows, without substance or foundation. A few days on the Pacific coast among colleagues would put him right. The train had been a good choice. He thought with pleasurable anticipation of the lakes, the prairies, the mountains to come. It was after all no small thing to be a successful citizen of this country, *his* country, entitled to sit here, drink, food and berth to hand, as it unrolled its splendour for him.

Yes, this strange fear would pass – which was just as well! His behaviour during the past few weeks must surely have struck people as peculiar at times – to say the least! Oddly enough, no one had commented on it, not even his own family. He stirred uneasily. Why? he wondered. Surely, if they had cared enough . . . He remembered how he had turned and looked for them as the taxi drew away, the light on the empty patio. He felt the fear surging back.

And then it was gone; the drowsiness returned. It was all part of the sickness: this getting upset over trifles. That moment with Clare in the bathroom, the children's reluctant appearance – these meant nothing. He had always had this light, cool relationship with his family – encouraged it. Clare's response to that sudden mad suggestion of his that they all come away with him, had been just right: sensible, cool. At work, he liked things to go along evenly, without fuss. He thought of his grey office, the grey broadloom carpet, the telephone with its rows of lights, his secretary within calling distance, his papers always immaculately arranged. Yes, tidiness, the well-ordered life, these things were satisfying. His thoughts moved ahead to the convention. This would be all pleasure. The hotel with its tasteful rooms; muted ochre early-morning light diffusing through heavy curtains; a glimpse of the Pacific. The men he would meet: all colleagues, friends. The award he was to receive. And behind him, his home: the house with the blue shutters on the quiet, maple-lined street. The leaves that blew with a soft insistence in summer and in fall crinkled in that special way that always made him think of barbecues and woodsmoke on October nights. As soon as he got back from the convention he would take the family up to the lakeshore cottage. He saw the days ahead in anticipation: the group on the porch, the chilled beer with beads of water gleaming on the cans, the pure white bow wave as his boat surged past, the voices of friends calling across the water. Then winter again, the snow, the ski slopes, that favourite hill of his above Lac Morin. Sleepily he thought of it now, with the wind whispering in the firs. Far below him, the other skiers: colours, cries and laughter all fading into winter twilight. He would join them; there below were friends, drink, log fires, rest. He crouched, adjusted his boots, stood and drove in his ski poles, pushed himself downwards . . .

He caught the scream in his throat. He was falling through black space. The trees, the colours, the uplifted faces: all were gone. He was tumbling over and over, falling through endless space. At one stage he saw himself, as though from a great distance: a tiny white doll, its arms and legs flailing at darkness. He wanted to cry out, to reach out and check its fall, but he could not move or speak . . .

Then it was over; his skis touched snow and he slid down the long white slope into a dreamless sleep.

He was wakened by a droning voice. An elderly man seated opposite him was making caustic remarks to a young companion about the muzak that flowed unceasingly overhead. 'Appropriate to our aseptic times. You know they edit it, I suppose? Nothing must remain that jars or stimulates. Leviathan must not wake.'

His voice was clipped, precise, but there was an undertow of heavy dreariness in it that went with the withered mouth, the dried academic features. Joe took him for a university lecturer, a professor perhaps; his companion: his son, or possibly one of his students. Joe caught the young man's eyes and looked away quickly. They were pale blue, cold, devoid of any human expression. Everything in their regard seemed to weigh the same. They flickered over Joe and he became one with the furniture, the scenery, the pale yellow and green afternoon light.

'Sweet music of reassurance,' rasped the old man. 'The nurse's croon. You shall not know pain. *Memento mori?* We'll see that you don't.' He paused. 'Yet even at this moment, we travel on the dead.'

The idea seemed to please him: a wintry smile etched the corners of his pale mouth. 'Yes, in the building of this stretch of track alone, I gather, a score of serfs lost their lives, in order that we might go on our significant ways.' He glanced out of the window at the interminable trees and yawned hugely. 'Bizarre contrasts,' he droned. 'Out there, a wilderness. In here . . .' He flicked a contemptuous hand at the coach's interior. 'Frontiers – once men lived at them, whether of earth, mind, or life itself. Life could only be realized fully at such outposts. *We* seek only oblivion: that is our frontier. Embalmed in our funkholes, wrapped in our foetal sacs, we pray that we will be spared any great intensity of feeling; that suffering, adversity, even love itself, will not break through to us. Provide us with small amusements, Lord, supply mindless preoccupations, allow us, if it be Thy will, to pass through varying degrees of anaesthesia to a painless and total extinction. Amen.' He paused and made a steeple of his fingers. 'What strange freaks must result from this trivialization of the spirit. What weird aberrations of behaviour we shall see as we submit to this slow paralysis . . .'

His voice tailed off. A look of insufferable boredom crossed his face. He gazed indifferently at his watch. 'Well, thank God, it seems it's nearly time to eat. You hungry?' Briefly his dead brown eyes met the cold blue eyes of his companion and they exchanged what might have been smiles.

The train had stopped. The line ahead was a single track, and they were waiting presumably for an oncoming train to go through. Joe took out the notes for the speech he was to make at the convention. He had prepared a rough draft of the speech already, but this now seemed inadequate. While the elderly man had been speaking, he had been pursuing his own line of thought, reviewing his life, his achievements. He ticked these off one by one in his mind and the results were satisfying. He would like to say something about them in his speech, introduce the personal note, express gratitude for his good fortune. And to whom? Why, surely to his firm, since they had been the principal providers. He started to jot down words and phrases: 'Believe me when I say that I am not ungrateful . . .' 'I am deeply and sincerely grateful for . . .' 'On my own I know that I would never have got to first base . . .' He stopped writing. His pen was wobbling, his hands shook. He felt tears in his eyes and emotions tracking through him out of all proportion to what he was writing. He shook his head irritably and wrote on: 'I am always conscious of the fact that our product brings us into relationship with the whole human family, of which I am privileged to be a . . .' He leaned back in his seat, eyes closed, seeing himself, hands spread, linking hands with men and women throughout the world. A sob racked his body. His hands went to his eyes. Oh Christ, what was wrong? He covered his eyes with his hands, afraid that he might reveal something to the men opposite, but they were preoccupied with their own shadows. He struggled for composure. What was going on? What was happening to him? He recalled other moments like this from the weeks since the fear had entered his life: exaggerated emotional reactions to small things. Watching his children playing in the garden, for instance, he would suddenly feel tears running down his cheeks; but more particularly when he was watching some silly soap opera on television, he would find himself leaning forward with a desperate yearning that all should end well, and he wept when it did. He had even known the same intensity of feeling while displaying his firm's products to a prospective client. Once he had gripped a customer by the elbow and shaken him when his response had been flat. He felt a keen sense of pleasure now recalling the fear in the other's eye.

He drained his glass of whisky. It occurred to him that this was his fourth in this pre-lunch period. He'd drink no more till this evening, have a nap in the afternoon. He would sit quietly now and do nothing . . .

He put down his pen and looked out of the window. They had stopped by a small lake, walled in on three sides by trees. A listless wind riffled its black surface. A pale lemon light filtered through the scraggy heads of spruce and pine. The light lay on the still water with a cold metallic gleam and fell in broken shafts across the grey upholstery of the parlour car, revealing a patina of dust, a dusty shabbiness Joe had not noticed before. The old man had dozed off. His mouth had fallen open revealing stained or decaying teeth; his Adam's apple was mottled with pale grey gooseflesh. Joe turned away. Under the lake's still surface he could see stumps of fallen trees turned ochre and black by their long immersion. They lay with an eerie stillness, like submerged monsters. He could imagine no life in that pool; for thousands of years it had lain there, lifeless recipient of dead growth.

He rose in sudden agitation and went up to the bar counter. The coloured attendant was polishing glasses.

'What's up?' said Joe. 'Why have we stopped?'

The man gave him a quick gleaming smile. 'It's all right, sir. Soon be on the move again.'

'Yes, but what's the hold-up? Why are we waiting here?' He was beginning to sweat. When he took out his handkerchief to mop his brow he could not conceal the shaking of his hand. The barman gave him a long, considering stare over a glass rim. Was there insolence in that stare? Joe wondered. 'Waiting for a train to pass, *suh*.' Yes, that 'suh' was deliberate, he was sure. Fury and fear mingled. Why had he not simply answered his question at once? His fear must be apparent. The other must have spotted it and decided to patronize him. Joe was shocked to find some furious racist epithet leaping to his lips. The effort to suppress it left him trembling. 'Okay, give me another Scotch. And make it quick!' He took his drink back to his seat and sat down, trying to control his shaking hands. Hell, no one could ever accuse *him* of colour prejudice! Didn't he always smile at the coloured workers in his firm who worked, so he believed, somewhere in the basement?

The trembling passed and was succeeded by an overwhelming listlessness. He tried to return to the notes for his speech, but when he read over what he had written, the expressions of gratitude to his firm, references to his own life, he was seized by a violent revulsion and screwed up the papers. He tried to recall the cheerful thoughts that had inspired them: his achievements, his family, his house, his possessions, and felt the same disgust. Again, his thoughts rushed ahead, seeking to hold on to one thing: the scenery, lakes, prairies, mountains . . . the hotel . . . the convention . . . his award – each sped past, were gone before he could grasp them. A black pall of utter indifference settled on him. At the back of his mind some dark thought was taking shape. He tried to ward it off, reaching out with a fending motion of his hand, as though it were palpable. 'No, no,' he whispered, but he could not stop it. It moved forward like a black scything wind and as it did so, it levelled his life. Roving desperately, back and forth, through childhood and youth, work and marriage, the years to come, he could discover nothing when the thought had passed that seemed of the slightest consequence.

Outside the glass the pool blinked in the cold sunlight like a great sardonic eye, and then a shadow crossed the water and seemed to gather it into the vast indifferent forest. This struck further terror into the watching man and he almost cried out, but observing the young man watching him, he struggled to render his features impassive.

The cold blue eyes stared at him, unblinking. There was nothing to distract this youth now. His elderly companion slept, the scenery discernible from the stationary train was soon absorbed. His hands moved up and down his thighs with irritable intensity. The eyes that regarded Joe carried a hostile gleam.

Then the train started to move again. Immediately Joe felt better. He stood up, smoothed down his suit and straightened his tie. He went to the washroom and sluiced cold water over his face. He washed and dried his hands carefully. The fear was ebbing; already he was forgetting what he had felt so recently. No doubt it was simply hunger! A good lunch, a bottle of wine would make all the difference. Indulge yourself, m'boy, he thought. You deserve it! He smiled at his reflection in the mirror. Aloud, he said: 'Take it easy, boy, huh?'

Wheels drummed steadily beneath him; power surged through him. After all, he was in pretty good shape for forty-five! A pink glow in the mirror flattered his face. He straddled the pedestal flush, leaning his head on his wrist against the wall. When he pressed the pedal an envelope of pale light interposed between his vision and the railroad ties. The track seemed to be tearing beneath him at some incredible speed. His vision blurred; he was mesmerized by light and flashing ties. When he straightened up his wrist was aching; he felt dizzy. How long had he been standing there? Or was it simply the whisky? Okay, no wine, then. 'No wine, boy, okay?' he said aloud. He turned away and as he did so, he caught a glimpse of his face in a chrome water pitcher. In it his features were rendered infinitely small; he saw a tiny smile playing about a tiny mouth.

The fear surged back; then everything went dark.

The moment passed and light returned. He found himself smiling at the reflection in the mirror. He stepped back, puzzled, as though he had encountered a stranger. As he did so, he trod on broken glass. He saw a smashed tumbler at his feet. It occurred to him he must have smashed it himself, literally picked it up and flung it. For some reason this did not alarm him. He felt very calm and still. He picked up the pieces carefully and placed them in the trash can, then he washed his hands again and returned to his seat in the parlour car.

He ordered another drink and sipped it slowly. A strip of light was widening at his feet like a fan. He stopped drinking and watched it with fascination. He felt as though he was on the verge of some insight or understanding, and he sat very still, waiting, listening.

They were leaving the forest behind and coming into a wide area, broken by a lake. Cabins were sprinkled along one edge and at the far end he saw what seemed to be a hotel by a wooden pier.

The train was slowing down. Light was filling the coach. Outside, the surface of the lake was stretched tight like the skin of a drum pegged to the earth's corners. A sullen yellow gleam lay heavily on the lake. Tied to the pier were two cabin cruisers, top-heavy with decks and flashing glass.

Joe stood up and walked to the door. 'I'd like to stretch my legs,' he said to the attendant.

'Only stopping here a minute, sir.'

'Let me out!'

He walked to the end of the platform. The train gushed steam gently. Nobody seemed to be boarding or leaving. The platform was deserted. At the end of the platform was a small red shed. Joe stepped inside it and watched the train through the cracks in the planks. The train seemed very far off or like a train in a movie. Light filtered through the cracks in the hut, spinning dust motes. He watched his attendant get down and glance anxiously up and down the platform.

'Leaving now, sir,' he called out. He hesitated and started to walk towards the shed. Joe moved back into the shadows and crouched behind some boxes. The attendant stood in the doorway, peering into the gloom. 'You in there, sir?' He stood uncertainly, then set off towards the head of the train. Joe could see him having an altercation with the engineer. There was much waving of arms, then the attendant returned to the coach, boarded it, and after one long puzzled look up and down the platform, waved to the front of the train.

Joe waited until the train was out of sight, then walked on towards the hotel. It was new, cheap, half-painted, fresh planks still stacked to one side. The woman at the desk was French-Canadian. There was a lop-sided look about her face, due probably to lipstick which had been smeared on heavily and askew. She had a black eye and was screaming at someone behind her: '*Bête! Salaud!*' She turned back, still scowling.

'Yeah?'

'I'd like a room.'

'Yeah? How long? One, two hours?'

'What? Why, a night, I guess.'

The scowl deepened. She threw him a key.

'You have room twelve.'

The stairs creaked with newness, the walls of his room were made of fibreboard. He could hear the rhythmic creaking of springs from the next room. Presumably the rooms were rented out for an hour or two at a time to randy couples off the boats.

He lay down on the bed. Circles of light concentrated and spread on the ceiling. He could feel the dull weight in his bones; he did not think he would be able to move again, but he was uncomfortable, his temples thudded. He raised himself off the bed and went downstairs. He bought a bottle of whisky and took the bottle and a glass into the beer parlour. The room was full of afternoon drinkers, mostly men. By their faces and paunches he could tell they were mostly city dwellers like himself, come here to hunt for game they did not need, fish they would not eat. They spoke too loudly and waved their arms to demonstrate their masculinity. His business suit attracted one or two hostile glances, like the young man's on the train. These hostile glances gave him an intense secret pleasure. He poured a tumbler of whisky and drank slowly. The clamour in the room was continuous, but softly behind it he became aware of an insistent soft thudding. At first he took this to be the thudding in his temples; then he noticed that the room was growing dark, though it was not yet mid-afternoon, and when he looked up at the windows he could see the flyscreens beyond them covered in a mat of winged insects. Their numbers were being increased all the time and as they piled on the lintels or were caught in the wire mesh, they gradually inched out the light, introducing a pale green dusk to the bar. In this half-light the figures at the tables with their gesturing arms and wide mouths looked like circus clowns or men waving from a green sea before they drowned.

A woman joined him. She was thin, almost scrawny, with a tired, apathetic face. She wore pink shorts, a black singlet.

'Hi. You alone?'

She sat down, not waiting for his assent. 'Tha's okay, then.' She slurred her words and her eyes slid around the room as though trying to concentrate on a pitching horizon.

He scarcely noticed her. He drank slowly and watched the faces around him with mesmerized revulsion.

'Goddam mayflies,' she said, waving at the windows. 'See no point in it, d'you? Get born, fly around coupla days, 'n tha's it, all finished, dead. You unnerstand that? Mind if I try some've your whisky?'

He pushed the bottle towards her.

'I'm trying to kick the habit, but what the hell . . .'

Her hand shook slightly as she poured. 'So where yer from?'

'Nowhere.'

'C'mon, that's not nice! Jus' tryin' to be frenly.'

Gradually he became aware of her drunken unwavering stare and briefly panic returned. Like a patient waking from an anaesthetic he stared wildly around; his hands went to his pocket desperately as though seeking a card of identity. He felt compelled to say: 'I'm just passing through. Like, this is a stopover. On my way to a convention.' 'Convention' suddenly seemed a very amusing word. He giggled and repeated it slowly: 'Con-ven-shun.' Now he could feel the sob tearing at him again, tears stinging his eyes; then that mood passed and he felt enormously calm again.

'Wha's the joke?' she said.

'Nothing.' She continued to watch him, and he put a hand on her thigh.

'Hey, what do you think I am?' But she did not move away. When he looked down he could see his hand lying there, like the hand of a stranger. He looked curiously at the gold ring, the stretched fingers that revealed white cuffs, the strong black hairs on the back of the hand. He felt a powerful surge of sexual desire, but this passed almost at once.

He stood up abruptly, unable to tolerate the succession of emotions tracking through him, and went outside.

The pier was thickly carpeted with dead or dying mayflies. At times he was ankle deep in them and as his feet crunched among them, a rank fishy odour rose from the seething bodies. And still they were flying in from the lake's edge, swarming males seeking swarming females, some beaten to death against the hotel before they could meet and couple for the first and last time in their brief lives. Some at his feet were still going through the last frenzy. The male would die soon after and the female in a day or two, once her eggs were laid. Then the cycle would begin again: the pupation among the slime and rock of the lake bed, the slow rise towards the sun, the wings forming and spreading for this brief flight and single ecstasy.

Thunder was rolling over the forest. Across the black frieze of trees a pennant of yellow light stretched against a greying sky. The skin of the lake was still taut, stretched to break point. Distantly it was pierced by a rapier of lightning, once, and again, and now in a dozen places, nearer and nearer. His head ached. Feet crunched behind him. He turned and saw the woman. A man called from one of the boats: 'Hey, Ellen, you're going to get wet. C'mon board!'

'Ah, screw off!'

She joined Joe. 'What you doin' out here? I thought you'd gone to the john.' She clasped her arms about her and shivered. 'Place gives me the creeps.'

He closed his eyes as a brilliant flash smote the lake's surface. For the duration of the flash he felt a rising expectancy, the onset of a kind of jubilation. Life's potential seemed about to declare itself to him. He smelt the rain in the air, heard frogs croaking in the marshes, as he had done as a boy. When he opened his eyes the moment had passed. The ache in his head persisted. The lake shone with a dead lustre. Aloud, he said: 'I do not see things properly.'

'How was that?' she said.

'Nothing.'

'You're a funny guy.' The woman moved closer to him, touched him with her whole body. He felt her thinness and something like pity stirred in him.

'I've got a room,' she said. 'Why don't we go there?'

He followed her inside and upstairs. She undressed and watched from the bed as he folded his clothes and stacked them neatly one by one. All this was happening away from him, to a stranger in a foreign room. From time to time he would pause, as though listening for something.

'For Chrissake!' she said.

He looked across at her. Reflections of lightning rippled around the room like barographic lines. They rippled across the thin naked body with small sagging breasts, lying in the half-light. A shadow swept across the floor and the light that followed it was like a powder flash that left the room virginal, pure.

Soon it would be all right. Gradually the emotions that had ravaged him over the past few weeks were becoming one. He stood quite still and when he was utterly calm and sure, moved towards her.

The first rain began to fall as he lay down beside her, slowly at first, then with a sustained roar. He might have said, if anyone could have asked him later, that when he first pulled her towards him, he had felt nothing but a tenderness so powerful it was as though it had been damming up for years. He could not have said when the tenderness changed to something else, or even if it had changed at all. Nor could he have said when the power took over and his arms were no longer his arms, his hands not his hands.

It was nearly dusk when he left the hotel and started walking towards the forest. The storm had passed, the air was fresh. He walked with the air of a man who has suddenly discovered aim and purpose. He followed a narrow trail into the dark line of trees. A light wind stirred the branches overhead with an incessant hissing sound. The path was rough and sometimes he stumbled, but he kept up the same speed and the fixed look of purpose on his face did not change. Soon the path petered out and with its termination the light too faded quickly. Dead branches strewed his way and he often stumbled and fell. Each time he brushed down his clothes before starting again. At one point his wallet dropped from his pocket. He did not bother to pick it up.

It was dark when he reached the pool. He sat down by it and stared at the black still water. The wind died, the darkness intensified, but however dark the night, the pool was still blacker. It turned cold, but he did not move for a long time; he sat quite still, staring at the black water. Then he stood up and started to walk.

It was a month later that the patrol car pulled off the dirt highway a few miles from the hotel. Constables Willis and Donnelly were bored and this had allowed a mutual antipathy to intensify. They had reached the point where they were not speaking, save on official matters, and Willis was glad to use the call of nature as an excuse to get away from his colleague for a while. He walked as far into the forest as caution counselled. He knew the dangers of going too far. A couple of hundred yards would do it, just far enough to lose the sound of traffic, then the forest had you; you could start walking in circles, never be found again. He'd known that happen to men before.

So he kept within earshot of the pop music Donnelly had switched to and delayed his return by sitting for a while on a fallen branch, listening to the wind high in the trees and looking casually around.

He was at the top of a slope. At the bottom was a small pool. Beyond it he could visualize the forest stretching for a thousand miles: nothing but an infinite repetition of lonely pools, dense trees. He shivered, and strained to hear Donnelly's music. Already, after only a few minutes, the loneliness of the place was oppressing him. Already he felt the need of a voice to break the silence. Even Donnelly's! He stood up to go, glancing back once more at the pool before he did so. His eye was caught by something there, among the fallen timber, and he called through the trees to his companion.

They scrambled down the slope together. 'Thought at first it was just another dead branch,' said Willis, bending over the body.

They went through the pockets. 'No identification. Nothing,' said Donnelly. 'What's a well-dressed bastard like this doing here? Can't have come off the road. His car would still be there.'

They studied the trail of footprints that had worn a path round the pool. 'Wonder what he found so fascinating about this goddamned puddle,' said Donnelly.

'Lost,' said Willis. 'You know how it is in the bush. You walk in circles. Maybe some guy at the hotel thought he'd have an evening stroll.'

'Hey,' said Donnelly, 'you don't think he could have had anything to do with that woman who was strangled, do you?'

Willis glanced at the dead man's face. 'Not this one,' he said. 'C'mon, let's get him into the car.'

They were silent as they carried their burden through the trees, but once they saw the road and their patrol car, they began to chat easily and crack the odd joke. The incident had drawn them together. They were, after all, two men engaged in responsible, important work. Their lives had shape and purpose.

Willis found himself whistling as they stowed the body in the trunk of the car and readily agreed to do a little hunting with Donnelly at the weekend.

# A Sleeping Pill for the Doctor

## LIONEL SEEPAUL

AGAIN, NOW FOR the third time within ten minutes, the black telephone just outside the doctor's darkened bedroom was ringing.

'Who is it? Why don't they say something at least?' Then, she thought, 'Perhaps it's he . . .'

When the first call had come, Merna, the twenty-seven-year-old wife of Dr Balroop Moonee, was in the bathroom – naked. Though alone in the house, she feared suddenly coming upon some intruder. This was the feeling that suddenly clutched her whenever she was naked, which often she was before the tall, elongated mirror mounted on the bathroom door.

The first call might have lasted two minutes. It had seemed longer however than the second call, coming three minutes later and lasting less than a minute. But this, the third call, was unceasing; on and on the telephone kept ringing like a persistent bore.

Frantic, beside herself with rage, Merna rushed out, clutching the flowered skirt she had hopped into. Above, waist up, she was naked; but ignoring that uncanny feeling someone might be spying on her large breasts with enlarged nipples, she grabbed the phone, crushing the black, coiled cord as though it were some obstinate serpent.

'No, I'm not the maid – I'm the doctor's wife!' she shouted, releasing the cord which went limp at her naked feet. Then, quickly, in an acidulous tone:

'This is not the police station, you know, this is the doctor's residence . . . Eh? What you damn Trinidad people think that this is, some bloody police station that you can call and hang up any damn time you well please . . .'

She paused, nervous: still no voice on the other end.

'Look, whoever you be, the doctor would be home any minute now. He has an office, if you want to know. Don't you think the doctor is entitled to a little peace of mind in his own castle? He already working his tail out for you people at his office. Then he does overtime at the public hospital. The doctor driving himself so hard that – that he has to take a sleeping-pill to go to bed . . .'

Pausing again, Merna slowly sucked in air, looking down her almost athletic body and struck by an odd thought: a skirt somehow showed up less wrinkles than a dress.

'What you people think you paid the doctor's medical school fees that you could take up a phone and ring him – just like that.'

Her tone was decidedly comic, but it progressed into studied sarcasm: 'Another big mistake – the first was granting Independence – was to give every Tom, Dick and Harry a telephone in Trinidad.'

Merna slammed the phone. She bit her moistened lips, neatly edged, and stood back to consider the effect of her speech. She had certainly recited the words drily, forcing some drama, but really suspecting that on the other end of the line the caller might indeed be her husband, Dr Moonee himself.

Were it really the doctor, this outburst she thought might well lessen, though not quite completely erase, his suspicion. He was, she had observed lately, not quite himself. He was rash, irritable, and impulsive. In this mood he had without warning dismissed the maid; and, if this were not enough, sold the red sports car, a gift from her father.

'Wait till Papa hear about this.'

This too, Merna might complain about. Pretending he was searching for termite in the dusty flooring, Dr Moonee would inch up surreptitiously while she was speaking even with her father. Then Dr Moonee had torn open a letter addressed to her from the Horticultural Society, confessing later it was an innocent error.

'People still can't write clearly – why don't they print instead.'

Not that his remark quite mattered to her. Dr Moonee remarked on almost anything; everything and everybody was in need of some improvement, most of all, his wife. Not that that too quite mattered to her. But last month, when in a rash display of impatience he dismissed the maid for merely overcooking the potatoes, Merna felt threatened.

'What he think that a maid so easy to get? Since this island turn Independent, the maids turn independent too. You hire them and the next thing you know the maid's turning around and giving you, the madam, orders left and right. And telling you too, what day they taking off. The doctor must be think I could run down by the public market and pick up a maid like a pound of potatoes,' she said aloud, bitterly and angrily.

An oil reproduction of a wild mare rearing against a background of darkling foliage, bought by her husband a year ago in a basement sale, teased a remote comparison.

'Better I were in a paddock,' she lamented. 'Already I was in a convent school for five long years. It would have been six if Papa didn't – didn't take me to the airport to see this – doctor! This house is worse than a jail, worse than the convent . . . No maid, no car.'

The coolness of the afternoon, with its slight breeze flapping an originally bright orange-coloured curtain but now speckled with dust, suggested the hour. It might be nearly six. Sometimes, though not always, Merna could guess the hour from the darkening corners of her high, two-storeyed, concrete house. She had acquired this habit from practice, by not rushing every moment into the doctor's darkened bedroom to look at the quaint clock, the final gift of his deceased mother. When Merna did, she somehow found the day seemed longer, the hours more drawn out.

She sighed and bent her pear-shaped head till above the tip of her pointed nose she saw again her pair of breasts, solid but erect. With slender fingers she fondled them maternally, passing both hands simultaneously along the side of her smooth body till both hands firmly clutched her narrow waistline. She exhaled, pleased with her shape.

Again she sighed but it was more like a groan from the inner recesses of her soul. How aged she felt; jaded at barely twenty-seven. And when the feeling became intense she would rush into the doctor's bedroom – her own too – and ransack the medicine cabinet, among the litter of bumpy tubes, plastic phials, varied laxatives, a hoard of sample drugs, the sleeping pills he had prescribed for her sudden insomnia – for a jar of baby-cream.

Footsteps, the doctor's – who else? Briskly she put on her tight, red shorts and red jersey with its armless sleeves and prostrated herself on the faded couch jammed against the gritty concrete wall. She closed her large, brown eyes; put her right hand slackly on her flattened stomach; crooked the left leg, counting the footsteps.

The usual words, 'These deadly bacteria we doctors are exposed to,' she heard him say with unforgettable importance. Then he was brutally rasping his shoes away on the brittle brown mat. 'But such cannot survive this deadly spray.'

Merna heard a sound like the one from the can of aerosol spray she used in the kitchen; and, the next day, she would garner cockroaches lying belly-up along the red kitchen counter, and some on the tiled floor with pale burnished wings quivering perhaps in their final futile struggle for life. 'The wings of Azrael,' which recalled her convent religious instructions.

Dr Moonee announced his presence by spanking louder on the flooring.

'Eating and sleeping. No exercise. No wonder you can't sleep at night, Merna. No wonder those powerful sleeping pills I prescribed have no effect on you.'

Even tighter Merna closed her eyes, hearing, 'You be

careful with those pills, Merna,' the doctor's tone was casual though less caring; 'even a doctor's wife can become addicted to them, you know.'

Just then the telephone began ringing.

Slowly, as one coming to from a long sleep, Merna opened her eyes. Dr Moonee stood swinging his bulging briefcase; the motion was deliberate and slow. On either side, etched in silver: Dr Balroop Moonee, MD.

So metallically, so persistently the telephone whirred, that Dr Moonee swung sharply around, almost thrown off balance by his heavy briefcase.

'You answer that bloody phone, Merna, before I rip it off the wall. Like everybody timing me, to see when I come home.'

Merna sprang both slender arms up, cupping both ears, pierced a few days ago.

'Put away that damn baby-cream. You're brown already. What you want to add another shade on your skin. Leave that sort of thing for the English girls. They don't have all-year-round sun like us so they spend long hours under sunlamps, and using all kinds of skin creams to get a tan. But you have this baby-cream driving me crazy, Merna.'

Merna rubbed her large, brown eyes, blinking and rolling them about while she shoved the jar of cream under the faded couch. He observed her somewhat in a professional manner now. Something medical was sure to come from him, she thought, posturing like a woman slowly awakening.

'Are you deaf, woman? The phone, the phone.'

'One of your patients, I'm sure,' she said crossly. 'Maybe that mysterious caller or that woman again.'

'Woman, eh?' he said. 'Then let her keep ringing till she get fed up.'

The phone stopped ringing.

Merna snickered; Dr Moonee scowled darkly: poor timing on his part. Somehow he was always saying things that never seemed to work out in his favour.

'Why', he asked, 'do you let the phone ring for so long? A call to us doctors can mean life or death. All the way up the steps I was counting. I'm sure I counted ten rings at least.'

'You counted ten,' she countered, lifting her slender arms and her fingers fanning out towards him. 'But that was only for one call. What about the more than ten calls during the day? I feel like some maid –'

'You are a doctor's wife,' he curtly corrected.

'A doctor's wife or servant,' she replied with deep offence in her voice.

Dr Moonee played theatrically with his stethoscope for a while; it was still round his short neck where it hung while he drove his huge American car to and from his office.

He took off his brown chequered coat he brought back from England and hung it over the back of one of the four metal chairs. And while he stuck the stethoscope into the left pocket, he asked rather softly but shrewdly, 'When – what time did the call before this last one . . .'

Merna squinted, and lifted a naked wrist.

'If you were wearing the watch I gave you for our fifth wedding anniversary you would have known,' he scolded.

'I haven't sold it as you did the red sports car Papa . . .'

Dr Moonee grunted; he pinched up his frayed sleeve and studied his own watch.

'I was expecting a call from Dr Fen. He was going to call and leave a message with you, Merna. But you had to have your Roman bath,' he sulked.

'Hmnn, Dr Fen . . .' Merna stretched her legs, threw back her head and yawned; yawning a second time so widely that her white teeth showed an evenness the doctor perhaps was seeing for the first time.

Dr Moonee walked across to the round table, heaved the briefcase on the top, murmuring to himself: 'Five years, and this woman doesn't understand yet that answering the phone promptly can mean life or death to some patient.' He turned and faced her; his eyes were accusatory, his tone somewhat cryptic.

'All day long it seemed this house is busy.'

'Your patients, doctor. I warned you not to give every Tom, Dick and Harry your home number . . . This In-dependence spirit going to kill us sooner or later,' she said, levering herself up from the sagging surface of the couch, groping with the free hand for the jar of baby-cream.

Their eyes clashed; his reddened ones were fixed on her. The penetration revived a certain fear located in a revolver Merna had discovered a few days ago under the doctor's pillow. He had explained its presence only because the revolver was bought privately and was unlicensed. 'No son-of-a-bitch going to get Dr Moonee's cash without a couple of bullets in his head.'

Quietly she lay back; she was hardly pacified even though he had afterwards conspiratorially confided this secret to her. Twisting her body somewhat, she unscrewed the white plastic cap from the jar, scooped two fingers in and applied the cream to her elbows.

'Dammit, to have missed Dr Fen's call,' he swore, stamping. 'Dust – dust,' he complained.

Merna sneezed. Afterwards she smiled a wavering smile; her voice, too, was wavering: 'Since when you and Dr Fen are bosom-bodies?'

Fiercely – 'We are colleagues – medical doctors together,' he defended. 'Never mind our differences.'

'You mean – competition.'

He cut her short; enraged, he stamped again. But Merna repressed a sneeze.

'We doctors are forming a scuba-diving club,' he looked down at the spot he had stamped on.

'Scuba-diving club,' she moaned, bending over to massage her thigh.

Dr Moonee, discerning the frilled edges of her underpants, grunted. 'Dust. I don't know why I left England to come back to this small, dusty island – but then I could not take up scuba-diving in the chilly English waters.'

'You already work six whole days in your office, doctor. Then you do overtime at the public hospital. Couldn't you stay home on Sundays – just one day. Doctors need rest too.'

Her tone might have been genuine; Dr Moonee could detect a trace of pleading.

'Rest?' He laughed a casual but forced laugh. 'Doctors need

rest but also recreation,' he added with emphatic self-concern. 'Besides, why do I need rest when all day long you're resting for both of us, Merna.' And again he laughed.

His hollow laugh was effective; Merna winced, pressing her palms together, she fixed her large, brown eyes on the ceiling, flat and flaked.

Dr Moonee was waiting, expecting some response to his thrust. But Merna was prepared for silence, at least for the moment. She was staring now at the four metal chairs around the round-top table where Dr Moonee was bending over now, fumbling in the coat-pocket for the keys of his bulging briefcase.

In that stooping posture he resembled a dwarf. And when he stamped again, having not yet found the key, Merna mocked, 'One day you would put your big foot through the floor like Rumpelstiltskin.'

Slowly he straightened. 'My house, Merna,' he said sharply; 'I could stamp through the flooring or even build a fire in my backyard. But at least I would sweep the dust away.'

'The doctor knows the story, I see,' she teased.

'You go on, Merna,' he warned. 'One of these days I am going to forget I am a medical doctor and – and put my foot in – in,' he stammered, fitting the key into the slot just above the etched MD.

So startled by his reaction was she that she decided against accentuating the point about the lonely dwarf's intense desire for company, the Queen's first-born. She lay still, studying her husband.

In the light of the naked bulb hanging by a black but knotted cord over the table, Dr Moonee's squat form showed an unevenness. His waist billowed; the spotted bright yellow shirt could not quite conceal the wobbly fat. He was short, could have appeared athletic, but he was definitely an un-exercised man. He was content to drive; to be seen walking was humiliating: an activity for the poor and pariah of the island, not for a medical doctor for whom walking was degrading – something beneath what he thought people expected of him.

Merna drew up her legs; the couch squeaked. Again the frilled edges of her pink underpants lay exposed to Dr Moonee's view. But he would not look up. He was concentrating on bricks of blue and green notes held by thick rubber-bands which as he snapped off sent thick low sounds resonating through the room.

'Like some damn little boy who wanted a toy-guitar,' Merna thought, rustling her red top, blowing down her high bosom, rendered higher by full-grown breasts.

Aware perhaps of her irritation, Dr Moonee twanged and snapped the rubber-bands.

Merna dropped the jar of baby-cream.

Sensing she had deliberately dropped the jar, he sensed too that she was deliberately ignoring him. So with some forced alarm he spoke, not however looking at her.

'Woman, you could get a damn bullet through your skull if you do that foolish thing when I am counting my day's earnings. I didn't pay money for nothing for that revolver. I intend to get my money's worth. The day some of these newly-freed people think they could march through those doors for my hard-earned money, I am going to shoot their arse left and right. Independence or no independence. I working too damn hard for my money for any son-of-a-bitch to grab it, just because they think independence make them free. Free for everything – for taking, for begging – not for working. Ah, when I was bursting my brains in England, studying to be an MD – a medical doctor – it was hard, hard work. That what freedom is, Merna. Not this daily siesta you're having, Merna; lying your tail down on the couch and dropping baby-cream jar to startle me.' Finally he glanced at her. 'Next time I'm going to put the revolver on the table next to me.'

She almost sniggered; such a threat merely brought out the comic in him, equally accentuated by the manner in which he strained his chin in her direction.

'If you want to make yourself useful, woman – get up and close the door.'

Reluctantly, she bolted the door; the frosted glass-panes rattled in their frames.

'Leave the window open,' he commanded. 'Let the breeze come through.'

Merna said, 'I don't know why you couldn't put your money in the Night Safe at the bank.'

'My money is just as safe here as in the bank. Why should I put my own money in the bank when every time I turn around the bank increasing their rental fee.'

Merna asked with grave concern, 'Suppose someone followed you home one day . . .'

'In which case . . .' He paused, then blurted, '. . . the newly-freed man shall get a free post-mortem from Dr Moonee.'

After a prolonged chuckle, Dr Moonee stripped waist up. The wind whipped the tangled curtains; and the curtains rasped away at the frosted window-panes also slack in their wooden frames. The room was humid. Merna saw again the man she was coerced into marriage with. He was still crude and awkward, yet not unrefined.

Like a crane lifting some delicate piece of cargo, Dr Moonee hoisted a stack of notes and placed it carefully on the others, neatly arranged before him.

'Hmn, everybody want to see about my money now. But nobody cared two cents for me when I was burning the midnight oil. They think an MD' (tracing with his eyes the etchings on his briefcase) 'was given me on a silver platter. But let them know that I wasn't born with any gold spoon in my mouth – no spoon at all, not even a damn toothpick if you ask me. But they don't know – these banks and free people – how I grew up. But I grew up,' he added pompously, at which Merna, turning on her side, humping her splendid hips, yawned.

'Yawn on me, woman,' he said acidly. 'But I am one man not ashamed to say how poor I grew up that for dinner I had to throw a fishline in the muddy river, and after school, late in the afternoon, run back to see if the line had a fish. No fish, no dinner. Yet I grew up.' He pushed out his hairy chest and knuckled it. 'The same, self-same Balroop Moonee, now Dr Balroop Moonee . . . he was so poor that he had to run barefoot to school, barehead too in the hot, hot sun, with one exercise book and a small piece of pencil tied to a yellow string round his neck. Yet despite all that was said and done me . . . I made it.' Solemnly he was nodding, blinking as if he were about to doze off.

Merna looked away at the phone, gleaming in the shadows of the corridor which the bedroom door opened on. With thick green curtains always drawn, the room was somewhat cooler than the living room but stifling and sombre.

'He must think we have winter in Trinidad, always keeping the curtains pulled,' Merna sulked.

Brusquely he scraped the metal chair.

Indignantly – 'Do you have to?'

'You raise that voice at that rich father of yours, woman.'

Merna lowered her eyes with derision, dropping her voice: 'The once poor, barefooted boy . . . Why don't you finish the story about the great doctor who once slept on a sack on the mud floor with six or seven children, brothers and sisters. Bitten by fleas, stung by mosquitoes, suck by bedbugs, the poor boy rose early in the morning and milked the cows and tied out the bull in the fields that he came back, all ten toes with jiggers. And then on Saturdays and Sundays, the same poor boy selling potatoes and onions and bananas in the public market and on the wayside –'

'Shut up, woman!' shouted Dr Moonee, gritting his teeth, somewhat stained at the base. 'Shut up, once and for all,' he screamed belligerently.

'Imagine,' with a look of incredulity she said, 'that the doctor – and not the poor, poor boy – is shouting and is screaming.'

Dr Moonee fidgeted; he was pointing an index finger directly in her face.

'The society madam is going to teach me some manners, how I must purse my lips and regulate my voice. I who lived and studied in England don't know about refinement. But this kiss-my-tail small island woman will. She knows everything, ectually almost eeverything.' Dr Moonee clapped his incipient paunch, and in an accent that went heavily English now, 'I say,

Merna, if I make two-three hundreds I call that good going.'
He tapped at his mound of money. 'Say, do you think your
father could ever earn that in one day?'

But her expression had hardened; she was staring vacantly
ahead. The phone seemed as though it might ring any
moment. Merna twitched a bit, somewhat nervously for the
first time: the revolver under the doctor's pillow might be
unsettling on her nerves.

Her voice was exaggerating. 'Nobody in this island but you
doctor ever see and touch so much money at once.'

'Don't you forget that. And remember this also: I, Doctor
Moonee, could put your father and ten like him in my back
pocket. I can buy them out in two twos. Wait till you see the
money rolling in, left and right. They'll eat their words, your
father included. Didn't he once remark that nothing but a
first-class quack could come out from the sugar plantations.
"Only drunks and bastards come out from the plantations" –
were not those his very words?'

The poor, poor boy, she thought; now he would be
describing how late at nights he caught frogs and dissected
them.

Dr Moonee seemed to have sensed her sarcasm.

'I could put your father and this whole island in my back
pocket one day. Just give me the chance. Not so, Merna?'

His sharp tone was demanding an answer. How was she to
respond?

'Yes, you could put everybody in your back pocket and –
and make them fit too,' she said sardonically, which made the
doctor scowl darkly. 'But – but –'

'Don't stammer, woman,' he ordered her.

She burst out: 'Wait till Papa hear how you sold the red car.
Papa paid real money too. Not money he shake down from
some mango tree in the backyard.'

Dr Moonee flickered a smile; it was tinged with triumph.
Her tone was less mordant; he thought he detected a pleading
in her voice, thinned out on the final consonants, ending like
dronings.

She rose and went to the window. It was almost six-thirty;

the twilight had thickened into sudden darkness, so sudden the change without any discernible transition: the tropical wonder.

She slammed the window shut. The window needed force to fit in the sagging frame. The doctor grunted.

'Tea, doctor?' Her tone was studied.

Dr Moonee felt flattered, charmed by her unusual formality.

'Yes, my dear,' he replied, punctiliously, with a certain flavour of an English background. 'You never cease to amaze me, Merna. Wonder shall never cease,' in a tone more English than he cared to admit.

Merna sucked air through teeth: an expression of light contempt.

'Sucking your teeth, that's not polite,' he said, rising gently, not scraping the metal chair, then suddenly slumping down, almost scraping the floor. The next moment he was pawing his paunch so reminiscent of a pregnant woman groping for the head of her baby.

'What sort of tea – doctor?'

Her tone was capable of reflecting more patronage than his, which deflated him. He was vulnerable to her ridicule; her snides wounded promptly.

'You may as well do something useful, woman.' But his tone was depression itself.

And sensing his dejection, Merna hurried away to the kitchen. The kitchen smelled of disinfectant, which made her eyes smart. Even the kitchen generated despair in Merna; the doctor had even imposed his taste there. One day he had brought home a can of red paint, and repainted the white counter and blue walls – in red. The thought flashed through her mind that Dr Moonee might have inserted only red bulbs had not a house not far from theirs, operating as a clandestine brothel, been using a large red bulb in its porch as a mark of identification.

'Like you gone to England to brew me a cup of tea?'

His impatient voice impinged on her tender ears, like the scraping of the metal chair.

While she poured the tea with the same haste as she had hurried back, a few drops were spilled in the plain plastic tray with its flowery sugar-bowl.

'Your nerves are going to pieces, Merna. Better take a double dose of those sleeping pills.'

Merna shifted the tray; some more tea, like a little splash, spattered against the sugar-bowl.

'Ah, good tea,' he gurgled indulgently.

'When you scald your throat, don't blame me,' she said with some concern.

'Pour me another cuppa, woman. You forget I am a medical doctor. I know what's good for me.'

She scratched her left breast.

'Some respect, Merna, don't mind I am used to all sorts of women undressing in my office.'

'Plantation value,' she hissed.

Dr Moonee chuckled.

They might have quarrelled again; inevitably they did when Merna scathed him with remarks about his impoverished origin. But just then the phone began ringing.

Briskly, she ran to the phone, saying, 'I'm sure it must be Dr Fen,' but thinking, It might be Jeevan – how would he know the doctor had given up his Night Safe at the bank and was coming home an hour earlier.

'Woman, the doctor cannot come to the phone,' Merna declared, deadly serious. 'No, Dr Moonee does not make house calls, he has an office, you know. Besides, there is a public hospital.'

From the corner of her eyes, Merna saw the covert smile of Dr Moonee, cleft chin propped in his right hand.

Her tone was lightly abusive: 'You Trinidad people spiteful, if you ask me. You have the whole damn day to get sick, but you waiting till nightfall when the doctor so tired that he has to take a sleeping pill to get some rest – is then all kind of diseases take you all.' Merna paused, fretting, but mainly to study the amused expression on Dr Moonee's face, radiating with pleasure.

'Yes, I am the doctor's wife. But don't describe any

symptoms to me – I am not the doctor. Neither are you. So how can you know your mother has a heart attack. I know you people well. You drink rum whole day and then bothering the doctor with talk about heart attack. I tell you Dr Moonee is in bed. What you want to hear him snoring, to believe me?' And abruptly Merna put down the phone.

She was gasping, not looking at the doctor; looking distractedly however at the wild mare with its forelegs rearing against the darkened horizon.

Dr Moonee was essentially delighted.

'You have more brains than I can give you credit for. You pull that one off cleverly, very cleverly,' he said, lapsing into his affected English accent.

But with a martyred expression and with a bitter voice, Merna replied: 'You have me lying . . . lying to your patient, doctor.'

He ignored her complaint; still praising her.

'If I could have handled that woman the way you did, I would not have had so much trouble. That woman almost caused trouble between me and Dr Fen.'

Merna said, 'That woman ringing this house whole day today. No peace for me.'

'That woman gives nobody peace, Merna. She was a patient of Dr Fen before she came to me.'

'Why did she leave Dr Fen?'

'That's a long story, Merna.'

'Why did she come to you?' asked Merna pointedly.

Dr Moonee was annoyed.

'For assurance, woman,' he snapped.

Again, Merna asked about Dr Fen; and Dr Moonee perhaps to relieve himself said: 'That woman was fed up with Dr Fen and his bargain medicine. So she came to me –'

'For sample medicine?'

'For assurance, Merna – and stop interrupting me like some of these patients of mine.'

The dim light blurred, brightened, dipped low again. Merna plopped down on the couch and resumed pasting her flattened stomach with baby-cream.

'I am not one of your patients, doctor.'

'Very well,' he admitted. 'Now would you let me tell you what this woman said about Dr Fen and – and me, too.'

'What did she say about you?' Merna spiritedly asked.

'One thing at a time.' And he gestured, almost knocking down the mound of money. 'I am ten times a saint to Dr Fen . . . Dr Fen has a package deal. It's like this: you pay five dollars less if you let him fill out the prescription he gives you. You see, Dr Fen got some jars from his father, who runs a grocery. These jars contain antihistamines, vitamins in different colours, laxatives – even sleeping pills. And black is white, Dr Fen only prescribing those drugs for his patients. He even prescribing an aphrodisiac – a sex stimulant, Merna – some kind of distilled water Dr Fen father importing from China. Is when he recommended this water for the woman that she got damn mad and came to me. Medically speaking, the woman's case was purely domestic; in Trinidad we would say she has "man troubles". So I frankly told her if she wasn't satisfying her man and another woman was . . . why should she bother.'

Merna sneezed, then coughed.

'It's then the woman left me, ran back to Dr Fen, accusing me of not only meddling in her private affairs, but selling her – sample drugs.'

'Medical ethics . . .' Merna muttered. 'Dr Fen, on one hand, opening a pharmacy in his office; and you . . .'

Dr Moonee springing to his feet, pointing his finger at Merna: 'You stop that talk right here, woman.'

She followed his hand so as not to see his repulsive armpit, which hand fumbling in the coat pocket fished out a tube of medicine.

'By itself,' Dr Moonee hotly explained, showing the silvery tube as a visual aid, 'this tube is useless till it is prescribed by a medical doctor. This tube like all the other sample drugs is like rubbish in a salesman's or for that matter, in that woman's hand. So when I gave her a tube of medicine, with my medical advice, only then was the tube worth anything. In other words, Merna, the woman like all the other patients is paying for my medical advice.'

He sat down, abashed. It was strange, perhaps more so to herself, that Merna had listened to her husband and not interrupted him. He wondered about this; he wondered too, if she asked why he pasted over his own label on the sample drugs, what he might possibly tell her.

'Medically speaking, though this woman needed no medicine – I still had to. If I didn't the first thing as she run out my office would be to tell people that I was some plantation quack, getting she money, giving she plenty talk, but no medicine. Even the obeahmen and bush-doctors giving some bush mixture in this island.'

'Poor woman . . . you could at least have given her the sample free,' Merna said, commiseratingly.

Her tone, as usual, rasped away at the doctor with its punishing irony.

'You stop that poverty-syndrome talk with me, Merna. Poor woman. You should see the thick gold jewellery round her neck, her wrist, and those rings round her fat fingers. She doesn't look starved. Plump and rosy, it seems she has a life of leisure: three square meals and a daily siesta. And you should smell her, like some Evening Lady as they would say in Europe, with all that perfume on her.'

He completed this moving speech with nondescript gestures. But Merna merely smiled, nodded, uncrossed her legs, and propped her head somewhat brazenly on the armrest of the couch: a teasing posture. She was sly and silent; he was watching her. In her rounded, distinct face there was mockery; and in the parted lips, scorn. Such concerted condemnation was humiliating to him.

Dr Moonee yawned. Merna coaxed him to go to bed. He was startled yet pleased by this show of affection. He was too tired to examine motive; but he suspected this tender feeling was hollow. Merna had lifted his brown coat and his stethoscope while tardily Dr Moonee packed his earnings in the briefcase.

'Don't forget my cuppa in bed,' he reminded her.

'Of course not, doctor.' And off to the kitchen she hurried.

While he lay in bed, awaiting the tea, his mind grew hazy. It was fading away when gradually on the horizon there appeared a thirty-room bungalow with Roman columns and arched hallways lighted up by ornate chandeliers. Around this enormous bungalow – each window canopied with variegated awnings to shut out the rays of the sun – he pictured rich, green lawns, cropped and even, level as the multicoloured Persian carpet spanning each room even the bathroom of this majestic bungalow, surrounded by choice tropical trees reflecting their floundering tops in the placid chlorinated water of his turquoise-coloured swimming pool.

'No riff-raff going to dip their bodies – only – only . . .'

'Only what?' asked Merna, laying the tray near the bed.

He was dazed, still not fully recovered from his reverie – annoyed at her sudden invasion. He lifted the teapot, peeped in.

'Too weak. Don't skimp with the teabag,' he snapped, anxious to be alone, still with the impression of his dream bungalow strongly implanted in his mind.

Dr Moonee was gasping.

'You are very tired, doctor.'

But he gestured towards the kitchen where Merna, puzzled by the glazed silly look on his face, hurried to.

There was a remnant of his vision yet to be articulated. Once again he saw the bungalow with its pyramid-shaped roof of shingles – shingles imported especially for him from some remote country where artisans still took pride using their skills. But inside the thirty-room bungalow on walls panelled with Canadian cedar dangled masterpieces, paintings by Constable and Titian.

There was a knock on the door.

'You don't have to knock, Merna. Come in.'

Merna bit her lip and bowed her head; her hair almost covered her eyes, looking down. She was nervous, almost dropped the teapot.

That telephone again.

'Damn pest.' Dr Moonee gritted his teeth; he was under the flowered sheet as though still mesmerized by his fantasy.

The door was ajar.

'No, for the hundred time you cannot speak to the doctor. Look, I couldn't care less about grammar now. Whether "to" or "with" the doctor – the answer is still the same. The doctor has just fallen asleep. He's just taken a sleeping pill.'

Pausing, Merna heard the indulgent cackle of her husband; he was choking on the tea, perhaps. She gave the door a surreptitious kick; it slammed shut as though by a sudden gust of a mysterious wind.

Sharply Merna whispered, 'I don't know whether the doctor is finding out about us, Jeevan. He's acting suspicious, asking me all sort of questions about a "woman" caller.'

Again she paused, held her breath.

Did she hear footsteps approaching? She pressed her tender ears against the walls of the bedroom.

She was loud again, shouting into the phone: 'No, no, I don't care whether you are dying. The doctor is flesh and blood too – he needs his rest. No, I can't; he's just taken a sleeping pill.'

After listening intently for any footsteps, only hearing the excited beatings of her own heart, she whispered, 'Jeevan, the doctor gave up his Night Safe. He even dismissed the maid or she would have told you. Oh, how the doctor is humiliating me. After some woman went to his office and told him she saw a red car parked near your place, the doctor got rid of the car, the car Papa bought me.'

There was a squeak, not sudden but quite gradual as if the bedroom door-knob was being stealthily turned.

Merna was fidgeting with the black, coiled cord of the telephone.

'You patients think you paid Dr Moonee's medical school fees, eh? You want charity, madam, then go to the poor house. Yes, madam, the doctor needs his sleep too so that he can see you in his office in the morning.'

The door was opened. Dr Moonee with a malicious grin on his face was nodding his head.

But wildly Merna went on speaking: 'His office hours are from eight to five. Don't ask me why the doctor opens his office an hour earlier than all the other doctors.' And she slammed the phone.

'I lose all my sympathy for that woman . . . she again, who else? She wants to know why the doctor this and the doctor that . . .'

'Well.' He stood shakily, rubbing his hands. 'Why the doctor this and the doctor that . . . Well, tell her the doctor needs his tea warmed a trifle bit, with a trifle bit of sugar, if you please.'

'Yes, doctor,' said Merna, curtseying.

Merna was somewhat longer in returning.

Slower than the maid, thought Dr Moonee, propping his pillow after having checked his revolver.

As soon as she came into the bedroom, Merna blurted – 'So that you can have a good sleep, I – I took the phone off the hook, doctor.'

'You have more sense than I praise you for, Merna,' the doctor said, smiling tiredly, yawning widely.

Merna, curtseying like a maid indeed, watched the doctor slowly sipping his tea; heard him make satisfied noises.

'Just right,' he murmured.

She thought his English accent perfect, perhaps induced by the extra-strong tea.

'Just right,' he said again, smacking his lips. 'But – but a trifle bitter, if you asked.'

Pity, she thought, mockingly, fluttering her eyes.

She was prepared to pour another cup, but he beckoned her to draw closer; he was groping for her wrist. What could he mean? He was smiling too. But he always did smile that silly smile.

'You like my baby-cream . . .'

His lips moved queerly and his eyes seemed heavy. A broad smile was left incomplete. She waited a while, her eyes fixed on him.

'An-oth-er cup-pa, doc-tor?'

A groan, and he mumbled something, something in-coherent.

She grew afraid. She tried to imagine the effects of those sleeping-pills he had insisted she take in his presence. They were so strong and bitter to the taste that she suspected the doctor might have been trying to rid himself of her.

Merna stood petrified. The doctor lay still, almost lifeless. She thought his lips looked a bit bluish. Her first impulse was to take him by the wrist; but, this art of feeling for his pulse was beyond her. She had seen how people pressed their ear against the heart – but, in her panic, she had forgotten whether the heart was on the right or on the left. And she had forgotten, too, about putting a mirror to his mouth.

In her alarm, suspecting she might have dissolved the wrong pills in his tea, Merna began ransacking the medicine cabinet. A jar of baby-cream toppled to the floor.

There was a slight groan from the doctor. He moved vaguely. Both hands were spread out; a leg was crooked under the sheet. After a while she heard his breathing, his loud snoring coming on with regularity.

Once more Merna gathered her thoughts. She glanced at the clock before entering the bathroom. She fixed her hair, growing very excited. The pair of red shorts unzipped hurriedly crumpled at her feet. She lightly stroked her smooth thighs, and was amazed at the splendour of them. Briskly she slipped into a flowing, flowery skirt.

When she re-entered the doctor's bedroom, he was snoring thunderously. A flicker of some enigmatical smile was trapped around the corners of his lips.

Should he perhaps get up before she returned home, Merna left a note for the doctor: Gone to visit Papa.

# Good Friday, 1663

## HELEN SIMPSON

*We have a winding sheet in our mother's womb, which grows with us from our conception, and we come into the world, wound up in that winding sheet, for we come to seek a grave.*

MY RUSTIC HUSBAND, preferring to be fifty years behind the times in church matters as in all else, has ordered Parson Snakepeace to preach only sermons from the old dead Divines, and to read them aloud without comment. This being Good Friday, he has chosen the horridest sermon he could find, all to do with death and earthworms.

Lord, I'm sure I am grown quite melancholy at that old barbarous tale of the thorn crown and the sponge in vinegar. Ha, ha, ha!

This church is as cold as the grave. You would not know the air was so gentle outside, all the daffodils kissing the air and the apple trees like brides.

Here, by my pew, lies my husband's mother, Myrtilla Fanshawe, twenty-six years old, d. 1634, boxed up in fine Carrara:

God's goodness made her wise and well-beseeming
Her wifely virtues won her much esteeming,

Earth would not yield more pleasing earthly bliss
Blest w'two babes, though Death brought her to this.

That shallow space over there, beneath the window showing
St Catherine, is reserved for *my* tomb. I insist on a chaste
design. None of your beastly seraphim, mind; I never could
endure your marble flittermice.

Myrtilla died in childbed, bearing that blockhead my
husband. He sits beside me now pretending to listen to the
sermon, his mouth catching flies, a pure clown, mere element-
ary earth, without the least spark of soul in him. That he
should have claimed *me* for his wife! He would be more fitly
mated with some silly, simple, peeking, sneaking country
girl, one that goes with her toes in, and can't say boo to a
goose.

I cannot endure him near me, with his sweating, snoring,
scratching, snap-finger ways. He'll sit and yawn, and stretch
like a greyhound by the fireside, till he does some nasty thing
or other and so gives me an excuse to leave the room. When he
has blown his nose into his handkerchief, he looks into it as if
there were a diamond dropped out of his head.

*There in the womb we are fitted for works of darkness, all the while
deprived of light: and there in the womb we are taught cruelty, by
being fed with blood, and may be damned, though we be never born.*

To confine a woman just at her rambling age! take away her
liberty at the very time she should use it! O barbarous aunt! O
unnatural father!

My aunt Champflower is a very violent lady. She will fall
into a fit or fly at you for the least piddling insignificant thing.
In her day she was a beauty, but now she washes her face and
hands in lead varnish to hide the dismal hollows of eight and
thirty years.

The patches on her white lead face, some big, some little,
look like so many raisins and currants floating in a porringer of
rice-milk.

Lord, what a difference there is between me and her. How I

should despise such a thing if I were a man. What a nose she has! what a chin! what a neck! She desired my ruin with all her little heart. She danced for pure joy at my wedding.

My father never would have heard Scandal's buzz had she only kept it from him. He would have let me look where I pleased for a husband. I have a tidy fortune. But no, I must be thrown away in haste to this clodpole squire.

My aunt calls me to her room and talks of Honour and Reputation with a long face like the beast of the Nile.

'Aye, aye,' says I. 'But what has such talk to do with me?'

'What indeed!' cries she in a passion.

She pauses. She trifles with a lace some time before she speaks next, making play with a certain letter, reading it to herself with a careless dropping lip and an erected brow, humming it hastily over.

I recognize the hand. It is from my Celadon.

'Well, niece, this galloping abroad and allowing young fellows to fool with you has given your reputation no very good complexion.'

'Madam, I seek only to follow your example. Besides, I have heard it said often and often when I was with you in London, that a lady's reputation ought to be a sort of brunette; then it has an attraction in it, like amber. A white reputation is as disagreeable to men, I am sure I have heard you say twenty times or more, as white eyebrows or white eyelashes.'

'Pooh pooh,' says she with a sort of snarling smile. 'You can talk in that airy impertinent way until Domesday but it will not save you. I have other letters. Your fop delights in nothing but rapes and riots, as all the world well knows. I have heard certain tales. I have ocular proof.'

'Madam,' says I, though I start to feel a little uneasy now, 'there are some persons who make it their business to tell stories, and say this and that of one and t'other, and everything in the world; and,' says I . . .

'And your father shall know all,' she finishes.

*Our birth dies in infancy, and our infancy dies in youth, and youth and the rest die in age, and age also dies, and determines all. O,* huzza, Parson Snakepeace; cheerful matter for an April morning! *Our youth is hungry and thirsty, after those sins, which our infancy knew not; and our age is sorry and angry, that it cannot pursue those sins which our youth did.*

I shall never more see the playhouse, nor go to Ponchinello nor Paradise, nor take a ramble to the Park nor Mulberry Garden. I could as soon persuade my husband to share a sillybub in New Spring Garden or to drink a pint of wine with friends at the Prince in the Sun as I could fly.

My aunt Champflower took me with her to London last year for a spring holiday. We lodged near by St James's, and I never was so happy in all my life.

I dote upon assemblies, adore masquerades, my heart bounds at a ball; I love a play to distraction, cards enchant me, and dice put me out of my little wits.

On our third evening, then, we saunter to the pleasure gardens at Ranelagh for the sake of the Chinese lanterns and to taste a dish of oysters.

There we happen to meet again with a certain merry sharking fellow about the town, who has pursued us diligently from chocolate house to milliner to the Haymarket since our arrival. He has with him a friend; and this friend is Celadon.

'I came up, Sir, as we country-gentlewomen use, at an Easter Term,' explains my aunt demurely, 'to the destruction of tarts and cheesecakes, to see a new play, buy a new gown, take a turn in the Park, and so down again to sleep with my forefathers.'

'We see you have brought your sister with you in kindness,' says Celadon, giving me a mighty wink.

The two fine gallants pay her gross and lavish compliments, ogling and glancing and watching any occasion to do forty officious things. They have all the appearance of gentlemen about them. I notice that Celadon's eyes look sideways on me like an Egyptian drawing. He wears a fine long periwig tied up in a bag.

My aunt curtseys at last. Down goes her diving body to the ground, as if she were sinking under the conscious load of her own attractions; then launches into a flood of fine language, still playing her chest forward in fifty falls and risings, like a swan upon waving water.

Hang me if she has not conceived a violent passion for the fellow.

*. . . when my mouth shall be filled with dust, and the worm shall feed, and feed sweetly upon me, when the ambitious man shall have no satisfaction, if the poorest alive tread upon him, nor the poorest receive any contentment in being made equal to Princes, for they shall be equal but in dust.*

I look down now at my arms and see the fine eggshell skin with a pretty sparkle from the sun, and the violet-coloured veins at my wrist. I cannot think I am dust and worms' meat.

The carnation dew, the pouting ripeness of my honeycomb mouth, he said; and that my face was a swarm of cupids.

I do love Love. I would have all the Love in the world. What should I mind else, while I have any share of youth and beauty? When I went to Court all eyes were upon me, all tongues were whispering that's my Lord Spatchcock's fine daughter; all pressed towards me and bowed, only to get half a glance from me. When I went to the playhouse, some stood gazing on me, with their arms across their heads languishing as oppressed by beauty. The brisker fellows combed their wigs and prepared their eyes to tilt with mine. Ah, flattery was my daily bread.

Celadon is so agreeable a man, so eloquent, so unaffected, so particular, so easy, so free. All his finery is from the best in Paris – his shoes from Piccar and his gloves from Orangerie. He wears his clothes with so becoming a negligence that I can barely wish him out of them. He even soaks his handkerchief in rose water.

He had the greatest skill in arranging assignations that ever I saw; and all the while he flattered my aunt with a thousand honeyed words and promises, until I was ready to burst with laughing.

My hair was dressed in flaunting little ringlets and crimped serpentaux puffs. I wore my new under-petticoats of white dimity, embroidered like a turkey-work chair with red, green, blue and yellow, with a pin-up coat of Scotch plaid adorned with bugle lace and my gown of printed calico.

I carried my claret-coloured velvet coat with gold fringes to protect me from the dangers of the night air. Even in spring, jaunting abroad at four in the morning strikes a chill into the bones.

Parson Snakepeace has conceived the pretty notion of keeping a skull upon his desk.

I can never persuade myself that religion consists in scurvy out-of-fashion clothes and sour countenances, and when one walks abroad, not to turn one's head to the right or left, but hold it straight forward like an old blind mare.

'O that I were your lover for a month or two,' he murmured in my ear like a bumble bee.

'What then?'

'I would make that pretty heart's blood of yours ache in a fortnight.'

*That God, this Lord, the Lord of life could die, is a strange contemplation; that the red sea could be dry, that the sun could stand still, that an oven could be seven times heat and not burn, that lions could be hungry and not bite, is strange, miraculously strange, but supermiraculous that God could die.*

The most unnatural spectacle to be seen in Somerset since the Flood was surely my union with Squire Clodpole here. A dainty girl of seventeen yoked to a greasy, untoward, ill-natured, slovenly wretch! We were the laughing stock of five counties.

Now it is five months since our wedding, which I should rather call a show of Merry-Andrews, with nothing pleasant about it at all but the foolery of a farce.

The nuptial banquet was crammed with baskets of plum-cake, Dutch gingerbread, Cheshire cheese, Naples biscuits, macaroons, neats' tongues and cold boiled beef.

My new husband had drunk heartily. The guests cried out for a speech. He staggered to his feet.

'My head aches consumedly,' said he; 'I am not well.'

'Good-lack!' said I, 'if those fellows in France don't press all the grapes with their filthy naked feet. No wonder we are poisoned with their wine.'

He raised his glass to me, then toppled over behind the table.

There was such a laughing, they roared out again. The ladies teehee'd under their napkins. The teehee took a reverend old gentlewoman as she was drinking, and she squirted the beer out of her nose, as an Indian does tobacco.

By the time the bashful bride, meaning myself, was brought to bed, this numbskull had in some wise recovered his wits.

He called for a mouthful of something to stay his stomach, a tankard of usquebaugh with nutmeg and sugar, if you please, and also a toast and some cheese.

Faugh, the filthy brute.

'Supper, sir!' said I. 'Why, your dinner is not out of your mouth yet; at least 'tis all about the brims of it.'

That sharp comment confounded him, so that he cursed, and rolled about the bedchamber like a sick passenger in a storm; then he comes flounce into bed, dead as a salmon in a fishmonger's basket, his feet cold as ice and his breath hot as a furnace.

His head is a fool's egg which lies hid in a nest of hair. He hangs his nose in my neck and talks to me whether I will or no. What a poor sordid slavery there is in the state of marriage.

During our brief courtship, he wailed out some songs of love.

> 'I have a mistress that is fair
> And as sweet as sugar candy,
> Had I ten thousand pounds a year
> I'd give her half a pint of brandy.'

And all the while he gazes on me like a sick monster, with languishing eyes.

I burst into laughter: 'Lord, sir, you have such a way with you, ha, ha, ha!'

*At night He went into the garden to pray, and He spent much time in prayer. I dare scarce ask thee whither thou wentest, or how thou disposedst of thy self, when it grew dark and after last night.* That has set my husband a-tittering. Now he nudges me with his elbow, the filthy fellow. I have no stomach for him. *About midnight He was taken and bound with a kiss, art thou not too conformable to Him in that? Is not that too literally, too exactly thy case? at midnight to have been taken and bound with a kiss?*

Yes, yes, Parson Snakepeace, I was taken captive in a garden, at my lady Wildsapte's last summer *fête champestre*, though I cannot see why you should make a sermon of it, for it had nothing to do with you or your talk of the grave.

We went chasing off by the light of torches down an alley of trees, shamming to fight each other with long hazel twigs.

My lady's grounds are full of little pagan temples and other fancies, and at last we fell down breathless at the foot of a pretty Egyptian obelisk brought back by her son from his late stay in Rome. Screened by the friendly shade of some low bushes, we fell breathless upon the ground together; the leaves around us were of the crimson flowering currant for I can still recall the sharp smell when we bruised 'em by lying upon 'em.

'Cherubimical lass,' he called me, and gazed on me devouringly. Our eye beams were in that moment tangled beyond redemption, and I could not bring myself to draw away when he caught me by the hand, wringing and squeezing at it as if he were mad.

He offered me no other rudeness at first, but we only gazed on each other with half smiles; and our breathing grew laboured when we twisted and knotted our fingers together as if in combat. Then indeed my bounding blood beat quick and high alarms.

He swore that he would come down from London in a fortnight, and marry me.

And so we progressed until, with broken murmurs and heart-fetched sighs, he so mousled and tousled me that I cried, 'Sweetheart!' and he clapped a hand over my mouth to save us from discovery.

Good gods! What a pleasure there is in doing what we should not do.

Then were we animated by the strongest powers of love, and every vein of my body circulated liquid fires; until we came at last to that tumultuous momentary rage of which so much has been whispered since the world began.

O Jesu, when I think back to the heat of his sweet mouth and the smell of his skin, I could weep for weeks together.

Hang him, let him alone. He's gone.

*Hast thou gone about to redeem thy sin, by fasting, by Alms, by disciplines and mortifications, in the way of satisfaction to the Justice of God? that will not serve, that's not the right way, we press an utter crucifying of that sin that governs thee; and that conforms thee to Christ.*

Well, I am eight months gone with child. I may follow Mrs Myrtilla's example more speedily than expected. That would indeed be a convenient conclusion, to be dispatched by my own sin. That would provide matter enough for a month of fine long thundering sermons.

This husband sits beside me like a ball and chain. A pack of squalling infants will do the rest, forging my bonds link by link, and soon I shall inhabit as heavy a carcass as my sister Sarah's. Then will I keep company with the mid-wife-dry-nurse-wet-nurse-and all the rest of their accomplices, with cradle, baby-clouts and bearing clothes, possets, caudles, broth, jellies and gravies. Pish, I grow nauseous when I think of them.

I may build castles in the air, and fume and fret, and grow pale and ugly, if I please; but nothing will bring back my free and airy time.

Outside this church it is almost summer; see how the sun struggles through these coloured glass saints to fall in jewels onto my gown.

I will not die of the pip, so I will not.

*O merciful God, who hast made all men, and hatest nothing that thou hast made, nor wouldest the death of a sinner, but rather that he should be converted and live; have mercy upon all Jews, Turks, infidels, and Hereticks, and take from them all ignorance, hardness of heart, and contempt of thy Word; and so fetch them home, blessed Lord, to thy flock, that they may be saved among the remnant of the true Israelites, and be made one fold under one shepherd, Jesus Christ our Lord, who liveth and reigneth with thee and the Holy Spirit, one God, world without end. Amen.*

# A Trinity

## WILLIAM TREVOR

THEIR FIRST HOLIDAY since their honeymoon was paid for by the elderly man they both called Uncle. In fact, he was related to neither of them: for eleven years he had been Dawne's employer, but the relationship was more truly that of benefactor and dependants. They lived with him and looked after him, but in another sense it was he who looked after them, demonstrating regularly that they required such care. 'What you need is a touch of the autumn sun,' he had said, ordering Keith to acquire as many holiday brochures as he could lay his hands on. 'The pair of you are as white as bedsheets.'

The old man lived vicariously through aspects of their lives, and listened carefully to all they said. Sharing their anticipation, he browsed delightedly through the pages of the colourful brochures and opened out on the kitchen table one glossy folder after another. He marvelled at the blue of the Aegean Sea and the flower markets of San Remo, at the Nile and the pyramids, the Costa del Sol, the treasures of Bavaria. But it was Venice that most vividly caught his imagination, and again and again he returned to the wonder of its bridges and canals, and the majesty of the Piazza San Marco.

'I am too old for Venice,' he remarked a little sadly. 'I am too old for anywhere now.'

They protested. They pressed him to accompany them. But as well as being old he had his paper shop to think about. He could not leave Mrs Withers to cope on her own; it would not be fair. 'Send me one or two postcards,' he said. 'That will be sufficient.'

He chose for them a package holiday at a very reasonable price: a flight from Gatwick Airport, twelve nights in the fairyland city, in the Pensione Concordia. When Keith and Dawne went together to the travel agency to make the booking, the counter clerk explained that the other members of that particular package were an Italian class from Windsor, all of them learning the language under the tutelage of a Signor Bancini. 'It is up to you if you wish to take the guided tours of Signor Bancini,' the counter clerk explained. 'And naturally you have your own table for breakfast and for dinner.'

The old man, on being told about the party from Windsor, was well pleased. Mixing with such people and, for just a little extra, being able to avail themselves of the expertise of an Italian-language teacher amounted to a bonus, he pointed out. 'Travel widens the mind,' he said. 'I deplore I never had the opportunity.'

But something went wrong. Either in the travel agency or at Gatwick Airport, or in some anonymous computer, a small calamity was conceived. Dawne and Keith ended up in a hotel called the Edelweiss, in Room 212, somewhere in Switzerland. At Gatwick they had handed their tickets to a girl in the yellow-and-red Your-Kind-of-Holiday uniform. She'd addressed them by name, had checked the details on their tickets and said that that was lovely. An hour later it had surprised them to hear elderly people on the plane talking in North of England accents when the counter clerk at the travel agency had so specifically stated that Signor Bancini's Italian class came from Windsor. Dawne had even remarked on it, but Keith said there must have been a cancellation, or possibly the Italian class was on a second plane. 'That'll be the name of the airport,' he confidently explained when the pilot referred over the communication system to a destination that didn't sound like Venice. 'Same as he'd say Gatwick. Or Heathrow.' They ordered two Drambuies, Dawne's favourite drink, and then two more. 'The coach'll take us on,' a stout woman with spectacles announced when the plane landed. 'Keep all together now.' There'd been no mention of an overnight stop in the brochure, but when the coach drew in at the Edelweiss Hotel Keith explained that that was clearly what this was. By air and then by coach was how these package firms kept the prices down, a colleague at work had told him. As they stepped out of the coach it was close on midnight: fatigued and travel-stained, they did not feel like questioning their right to the beds they were offered. But the next morning, when it became apparent that they were being offered them for the duration of their holiday, they became alarmed.

'We have the lake, and the water birds,' the receptionist smilingly explained. 'And we may take the steamer to Interlaken.'

'An error has been made,' Keith informed the man, keeping the register of his voice even for it was essential to be calm. He was aware of his wife's agitated breathing close beside him. She'd had to sit down when they realized that something was wrong, but now she was standing up again.

'We cannot change the room, sir,' the receptionist swiftly countered. 'Each has been given a room. You accompany the group, sir?'

Keith shook his head. Not this group, he said – a different group; a group that was travelling on to another destination. Keith was not a tall man, and often suffered from what he considered to be arrogance in other people, from officials of one kind or another, and shop assistants with a tendency to assume that his lack of stature reflected a diminutive personality.

In a way Keith didn't care for, the receptionist repeated, 'This is the Edelweiss Hotel, sir.'

'We were meant to be in Venice. In the Pensione Concordia.'

'I do not know the name, sir. Here we have Switzerland.'

'A coach is to take us on. An official said so on the plane. She was here last night, that woman.'

'Tomorrow we have the fondue party,' the receptionist went on, having listened politely to this information about an official. 'On Tuesday there is the visit to a chocolate factory. On other days we may take the steamer to Interlaken, where we have teashops. In Interlaken mementoes may be bought at fair prices.'

Dawne had still not spoken. She, too, was a slight figure, her features pale beneath orangish powder. 'Mingy,' the old man had a way of saying in his jokey voice, and sometimes told her to lie down.

'Eeh, idn't it luvely?' a voice behind Keith enthused. 'Been out to feed them ducks, 'ave you?'

Keith did not turn round. Speaking slowly, giving each word space, he said to the receptionist, 'We have been booked onto the wrong holiday.'

'Your group is booked twelve nights in the Edelweiss Hotel. To make an alteration now, sir, if you have changed your minds –'

'We haven't changed our minds. There's been a mistake.'

The receptionist shook his head. He did not know about a mistake. He had not been told that. He would help if he could, but he did not see how help might best be offered.

'The man who made the booking,' Dawne interrupted, 'was bald, with glasses and a moustache.' She gave the name of the travel agency in London.

In reply, the receptionist smiled with professional sympathy. He fingered the edge of his register. 'Moustache?' he said.

Three aged women who had been on the plane passed through the reception area. Had anyone noticed, one of them remarked, that there were rubber linings under the sheets? Well, you couldn't be too careful, another agreeably responded, if you were running a hotel.

'Some problem, have we?' another woman said, beaming at Keith. She was the stout woman he had referred to as an official, flamboyantly attired this morning in a two-tone trouser suit, green and blue. Her flesh-coloured spectacles were decorated with swirls of metal made to seem like gold; her grey hair was carefully waved. They'd seen her talking to the yellow-and-red girl at Gatwick. On the plane she'd walked up and down the aisle, smiling at people.

'My name is Franks,' she was saying now. 'I'm married to the man with the bad leg.'

'Are you in charge, Mrs Franks?' Dawne enquired. 'Only we're in the wrong hotel.' Again she gave the name of the travel agency and described the bald-headed counter clerk, mentioning his spectacles and his moustache.

Keith interrupted her. 'It seems we got into the wrong group. We reported to the Your-Kind-of-Holiday girl and left it all to her.'

'We should have known when they weren't from Windsor,' Dawne contributed. 'We heard them talking about Darlington.'

Keith made an impatient sound. He wished she'd leave the talking to him. It was no good whatsoever going on about Darlington and the counter clerk's moustache, confusing everything even more.

'We noticed you at Gatwick,' he said to the stout woman. 'We knew you were in charge of things.'

'I noticed *you*. Well, of course I did, naturally I did. I counted you, although I daresay you didn't see me doing that. Monica checked the tickets and I did the counting. That's how I know everything's OK. Now, let me explain to you. There are many places Your-Kind-of-Holiday sends its clients to, many tours, many different holidays at different prices. You follow me? Something to suit every pocket, something for every taste. There are, for instance, villa holidays for the adventurous under-thirty-fives. There are treks to Turkey, and treks for singles to the Himalayas. There is self-catering in Portugal, November reductions in Casablanca, February in Biarritz. There's Culture-in-Tuscany and Sunshine-in-Sorrento. There's the Nile. There's Your-Kind-of-Safari in Kenya. Now, what I am endeavouring to say to you good people is that all tickets and labels are naturally similar, the yellow with the two red bands.' Mrs Franks suddenly laughed. 'So if you simply followed other people with the yellow-and-red label you might imagine you could end up in a wildlife park!' Mrs Franks' speech came hurriedly from her, the words tumbling over one another, gushing through her teeth. 'But of course,' she added soothingly, 'that couldn't happen in a million years.'

'We're not meant to be in Switzerland,' Keith doggedly persisted.

'Well, let's just see, shall we?'

Unexpectedly, Mrs Franks turned and went away, leaving them standing. The receptionist was no longer behind the reception desk. The sound of typing could be heard.

'She seems quite kind,' Dawne whispered, 'that woman.'

To Keith it seemed unnecessary to say that. Any consideration of Mrs Franks was, in the circumstances, as irrelevant as a description of the man in the travel agency. He tried to go over in his mind every single thing that had occurred: handing the girl the tickets, sitting down to wait, and then the girl leading the way to the plane, and then the pilot's voice welcoming them aboard, and the air hostess with the smooth black hair going round to see that everyone's seat belt was fastened.

'Snaith his name was,' Dawne was saying. 'It said "Snaith" on a plastic thing in front of him.'

'What are you talking about?'

'The man in the travel place was called Snaith. "G. Snaith" it said.'

'The man was just a clerk.'

'He booked us wrong, though. That man's responsible, Keith.'

'Be that as it may.'

Sooner or later, Dawne had guessed, he'd say 'Be that as it may.' He put her in her place with the phrase; he always had. You'd make an innocent remark, doing your best to be helpful, and out he'd come with 'Be that as it may.' You expected him to go on, to finish the sentence, but he never did. The phrase just hung there, making him sound uneducated.

'Are you going to phone up that man, Keith?'

'Which man is this?'

She didn't reply. He knew perfectly well which man she

meant. All he had to do was to get through to Directory Enquiries and find out the number of the travel agency. It was no good complaining to a hotel receptionist who had nothing to do with it, or to a woman in charge of a totally different package tour. No good putting the blame where it didn't belong.

'Nice to have some young people along,' an elderly man said. 'Nottage the name is.'

Dawne smiled, the way she did in the shop when someone was trying to be agreeable, but Keith didn't acknowledge the greeting, because he didn't want to become involved.

'Seen the ducks, 'ave you? Right champion them ducks are.'

The old man's wife was with him, both of them looking as if they were in their eighties. She nodded when he said the ducks were right champion. They'd slept like logs, she said, best night's sleep they'd had for years, which of course would be due to the lakeside air.

'That's nice,' Dawne said.

Keith walked out of the reception area and Dawne followed him. On the gravel forecourt of the hotel they didn't say to one another that there was an irony in the catastrophe that had occurred. On their first holiday since their honeymoon they'd landed themselves in a package tour of elderly people when the whole point of the holiday was to escape the needs and demands of the elderly. In his bossy way Uncle had said so himself when they'd tried to persuade him to accompany them.

'You'll have to phone up Snaith,' Dawne repeated, irritating Keith further. What she did not understand was that if the error had occurred with the man she spoke of it would since have become compounded to such a degree that the man would claim to be able to do nothing about their immediate predicament. Keith, who sold insurance over the counter for the General Accident insurance company, knew something of the complications that followed when even the slightest uncertainty in a requirement was passed into the program of a computer. Somewhere along the line, that was what had happened, but to explain it to Dawne would take a very long time. Dawne could work a cash register as well as anyone; in the shop she knew by heart the price of Mars bars and the different kinds of cigarettes and tobacco, and the prices of all the newspapers and magazines, but otherwise Keith considered her slow on the uptake, often unable to follow a simple argument.

'Hi, there!' Mrs Franks called out, and they turned and saw her picking her way across the gravel towards them. She had a piece of pink paper in her hand. 'I've been doing my homework!' she cried when she was a little closer. She waved the pink paper. 'Take a look at this.'

It was a list of names, a computer printout, each name a series of tiny dots. 'K. and H. Beale', they read, 'T. and G. Craven', 'P. and R. Fineman'. There were many others, including 'B. and Y. Nottage'. In the correct alphabetical position they were there themselves, between 'J. and A. Hines' and 'C. and L. Mace'.

'The thing is,' Dawne began, and Keith looked away. His wife's voice quietly continued, telling Mrs Franks that their holiday had been very kindly paid for by the old man whom they lived with, who had been her employer before they ever moved in to live with him, who still was. They called him Uncle but he wasn't a relation, a friend really – well, more than that. The thing was, he would be angry because they were not in Venice, he having said it should be Venice. He'd be angry because they were in a package for the elderly when he wanted them to have a rest from the elderly, not that she minded looking after Uncle herself, not that she ever would. The person in the travel agency had said the Windsor people were quite young. 'I always remember things like that,' Dawne finished up. 'Snaith he was called. G. Snaith.'

'Well, that's most interesting,' Mrs Franks commented, and added after a pause, 'As a matter of fact, Dawne, Mr Franks and myself are still in our fifties.'

'Be that as it may,' Keith said. 'At no time did we book a holiday in Switzerland.'

'Well, there you are, you see. The ticket you handed to me at Gatwick is as clear as daylight, exactly the same as the

Beales' and the Maces', the same as our own, come to that. Not a tither of difference, Keith.'

'We need to be conveyed to our correct destination. An arrangement has to be made.'

'The trouble is, Keith, I don't know if you know it but you're half a continent away from Venice. Another thing is I'm not employed by Your-Kind, nothing like that. They just reduce our ticket a bit if I agree to keep an eye. On location we call it.' Mrs Franks went on to say that her husband had also scrutinized the piece of pink paper and was in complete agreement with her. She asked Keith if he had met her husband, and said again that he was the man with the bad leg. He'd been an accountant and still did a lot of accountancy work one way or another, in a private capacity. The Edelweiss Hotel was excellent, she said. Your-Kind would never choose an indifferent hotel.

'We are asking you to get in touch with your firm in London,' Keith said. 'We do not belong with your group.'

In silence, though smiling, Mrs Franks held out the pink list. Her expression insisted that it spoke for itself. No one could gainsay the dotted identification among the others.

'Our name is there by mistake.'

A man limped across the gravel towards them. He was a large man of shambling appearance, his navy-blue pin-striped jacket and waistcoat at odds with his brown trousers, his spectacles repaired with Sellotape. The sound of his breath could be heard as he approached. He blew it through half-pursed lips in a vague rendition of a Gilbert and Sullivan melody.

'These are the poor lost lambs,' Mrs Franks said. 'Keith and Dawne.'

'How do?' Mr Franks held a hand out. 'Silly thing to happen, eh?'

It was Mr Franks who eventually suggested that Keith should telephone Your-Kind-of-Holiday himself, and to Keith's surprise he got through to a number in Croydon without any difficulty.

'Excuse me a minute,' a girl said when he finished. He heard her talking to someone else and he heard the other person laughing. There was a trace of laughter in the girl's voice when she spoke again. You couldn't change your mind, she said, in the middle of a package. In no circumstances whatsoever could that be permitted.

'We're not changing our minds,' Keith protested, but while he was explaining all over again he was cut off because he hadn't any more coins. He cashed a traveller's cheque with the desk clerk and was supplied with a number of five-franc pieces, but when he redialled the number the girl he'd spoken to couldn't be located, so he explained everything to another girl.

'I'm sorry, sir,' this girl said, 'but if we allowed people to change their minds on account of they didn't like the look of a place we'd be out of business in no time.'

Keith began to shout into the telephone, and Dawne rapped on the glass of the booth, holding up a piece of paper on which she'd written 'G. Snaith the name was.' 'Some sort of loony,' Keith heard the girl say in Croydon, the mouthpiece being inadequately muffled. There was an outburst of giggling before he was cut off.

It was not the first time that Keith and Dawne had suffered in this way: they were familiar with defeat. There'd been the time, a couple of years after their marriage, when Keith had got into debt through purchasing materials for making ships in bottles; earlier – before they'd even met – there was the occasion when the Lamb and Flag had had to let Dawne go because she'd taken tips although the rules categorically forbade it. Once Keith had sawn through the wrong water pipe and the landlords had come along with a bill for nearly two hundred pounds when the ceiling of the flat below collapsed. It was Uncle who had given Dawne a job in his shop after the Lamb and Flag episode and who had put them on their feet by paying off the arrears of the handicraft debt. In the end he persuaded them to come and live with him, pointing out that the arrangement would suit all three of them. Since his sister's death he had found it troublesome managing on his own.

In Interlaken they selected a postcard to send him: of a mountain that had featured in a James Bond film. But they didn't know what to write on it: if they told the truth they would receive the old man's unspoken scorn when they returned – a look that came into his eyes while he silently regarded them. Years ago he had openly said – once only – that they were accident-prone. They were unfortunate in their dealings with the world, he had explained when Dawne asked him; lame ducks, he supposed you could say, if they'd forgive the expression; victims by nature, no fault of their own. Ever since, such judgements had been expressed only through his eyes.

'You choose your piece of gâteau,' Dawne said, 'up at the counter. They put it on a plate for you. Then the waitress comes along and you order the tea. I've been watching how it's done.'

Keith chose a slice of glazed greengage cake and Dawne a portion of strawberry flan. As soon as they sat down a waitress came and stood smiling in front of them. 'Tea with milk in it,' Dawne ordered, because when she said they were going abroad someone who'd come into the shop had warned her that you had to ask for milk; otherwise the tea came just as it was, sometimes no more than a tea bag and a glass of hot water.

'A strike?' Dawne suggested. 'You're always hearing of strikes in airports.'

But Keith continued to gaze at the blank postcard, not persuaded that an attempt at falsehood was wise. It wasn't easy to tell the old man a lie. He had a way of making such attempts feel clumsy, and in the end of winkling out the truth. Yet his scorn would continue for many months, especially since he had paid out what he would call – a couple of hundred times at least – 'good money' for their tickets. 'That's typical of Keith, that is,' he'd repeatedly inform his customers in Dawne's hearing, and she'd pass it on that night in bed, the way she always passed his comments on.

Keith ate his greengage slice, Dawne her strawberry flan. They did not share their thoughts, although their thoughts were similar. 'You've neither of you a head for business,' he'd said after the ships-in-bottles calamity, and again when Dawne unsuccessfully attempted to make a go of dressmaking alterations. 'You wouldn't last a week in charge downstairs.' He always referred to the shop as 'downstairs'. Every day of his life he rose at five o'clock in order to be downstairs for the newspapers when they arrived. He'd done so for fifty-three years.

'The plane couldn't land at the Italian airport,' Keith wrote, 'owing to a strike. So it had to come down here instead. It's good in a way, because we're seeing another country as well!' 'Hope your cold's cleared up,' Dawne added. 'It's really lovely here xxx.'

They imagined him showing the postcard to Mrs Withers. 'That's typical, that is,' they imagined him saying, and Mrs Withers jollying him along, telling him not to be sarky. Mrs Withers was pleased about earning the extra; she'd been as keen as anything when he'd asked her to come in full time for a fortnight.

'Could happen to anyone, a strike,' Dawne said, voicing Mrs Withers' response.

Keith finished his greengage slice. 'Call in to Smith's for a will form,' he imagined the cross, tetchy voice instructing Mrs Withers, the postcard already tucked away among the packets of cigarettes on the Embassy Tipped shelf. And when she arrived with the will form the next morning he'd let it lie around all day but have it in his hand when she left, before he locked the shop door behind her. 'Silly, really,' Mrs Withers would say when eventually she told Dawne about it.

'I'd just as soon be here,' Dawn whispered, leaning forward a bit, daring at last to say that. 'I'd just as soon be in Switzerland, Keithie.'

He didn't reply, but looked around the teashop: at the display of cakes in the long glass cabinet that served also as a counter – apricot and plum and apple, carrot cake and Black Forest gâteau, richly glazed fruitcake, marzipan slices, small lemon tarts, orange éclairs, coffee fondants. Irritated because his wife had made that statement and wishing to be unpleasant to her by not responding, he allowed his gaze to slip over the faces of the couples who sat sedately at round, prettily arranged tables. In a leisurely manner he examined the smiling waitresses, their crimson aprons matching the crimson of the frilled tablecloths. He endeavoured to give the impression that the waitresses attracted him.

'It's really nice,' Dawne said, her voice still shyly low.

He didn't disagree; there was nothing wrong with the place. People were speaking in German, but when you spoke in English they understood you. Enoch Melchor, in Claims, had gone to somewhere in Italy last year and had got into all sorts of difficulties with the language, including being given the head of a fish when he thought he'd ordered peas.

'We could say we liked it so much we decided to stay on,' Dawne suggested.

She didn't seem to understand that it wasn't up to them to decide anything. Twelve days in Venice had been chosen for them; twelve days in Venice had been paid for. 'No better'n a sewer,' Enoch Melchor had said, not that he'd ever been there. 'Stinks to high heaven,' he'd said, but that wasn't the point either. Memories of Venice had been ordered, memories that were to be transported back to London, with glass figurines for the mantelpiece because Venice was famous for its glass. The menus at the Pensione Concordia and the tunes played by the café orchestras were to be noted in Dawne's day-to-day diary. Venice was bathed in sunshine, its best autumn for years, according to the newspapers.

They left the teashop and walked about the streets, their eyes stinging at first, until they became used to the bitter breeze that had got up. They examined windows full of watches, and went from one to another of the souvenir shops because notices said that entrance was free. There was a clock that had a girl swinging on a swing every hour, and another that had a man and a woman employing a two-handed saw, another that had a cow being milked. All sorts of tunes came out of different-shaped musical boxes: 'Lilli Marlene', 'The Blue Danube', 'Lara's Theme' from *Doctor Zhivago*, 'The Destiny Waltz'. There were oven gloves with next year's

221

calendar printed on them in English, and miniature arrange-
ments of dried flowers, framed, on velvet. In the chocolate
shops there were all the different brands – Lindt, Suchard,
Nestlé, Cailler, and dozens of others. There was chocolate
with nuts, and chocolate with raisins, with nougat and honey,
white chocolate, bitter chocolate, chocolate with fudge filling,
with cognac or whisky or Chartreuse. There were chocolate
mice and chocolate windmills.

'It's ever so enjoyable here,' Dawne remarked, with
genuine enthusiasm. They went into another teashop, and this
time Keith had a chestnut slice and Dawne a black-currant
one, both with cream.

At dinner, in a dining room tastefully panelled in grey-painted
wood, they sat among the people from Darlington, at a table
for two, as the clerk in the travel agency had promised. The
chicken-noodle soup was quite what they were used to, and so
was the pork chop that followed, with applesauce and chipped
potatoes. 'They know what we like,' the woman called Mrs
Franks said, making a round of all the tables, saying the same
thing at each.

'Really lovely,' Dawne agreed. She'd felt sick in her
stomach when they'd first realized about the error; she'd
wanted to go to the lavatory and just sit there, hoping it was all
a nightmare. She'd blamed herself because it was she who'd
wondered about so many elderly people on the plane after the
man in the travel place had given the impression of younger
people, from Windsor. It was she who had frowned, just for a
moment, when the name of the airport was mentioned. Keith
had a habit of pooh-poohing her doubts, as when she'd been
doubtful about the men who'd come to the door selling
mattresses and he'd been persuaded to make a down payment.
The trouble with Keith was he always sounded confident, as
though he knew something she didn't, as though someone had
told him. 'We'll just be here for the night,' he'd said, and she'd
thought that was something he must have read in the brochure
or that the clerk in the travel place had said. He couldn't help
himself, of course; it was the way he was made. 'Cotton wool

in your brain box, have you?' Uncle had rudely remarked the
August bank holiday poor Keith had got them onto the slow
train to Brighton, the one that took an hour longer.

'Silver lining, Keithie.' She put her head on one side, her
small features softening into a smile. They'd walked by the
lakeside before dinner. Just by stooping down she'd attracted
the birds that were swimming on the water. Afterwards she'd
changed into her new fawn dress, bought specially for the
holiday.

'I'll try that number again tomorrow,' Keith said.

She could see he was still worried. He was terribly subdued,
even though he was able to eat his food. It made him cross
when she mentioned the place they'd bought the tickets, so she
didn't do so, although she wanted to. Time enough to face the
music when they got back, better to make the best of things
really: she didn't say that either. 'If you want, Keithie,' she said
instead. 'You try it if you've a mind to.'

Naturally he'd feel it more than she would; he'd get more of
the blame, being a man. But in the end it mightn't be too bad,
in the end the storm would be weathered. There'd be the
fondue party to talk about, and the visit to the chocolate
factory. There'd be the swimming birds, and the teashops,
and the railway journey they'd seen advertised, up to the top
of an Alp.

'Banana split?' the waiter offered. 'You prefer meringue
Williams?'

They hesitated. Meringue Williams was meringue with
pears and ice cream, the waiter explained. Very good. He
himself would recommend the meringue Williams.

'Sounds lovely,' Dawne said, and Keith had it, too. She
thought of pointing out that everyone was being nice to them,
that Mrs Franks was ever so sympathetic, that the man who
came round to ask them if the dinner was all right had been
ever so pleasant, and the waiter, too. But she decided not to
because often Keith just didn't want to cheer up. 'Droopy
Drawers', Uncle sometimes called him, or 'Down-in-the-
Dumps Donald'.

All around them the old people were chattering. They were

older than Uncle, Dawne could see; some of them were ten years older, fifteen even. She wondered if Keith had noticed that, if it had added to his gloom. She could hear them talking about the mementoes they'd bought and the teashops they'd been to; hale and hearty they looked, still as full of vim as Uncle. 'Any day now I'll be dropping off my twig,' he had a way of saying, which was nonsense, of course. Dawne watched the elderly mouths receiving spoonfuls of banana or meringue, the slow chewing, the savouring of the sweetness. A good twenty years Uncle could go on for, she suddenly thought.

'It's just bad luck,' she said.

'Be that as it may.'

'Don't say that, Keithie.'

'Say what?'

'Don't say "Be that as it may".'

'Why not?'

'Oh just because, Keithie.'

They had in common an institution background: they had not known their parents. Dawne could remember Keith when he was eleven and she was nine, although at that time they had not been drawn to each other. They'd met again later, revisiting their children's home for the annual dance – 'disco', as it was called these days. 'I got work in this shop,' she'd said, not mentioning Uncle, because he was only her employer then, in the days when his sister was alive. They'd been married for a while before he became an influence in their lives. Now they could anticipate, without thinking, his changes of heart and his whims, and see coming a mile off another quarrel with the Reverend Simms, whose church occasionally he attended. Once they'd tried to divert such quarrels, to brace themselves for changes of heart, to counter the troublesome whims. They no longer did so. Although he listened carefully, he took no notice of what they said, because he held the upper hand. The Smith's will forms and an old billiard room – 'the happiest place a man could spend an hour in' – were what he threatened them with. He met his friends in the billiard room; he read the *Daily Express* there, drinking bottles of Double Diamond, which he said was the best bottled beer in the world. It would be a terrible thing if men of all ages could no longer play billiards in that room, terrible if funds weren't available to keep it going forever.

Mrs Franks rose and made an announcement. She called for silence, and then gave particulars of the next day's programme. There was to be a visit to the James Bond mountain, everyone to assemble on the forecourt at half past ten. Anyone who didn't want to go should please tell her tonight.

'We don't have to, Keithie,' Dawne whispered when Mrs Franks sat down. 'Not if we don't want to.'

The chatter began again, spoons excitedly waved in the air. False teeth, grey hair, glasses; Uncle might have been among them, except that Uncle never would, because he claimed to despise the elderly. 'You're telling *me*, are you? You're telling *me* you got yourselves entangled with a bunch of OAPs?' As clearly as if he were beside her Dawne could hear his voice, enriched with the pretence of amazement. 'You landed up in the wrong country and spent your holiday with a crowd of geriatrics! You're never telling me that?'

Sympathetic as she was, Mrs Franks had played it down. She knew that a young couple in their thirties weren't meant to be on a package with the elderly; she knew the error was not theirs. But it wouldn't be any use mentioning Mrs Franks to Uncle. It wouldn't be any use saying that Keith had got cross with the receptionist and with the people in Croydon. He'd listen and then there'd be a silence. After that he'd begin to talk about the billiard room.

'Had a great day, did you?' Mrs Franks said on her way out of the dining room with her husband. 'All's well that ends well, eh?'

Keith continued to eat his meringue Williams as if he had not been addressed. Mr Franks remarked on the meringue Williams, laughing about it, saying they'd all have to watch their figures. 'I must say,' Mrs Franks said, 'we're lucky with the weather. At least it isn't raining.' She was dressed in the same flamboyant clothes. She'd been able to buy some Madame Rochas, she said, awfully good value.

'We don't have to say about the old people,' Dawne whispered when the Frankses had passed on. 'We needn't mention that.'

Keith dug into the deep blue glass for the ice cream that lay beneath the slices of pear. She knew he was thinking she would let it slip about the old people. Every Saturday she washed Uncle's hair for him, since he found it difficult to do it himself. Because he grumbled so about the tepid rinse that was necessary in case he caught a cold afterwards, she had to jolly him along. She'd always found it difficult to do two things at once, and it was while washing his hair that occasionally she'd forgotten what she was saying. But she was determined not to make that mistake again, just as she had ages ago resolved not to get into a flap if he suddenly asked her a question when she was in the middle of counting the newspapers that hadn't been sold.

'Did you find your friends from Windsor, then?' an old woman with a walking frame enquired. 'Eeh, it were bad you lost your friends.'

Dawne explained, since no harm was meant. Other old people stood by to hear, but a few of them were deaf and asked to have what was being said repeated. Keith continued to eat his meringue Williams.

'Keithie, it isn't their fault,' she tentatively began when the people had passed on. '*They* can't help it, Keithie.'

'Be that as it may. No need to go attracting them.'

'I didn't attract them. They stopped by. Same as Mrs Franks.'

'Who's Mrs Franks?'

'You know who she is. That big woman. She gave us her name this morning, Keithie.'

'When I get back I'll institute proceedings.'

She could tell from his tone that that was what he'd been thinking about. All the time on the steamer they'd taken to Interlaken, all the time in the teashop, and on the cold streets and in the souvenir shops, all the time they'd been looking at the watch displays and the chocolate displays, all the time in the grey-panelled dining room, he had been planning what he'd say, what he'd probably write on the very next postcard: that he intended to take legal proceedings. When they returned he would stand in the kitchen and state what he intended very matter-of-factly. First thing on Monday he'd arrange to see a solicitor, he'd state, an appointment for his lunch hour. And Uncle would remain silent, not even occasionally inclining his head, or shaking it, knowing that solicitors cost money.

'They're liable for the full amount. Every penny of it.'

'Let's try to enjoy ourselves, Keithie. Why don't I tell Mrs Franks we'll go up the mountain?'

'What mountain's that?'

'The one she was on about, the one we sent him a card of.'

'I need to phone up Croydon in the morning.'

'You can do it before ten-thirty, Keithie.'

The last of the elderly people slowly made their way from the dining room, saying good night as they went. A day would come, Dawne thought, when they would go to Venice on their own initiative, with people like the Windsor people. She imagined the Windsor people in the Pensione Concordia, not one of them a day older than themselves. She imagined Signor Bancini passing among them, translating a word or two of Italian as he went. There was laughter in the dining room of the Pensione Concordia, and bottles of red wine on the tables. The young people's names were Désirée and Rob, and Luke and Angelique, and Sean and Aimée. 'Uncle we used to call him,' her own voice was saying. 'He died a while back.'

Keith stood up. Skilful with the tablecloths, the waiter wished them good night. In the reception area a different person, a girl, smiled at them. Some of the old people were standing around, saying it was too cold to go for a walk. You'd miss the television, one of them remarked.

The warmth of their bodies was a familiar comfort. They had not had children because the rooms above the shop weren't suitable for children. The crying at night would have driven Uncle mad, and naturally you could see his point of view. There'd been an error when first they'd lived with him; they'd had to spend a bit terminating it.

They refrained from saying that their bodies were a comfort. They had never said so. What they said in their lives had to do with Keith's hoping for promotion, and the clothes Dawne coveted. What they said had to do with their efforts to make a little extra money, or paying their way by washing the woodwork of an old man's house and tacking down his threadbare carpets.

When he heard their news he would mention the savings in the Halifax Building Society and the good will of the shop and the valuation that had been carried out four years ago. He would mention again that men of all ages should have somewhere to go of an evening, or in the afternoon or the morning, a place to be at peace. He would remind them that a man who had benefited could not pass on without making provision for the rent and the heating and for the replacing of the billiard tables when the moment came. 'Memorial to a humble man,' he would repeat. 'Shopkeeper of this neighbourhood.'

In the darkness they did not say to each other that if he hadn't insisted they needed a touch of the autumn sun they wouldn't again have been exposed to humiliation. It was as though, through knowing them, he had arranged their failure in order to indulge his scorn. Creatures of a shabby institution, his eyes had so often said, they could not manage on their own: they were not even capable of supplying each other's needs.

In the darkness they did not say that their greed for his money was much the same as his greed for their obedience, that greed nourished the trinity they had become. They did not say that the money, and the freedom it promised, was the galaxy in their lives, as his cruelty was the last pleasure in his. Scarcely aware that they held on to each other beneath the bedclothes, they heard his teasing little laugh while they were still awake, and again when they slept.

# Home Place

## GUY VANDERHAEGHE

IT WAS EARLY morning, so early that Gil MacLean loaded the colt into the truck box under a sky still scattered with faint stars. The old man circled the truck once, checking the tail gate, the tyres, and the knot in the halter shank, tottering around on legs stiff as stilts, shoulders hunched to keep the chill off him. He was sixty-nine and mostly cold these days.

A hundred yards behind him one window burned yellow in the dark house. That was his son Ronald, asleep under the bare light bulb and the airplanes. Whenever Ronald fled Darlene, the woman Gil MacLean referred to as the 'backpages wife', he slunk back to his father's house in the dead of night to sleep in a room lit up like a Christmas tree. To her father-in-law Darlene was the backpages wife because Ronald had found her advertising herself in the classified section of a farm news-paper, right alongside sale notices for second-hand grain augers and doubtful chain saws.

Dawn found the old man in a temper, a mood. It was the mare he had wanted when he rattled oats in the pail and whistled, but it was the gelding which had been lured. The mare, wiser and warier, had hung back. So this morning he had a green, rough-broke colt to ride. There was nothing for it, though. He needed a horse because his mind was made up to repair Ronald's fences. They were a disgrace.

Generally that was the way to catch what you wanted, shake a little bait. It was what Darlene had done with Ronald, but she hadn't fooled him, Gil MacLean, for a second. He knew how it was.

Four years ago his son and Darlene married after exchanging honied letters for six months. Ronald never breathed a word to him about any wedding. When Ronald's mother was alive she used to say Ronald was too much under his father's thumb. But the one time he slipped out from beneath it, look at the result. It happened like this. One morning Ronald drove off in the pickup. Twelve hours later he phoned from Regina to announce that he and his bride were bound for Plentywood, Montana, to honeymoon. Ronald was thirty-eight then, had never been married, had never been engaged, had never had a date that his father could recollect. It was a shock and a mystery. The way Gil figured it, Ronald must have proposed by mail before he ever met face to face with Darlene. Ronald didn't have it in him to offer himself in the flesh to someone with whom he was actually acquainted. He would be too shy, too embarrassed for that.

The old man folded himself into the cab of the truck, joint by joint. 'The best work, the worst sleep,' he muttered to Ronald's lighted window as he drove under it. In the east there were mares' tails on the horizon, fine as the vapour trails of jets, reddened by the rising sun.

It was Gil MacLean's speculation that his son married only to get his hands on land. Not land of Darlene's, she was a waif and a pauper and had none, but his land, Gil MacLean's land. He never entertained the idea that Ronald might have married out of loneliness, or lust, or any feeling the remotest kin to either. Just land. That was why he was sometimes troubled, wondering what share of responsibility was his to bear for Ronald's current unhappiness. Maybe he ought to have transferred the title sooner, but he had never trusted the boy's judgement. Events appeared to have confirmed his suspicions. Ronald had his own farm now, a wedding present. A married man needed land, so his father gave him the farm that the

MacLeans had always called the 'home place'. It gave Gil
satisfaction to see it pass from father to son and he thought it
might bring Ronald luck.

The home place consisted of the original quarter Gil's father
had homesteaded, the pre-emption, and another 320 acres
picked up cheap from a Finnish immigrant who went to pieces
when his wife ran off on him. Over the years the MacLean
family acquired other holdings but the home place was special.
Situated in a valley, it was a mix of rich bottomland and steep,
wooded hills. In the spring, down by the river, blizzards of
gulls floated in the wake of tractor and discer pursuing easy
pickings, while hawks rode the air high above the lean hills
and, shrieking, fell to plunder these lazy storms of white birds.
To Gil it had all been beautiful. It was all he had ever wanted,
to possess that place, those sights. A day spent away from the
farm made him restless, cranky. Returning to it, even after the
briefest absence, he acted oddly, dodging through the wires of
a fence in his city clothes to wade about in his crop, hands
running back and forth lightly over the bearded heads the way
another man might absent-mindedly stroke a cat. Or he might
suddenly strike off for the hills with all the energy and
apparent purpose of someone hurrying to keep an appointment, tie flying over his shoulder.

His wife used to say: 'Gil's gone off to satisfy himself that
nobody so much as shifted a cup of dirt on this place when he
was away.'

What Gil never confided to his wife was that he felt more
present in the land than he did in his own flesh, his own body.
Apart from it he had no real existence. When he looked in a
mirror he stood at a great distance from what he regarded, but
with the land it was different. All that he had emptied of
himself into it, he recognized.

The road to the home place ran due east without deviating a
hair, rising and falling regularly as a sleeper's breath as it made
its way over a succession of bare hills. The emerging sun drew
his eyes into a squint when he topped a rise; the blue shadows
in the hollows forced them wide again. In the back of the truck
the slither and clatter of iron shoes was unremitting. The colt

was either highly strung or lacked balance. If it lost its footing and fell it would be a task to get it on its feet again; the box was narrow and there was little room for manoeuvring. He'd have to go back and get Ronald out of bed to help him.

Turning Ronald out of bed was not an easy job. Despite his son's difficulties falling asleep, once he was gone he wasn't likely to stir. Often he didn't wake before noon. Gil, on the other hand, roused to the slightest sound. That first night the gritty scraping of the shoes on the stairs had been enough to jerk him out of a dreamless sleep. He'd never been one to lock doors, he had only himself to thank that a night intruder was climbing up to him. It was like the television and its stories of grinning madmen invading houses and arming themselves with drapery cords and butcher knives to strangle and to stab. The old man bunched up his pillow and held it out before him, ready to parry the first knife thrust. The footsteps, however, went on past his door. Only when the toilet flushed did he realize it had to be Ronald.

He simply shook in bed for several minutes, too angry and too relieved to ask himself what his son might be up to. Finally he grew calm and curiosity prodded him out into the hallway to investigate. The light was on in Ronald's old bedroom and the door stood ajar.

Ronald was lying flat on his back on the bed, staring up at his model airplanes. As a teenager, even as a young man, he had exhibited little interest in anything other than building models of airplanes from kits, squeezing tubes of glue, pasting on decals, and painting engine cowlings with brushes whose tips he sucked into needle points. The models had never been removed. Forty or more of them hung suspended from the ceiling on fine wires; his room was almost exactly as he had left it when he chose Darlene. Flying Fortresses, Mustangs, Zeros, Spitfires, Messerschmidts, a whole catalogue of war planes dangled there. The light in the bedroom was also as harsh, pitiless and glaring as it had ever been. When Ronald was fourteen he had unscrewed the bulb in the ceiling fixture and replaced it with a more powerful one. He also dispensed with the shade because he wanted the models hanging beneath the light bulb to cast their shadows on his bedspread and linoleum, in the way fighter planes and bombers passing between sun and earth print their images on country lanes and city squares. These shadows were repeated everywhere about the room, and in their midst lay Ronald, gazing up into the strong light, gazing up at undercarriages and silhouettes.

'What's all this, Ronald?' his father said. 'This is a hell of a time to pay a visit. It's past two.'

Ronald said: 'I can't stand it. I can't sleep there no longer.' He kept his eyes fixed on the planes as he spoke.

Gil knew there was talk going around town about his son and his daughter-in-law, all of it unfortunate. Darlene had come stamped with the word trouble; he'd seen it from day one. The old man sighed and took a seat on the straight-back chair beside the dresser. Ronald was not exactly the forthcoming type, he was prepared to wait him out.

After a considerable stretch of silence his son said: 'I should never have left.' Gil knew what he meant. Ronald wasn't saying he ought not to have left Darlene; he was saying he should not have abandoned this room and the comfort and solace of those planes that could not fly.

It was strange that, given all the worrying he had done about Ronald and Darlene, Gil had never seen the real danger. Now he did. The realization of what might lie ahead was like an attack of some kind. Before he could proceed it was necessary to relieve the pressure prodding his breastbone and robbing him of breath. He arched his back and squeezed his eyes tight until it eased and he could speak. And speak he did, urgently, for a solid hour without interruption and with a drying mouth. He said it was the government and the courts. They'd gone and changed the marriage property laws so that the women ended up with half of everything these days. Did Ronald know what that meant? Darlene could lay claim to a half share of the home place. 'No divorce, Ronald,' he repeated. 'No divorce. Don't let that bitch break up the home place. Don't you give her that satisfaction.' Only when he had wrung his promise out of Ronald did he cease arguing. For a moment he was overcome by his son's loyalty. He patted the back of his hand and murmured: 'Thank you. Thank you.'

In a month, however, Ronald came creeping back up the stairs. In fear of the future and baffled rage, Gil shouted through his bedroom door: 'Don't expect any sympathy from me if you won't try to adjust!'

Ronald explained that he had a problem going to sleep in the same room, the same house as Darlene. That's the reason he came home every once in a while, to relax and catch up on his sleep. Not that it was easy for him to get to sleep in his old room either, but there he could manage it. What he did was stare up at the glowing bulb and planes until the moment arrived when he could feel the sun hot on his back and suddenly he was winged and soaring, flying into sleep, released, sometimes for twelve hours at a time.

Ronald had been paying his visits to his father's to sleep for a year. About the time they started he commenced on improvements to the home place. This meant pushing bush and clearing land up top, above the valley, in the hills. Gil had pointed out this was nothing but sheer craziness. Marginal land like that was suitable only for pasture, cropping it would never repay the cost of breaking and if the hillsides were stripped of cover they would erode. But Ronald, who was usually willing to be advised, wouldn't listen to his father. A cunning, stubborn look stole over his face when he said: 'We'll see. I hired another dozer. Pretty soon the brush piles will be dry and ready to burn.'

All spring Ronald fired his huge, gasoline-laced bonfires of scrub oak and poplar. The gusty roar of flames was like constant static in his ears, heat crumpled the air around him and stained it a watery yellow, greasy black clouds mounted indolently into the purity of blue skies. The scars of the dozer blades fresh on the earth made the old man indignant. In places the soil had been cut so deep that streaks of rubbly gravel were exposed.

'You won't grow wheat in that,' Gil MacLean shouted. 'So what'll it be? Carrots?'

Smiling oddly, Ronald said: 'I'm not growing nothing. I'll open a pit and peddle gravel to the Department of Highways by the yard.'

'That's not farming,' his father returned, disgusted. 'That's mining.'

It was all Ronald had any interest in at present, pushing bush, clawing up roots, burning. His face appeared hot, scorched. His eyes were forever weepy and red, their lids puffy and swollen, lashes singed away. The ends of his hair had crinkled, crisped and gone white in the furnace-heat. Everything else Ronald neglected. He hadn't yet done his summer-fallow and his cattle were continually straying. This morning Gil was determined to mend Ronald's fences because he was ashamed of what the neighbours would think with his son's cows belly-deep in their crops.

The old man crested the last rise and the valley spread itself out at his feet. There were days when he would pull his truck over to the shoulder of the road and look with deep satisfaction at the slow river and sombre quilt of green and black fields, look until he had his fill. From such a height the home place looked fatter and richer than with your nose shoved in it. Up close dirt was dirt. There was no time for stopping and admiring this morning, though: he was in a hurry.

Gil entered his son's property by a little-used side gate because he didn't want Darlene spying his truck and reporting his doings to Ronald. He parked, unloaded the horse and slung a duffel bag of tools and a coil of barbed wire on the saddle. Within minutes he was riding down an old trail they had hauled hay on in summer and wood in winter in his father's time. Neither of those things would be possible now, encroaching wild rose and chokecherry bushes had narrowed it so a loaded wagon couldn't pass. The occasional sapling had taken root between the old ruts. Sunlight and sparrows strayed amid the poplar leaves overhead. Ronald's dozers hadn't reached this far yet, hadn't peeled all this back. Maybe his money would run out before they could, that was Gil's fervent hope.

It was eight o'clock before Gil located the first break in the fence. The wires were rotten with rust and would have to be replaced. He set to work. The old man ought not to have been taken by surprise. He knew the very nature of a young horse was unpredictability. It happened when he was playing out sixty yards of wire, lazy-man style, one end of the coil dallied round the horn, the horse walking it out. It could have been the sound the wire made hissing and writhing after them through the grass and weeds. It could have been that a barb nicked the gelding's hocks. Suddenly the colt froze in his tracks, laid back his ears, and trembled all over like a leaf.

Gil had been a horseman all his life, all his seventy years. He knew what was coming and he fought with all his strength to keep the gelding from pulling its head down between its forelegs. If the colt managed to get its head down it would be able to buck. It managed. An old man's strength was not sufficient. The horse squealed, wriggled, snapped out its hind legs. Gil's lower plate popped out of his mouth. The sky tilted. He fell.

It was bad luck to get snarled in the wire. The colt dragged him several hundred yards, the old man skipping and bounding and tumbling along behind like a downed water-skier – without the presence of mind to relinquish his grip on the tow rope.

When it had winded itself the horse came to a halt, stood rolling its eyes and snorting. The old man began to paw himself feebly, searching his pockets for a pair of fencing-pliers with which to cut himself out of the jumble of wire. Using the pliers, he had to move cautiously and deliberately so as not to excite the skittish colt. Nevertheless, when the final strand of wire parted with a twang the colt kicked him twice in a convulsion of fear before trotting off a stone's throw away. There it circled about anxiously, stepping on the ends of the dragging reins and bruising its mouth.

The old man lay still, taking stock. There seemed to be a lot of blood, the wire had cut him in many places. He sat up and the blood gushed out of his nose and mouth and spilled down his jacket front. He peered about him, dazed. The colt had dragged him to a desolate place. Ronald's dozers had been at work. Here there was nothing but bare, black earth engraved by caterpillar treads, piles of stones, and the remains of bonfires, charred tree trunks furred in white powdery ash.

While he sat up the blood continued to pour from his mouth and nose. It was better to lie back down. He was feeling weak but he told himself that was because he had taken nothing that morning but a cup of instant coffee. 'I'll rest and my strength will come back,' he told himself.

Gil closed his eyes and became aware of the powerful scents of sage, milkweed, grass. How was this possible in a place scoured clean? Then he realized they were coming from his clothes, had been rubbed into them by the dragging.

During the next three hours he tried a number of times to prop himself up, but the blood always ran so freely from his mouth he resigned the attempt. 'Not yet,' he muttered to himself. 'In a while.' He had little sense of passing time. There was only thirst and the stiff, scratchy ache of the wounds on his face, hands, legs.

When the sun shone directly down into his face he realized it was noon. The bright light in his eyes and the time of day made him think of Ronald. He would be waking now, looking up at his airplanes.

He had asked Ronald: 'What is it with you? Why do you stare up at those planes?' And Ronald had said: 'I like to pretend I'm up there, high enough to look down on something or somebody for once in my life.'

Gil had laughed as if it were a joke, but an uneasy laugh.

Suddenly the old man was seized by a strange panic. Making a great effort, he sat himself up. It was as if he hoped the force of gravity would pull everything he just now thought and saw down out of his head, drain it away. What he saw was Ronald's lashless eyes, singed hair, red burning face. What he thought was that such a face belonged to a man who wished to look down from a great height on fire, on ruin, on devastation, on dismay.

When the old man collapsed back into the wire he saw that face hovering above, looking down on him.

'You've got no right to look down on me,' he said to the burning sky. 'I came to fix your fences. I gave you the home place and showed you how to keep it.'

His vehement voice filled the clearing and argued away the

afternoon. It became harsher and louder when the sun passed out of Gil's vision and he could not raise himself to follow its course. The horse grew so accustomed to this steady shouting and calling out that only when it suddenly stopped did the gelding prick its ears, swing its head and stare.

# The Legs of the Queen of Sheba

## MARINA WARNER

WHEN IT WAS my turn to entertain in my room after the organized dinner and official proceedings were over, I fussed, I hid my underwear under a towel though it was still dripping from the wash, I shifted my spongebag to hide the anti-wrinkle cream and buttonback dispenser of pills, and zipped up my razor. Greg and I took the twin beds; Thomas found a niche on the hotel furniture. Soon, we were talking about legs.

'You're not a legs man, are you?' Thomas challenged Greg.

He acknowledged the truth of this, with a solemn swig of the duty-free malt he'd chosen at the airport. 'I don't know what you're meant to look for.'

Thomas grunted, 'Length, of course. Long legs, legs that go on and on.' He sketched this dream in the air, stopping at the cleft.

I turned my head to Greg alongside me on the other bed and said, 'But Danielle has the most beautiful legs ever, surely?' Danielle lives with Greg in Cambridge; she's my friend too, and as neatly turned as one of those ivory lay figurines of Chinese medicine, which women once used to point out to the doctor where it hurt.

'I know,' he sighed. 'So others say. But I don't understand what makes it so.' And he told us how Danielle, when she first

239

suspected this gap in his expertise, asked him to identify a pair of good legs. He had thought hard, and said, Anne. 'She was always full of Anne's praises, so I thought she'd be pleased if I chose her.'

'Anne!' Thomas hooted. 'Anne has treetrunks.'

'So it seems,' said Greg. 'Danielle says so too. She was mortally offended. And she hasn't forgotten.'

I said, pulling up my skirt, 'Now there, Greg, there's a pair of good legs. This is what's meant by legs. The knees should be round, and almost invisible when the leg is straight. So.' I demonstrated, flexing my knee and twirling one foot near Greg's face. 'The ankle should be slender, but not bony. The thighs should be . . .'

Greg looked, and drank, and shook his head.

'I know about arses,' volunteered Thomas. 'They should be high and hard.'

'Arses is it?' said Kevin, coming in. 'Makes a change from predicting the student intake in the natural sciences, as I've just been doing, adding the finishing touches for tomorrow's session, while you lot have been revelling by the looks of things.' He helped himself to a tooth mug of malt and found a perch on the radiator shelf by the window.

I went back to lying on top of the other bed, with Greg across the gap from me. 'My mother taught me,' I continued. 'She used to sit around discussing the points of her friends, like trainers sizing up bloodstock. That's what I used to hear when I was a child. "Have you taken a long hard look at her thighs?" – shrieks of laughter – "Her wrists, big like shackles?" – "tut-tut, they're not as bad as that" – "Her ears?" – hoots – "Those ear lobes would look better on a dachshund." Assassination, item by item, not of character, no, but of bodies. A kind of ritual dismemberment.'

Greg said, 'That's a bad strike against your sex, I'm afraid.'

Thomas said, 'Takes a woman to know one.' I drank up, waved the bottle at the boys, took some more.

'I like them smooth,' said Kevin, after a pause.

Thomas said, 'Since when do they come rough?'

'You know, hairy.' Kevin was sleepy, his lids heavy.

'Yeah, black fuzz flattened by the mesh of the tights, I know.'

A bit late, I grasped for loyalty to my own. 'Legs don't feel like they look. Black cats may saunter in and sidle up to Pretty Polly longlegs in the ads, and rub themselves against her – but you can't touch her in the ad, you can only see her. If you could, you might find you prefer unshaven legs. Like men's, they're softer. Down is nice. With shaving, there's a risk of stubble.'

Thomas grimaced.

Greg said, 'Danielle's always smooth. *And* I can get into Danielle's bath water after she's shaved her legs in it. I'm very proud of that. I don't mind the little black bits.'

'She must be good about doing it, often,' I said.

Thomas exhaled, noisily, to show his amusement. And I saw what I'd said; and stopped playing one of the boys.

When they had gone, I looked at my face in the mirror and watched the tears spring, with a certain grim pleasure that at least I could still feel. You stupid cow, I told my screwed-up mug. You think you can lie there, banter banter, girls this, girls that, you think it makes you liked and clever. Fool. Trade secrets, tell on your own kind, show your legs. Fool. Pretend you're in the know, keep up, egg them on, never dare show you're shocked, never protest. Where they lead, you'll follow. Drink, smoke, vie, boast.

Shame, slimy with tears, had her nails well and truly dug into the stuff of my soul and was clinging on tight, while her sisters, drink and no-sex, sank their claws into other parts as viciously. I hadn't even kept faith with myself. My mother with her scorecards of physical perfections had inflicted pain on me during my clumsy, plumpish, brainy adolescence, yet I'd pushed the memory away. My teacher's wisdom had taught me to keep women's codes from men because otherwise they use them to make women their pets, their dollies, their babies. I faced day by day in the classroom the need for girls not to want to please boys. So shame returned to scratch my face to a commotion of mirrored tears.

But I did not know then, as I went heavily to bed in the

conference hotel in Jerusalem, how closely I had brushed the Queen of Sheba that night.

The Queen of Sheba came from the south and proved King Solomon with hard questions. The sky of my city hangs like a blind and I had failed to issue any challenge. '*Nigra sum sed formosa*,' says the Shulamite, Solomon's beloved, in the Song of Songs, the love song of the Queen of Sheba and the King, according to commentaries on the Bible (*I am black, but comely*) – my closeness to her can't be found there either.

In Raphael's painting in the Vatican, she leaps up the shallow steps of the King's dais towards him, and he starts up from his throne to take her in his arms. She flings her right arm behind her to point to the servants in her company, some of whom, stripped like wrestlers to the waist, heave cauldrons of gold coin on their shoulders. One attendant is spilling the contents of his jar on the ground, and another stoops under the burden of an earthenware pot, filled with some precious distillation. Solomon's beard and hair escape in a grey fleece from the spikes of his oriental diadem. Male wisdom needs years to mature, but the Queen's springs green in her young limbs and eager embrace.

So I do not recognize myself here either.

The Queen of Sheba never grows old, unlike Eve. But Eve belongs to her story too, for when the first mother laid Adam out, there grew from the corpse the tree that would provide the wood of the Cross. The Queen of Sheba, daughter of Eve, recognized it many centuries later, in the foothills before Jerusalem, when she reached a bridge made from the tree spanning the stream of Gihon in the valley of Kidron, and refused to set foot upon the instrument of our future redemption. Instead, she forded the stream barefoot, as Piero painted in his fresco cycle on the legend of the Holy Cross in Arezzo.

So the Queen lifted her skirts and revealed her legs on the way to the Temple where Solomon would receive her.

The valley of Kidron lies to the south of Jerusalem, beneath the south-eastern corner of the walls of the Temple Mount, where we'd been shown by our official Israeli guide the commissure between the masonry of the Second Temple that Herod built and the massive stones hewn to equally formidable scantlings of the earlier, Hasmonean era. Today, tobacco grows there, wand-like self-seeded saplings, with perfumed yellow bells in spring. Behind the rampart of golden rose limestone stand the multiple arcades of the stables called Solomon's, which were used by the Templar knights for their horses when they occupied the holy site. Above, the dome of the Al-Aqsa mosque, the knights' own Temple, rises to twin the golden bowl of the Dome of the Rock; Al-Aqsa's used to be silver, but is now lead. George H., an old hand in Jerusalem, took me inside last time I was here; there was a smell like a boys' changing room.

The Queen of Sheba reached the valley of Kidron and looked up to this view of the city two millennia before tobacco travelled to the Mediterranean, one millennium before the Islamic dome rose over the most contested shrine in the world – but she would have seen her destination, the emplacement of the Temple, when she lifted her skirts to ford the water, and the Muslims, who later occupied the Judaic Holy of Holies and obliterated its precise location, still continue to tell the story of the Queen of Sheba's coming. Their story-tellers also claimed Solomon as one of their own, and aimed to magnify the wisdom and the glory of the King. A master of djinns, a wizard from whom nothing was hidden, the Solomon of the Koran and later Muslim lore could work prodigies of magic, unscramble the speech of birds, and eavesdrop on the gossip of camels.

Picnicking out in the desert of Judaea one day, under the green shade of Jericho's palms and fruit groves, Solomon summoned the birds, his eyes and hands abroad, to give news of his dominions and further afield. Only one bird did not come. In some stories, it's the hoopoe that is the culprit, in others the lapwing, perhaps a more fitting messenger in this context because of her cunning in survival. For the bird, when she finally answered the King's summons, calmed his rage – temporarily – by telling him of a great wonder she had found in the south, a woman who ruled her country on her own. This queen from the south was a beauty, and, like Solomon, clever. She was not quite as rich, but not threadbare either. Unlike the King, however, who kept his wives on the mountain of Silwan nearby, the Queen of Sheba was not married.

Solomon's rage against the truant bird gave way to curiosity. He ordered her to return to Sheba with a letter for its Queen, warning her he would advance against her people if she did not submit to his suzerainty. Then he struck camp, and returned to Jerusalem, to wait for her reply.

The djinns who served him advised that such a contradiction of the due order might be monstrous. They hinted that such a woman, beautiful, wise, not altogether poor, and unwed, might be a sorcerer's illusion, might have hidden diabolical features. Ass's hooves, they whispered; hairy legs, they tittered.

Solomon waited for her answer; he was impatient to know about her; his wives had made him an expert on the subject of women, and experts must prime their expertise to keep up their standards.

In Christian picturing, the Queen of Sheba represents the Church, her mission to submit to Solomon foreshadows the recognition of the Magi that Jesus was the Messiah and the King of Kings. The three wise men, and their forerunner the queen, an outsider like them from an equally exotic and mysterious eastern kingdom, announce the peace of Christendom, the union of different peoples under one faith.

In the Koran too, and in later Mohammedan embellishments on her story, the Queen of Sheba desired peace. She understood the finesses required by diplomacy, and answered Solomon's letter with blandishments and praise of his reputation and heaps of presents, arguing with her courtiers that she hoped to hold him at bay with such means, but feared that if he were a true potentate, he would not give in at such an early stage, but demand more. She wouldn't show enmity when he summoned her, but go to meet him, if they were in accord. They were; this was a womanly way of doing things, it has a long history – this is where I come in – and even though she was the ruler of her country, she was expected to know it too, by instinct. Presently, as she anticipated, Solomon refused her gifts and summoned her in person.

She was aware of the dangers he posed for her and for her people in her absence; she garrisoned the capital and strengthened the border, and concealed the national treasure, and its greatest jewel, her throne, in a deep cave behind seven doors, each of which she had locked with a combination code, to which seven different trusted colleagues, all unknown to one another, possessed the secret. But she kept back a single pearl –'an unpierced pearl' – and shut it in a casket in her luggage to give to Solomon. If she felt like it. Or so the Muslim chroniclers say. Then she loaded the caravan with gold and myrrh and oil and other produce of her southern country and chose a hundred Sheban children to follow in her train and see the land of Solomon and broaden their minds. But because she wanted them to return with her, and Solomon's appetite was famous, she proposed they should disguise themselves. Some of the fifty boys were to be dressed as girls, some of the fifty girls as boys, and she checked their appearance before the journey began, and satisfied herself that no one would be able to tell which was which.

The djinns, at their master's order, swarmed south, slipped the catch on the first lock, then on the second, then the third, and so forth, until they penetrated to the innermost chamber of the mountain hideaway, and shouldering the precious throne on their leathery bat-wings, they whisked it to Jerusalem, passing it on and landing it at Solomon's feet. The anomalous Queen was to learn who had mastery. Then Solomon issued another command, and the djinns again set to work pumping hard to bring the spring of Gihon from the valley of Kidron, where it gushes up from the earth's mantle, up through the underground tunnel that secretly connects the valley with the Temple. Once the jet spurted, Solomon ordered his demons to channel it into a stream flowing in front of his dais. They did so; he threw in crumbled biscuits to make sure fish were still present, and then, with a stern eye, froze the water hard as glass. The fish remained visible within it, trapped like ammonites in rock.

The security around the Temple, where Solomon expected the Queen's embassy, was tight. The hundred children in her train were taken aside separately and questioned; many of them had to identify their own baggage and order it down from the camels and open it under the eyes of Solomon's guards.

The Queen of Sheba fumed. She was kept waiting outside the Temple gates for the search of her entourage to be completed. Beside her, Solomon's guards chattered: but at least they did not submit her to the indignity of interrogation.

He wants to put me out of countenance, she told herself, I must not let him. He will gain the advantage if I become agitated and cross. Just hold on, think of other things. The sky here, is it a different colour? The light here, is it brighter, harsher? The men here, is their build different? Will he be handsome? Strange how the guards are all bearded; in our country only old men wear hair on their face. Will Solomon have a beard too?

Her nostrils and lips twitched at the thought of the scratchiness. Again, she rebuked herself for her drift, and stirred impatiently on the rug they had spread for her wait. She followed the pattern in the weave of hawkmoth heads, hung in tiers as in a collector's vitrine. It's standard practice, she continued, there's been trouble, everybody who enters the Temple must be searched, a man once pulled a dagger on the King, and if one of his bodyguards hadn't flung himself between the assailant and the King in time and taken the force of the attack, the King would be dead. As it was, the blade passed clean through the guard and its tip grazed the King's side all the same, it was so sharp and so long.

Perhaps it would have been better if he had been killed, thought the Queen, flexing her hands which were moist with the tension of her vigil. No, Solomon's successor might have been worse. Besides, she wanted to set eyes on him for herself, she'd been told so much about his power, his knowledge, his roomfuls of books and pictures from all over the world. She must keep calm: it was politics. A foreign power always displayed its muscle in front of the ruler of another, small, unknown neighbour, however grand a show she had put on to sue for peace as an equal. The Queen sighed. The spices and furs and gold and gems she had brought would have sustained Shebans for a long time; but she wanted to hide the poverty and difficulties suffered by her people: she knew men kick the dog that lies sickly in the street but pat the hound that leaps at the lead.

A guard picked out one of the young members of the Queen's train and lifted the curtain of a booth to usher her in. The Queen outside clasped her hands, and pressed her pulse down on her lap to steady her bloodrate; she was afraid.

Inside, the young woman soldier bunched up her fists like a child miming stone in a game of Paper, Scissors, Stone and passed them over the Sheban's body with practised speed. She traced the outside outline of her body, down over her hips, up the inside leg to the crotch, and fanned out over the back, shoulders and chest like a tailor drawing with chalk on a toile to mark adjustments. Underneath the Sheban livery of grey and primrose yellow pyjamas the boy's flesh shivered with shyness, with fear that she might become aware of his disguise, with pleasure as the rough girl's hands caressed him. But her features remained expressionless, and when she said, 'You're clear,' she spoke dully, as she pulled back the curtain of the green booth and showed him out.

Then, 'No body search today, for you,' she added. 'You're in luck.' Was there an emphasis, a touch of humour? He couldn't tell, and he flounced the panels of his tunic coquettishly, to share the joke with her, if she'd understood. But she was already ushering in another. (Later the guards would giggle together in the mess about the day, the wriggling girls in the men's searches, the stiff shy boys in the women's. But they didn't tell, because they were looking for concealed knives or hammers. Besides, they assumed the disguises were part of the visiting barbarians' outlandish customs.)

The Queen relaxed as she saw the children regroup undetained, and enjoyed the success of her ruse. Solomon was insatiable, she'd heard. What did that mean? He had a hundred wives, or more, it was said. How often could he do it? She tried to check her line of thought. He's an adversary, a danger, you must use all your powers to keep him sweet. Yet, she thought again, how often can he get around all of them? She imagined the chosen one rising from a gaggle of recumbent houris, tense, pleased, smoothing her dress, no, adjusting her hair, perhaps she doesn't wear a dress. The Queen shook herself, rapped herself over the knuckles, surveyed the bustling gates, one of the children waved to her, laughing. The time came for her to make her approach. Apprehension was clamped to her gut, and gnawing. She reminded herself, He is wise, they say, perhaps his wisdom will make him kind. The lines of attendants formed behind her; with a tap and a click, the baggage train began to move, and the Queen of Sheba and her train entered the enclave of the Temple.

Solomon was sitting on a throne, and he did have a beard; he was smaller than she had expected, slighter in build, and he looked eagerly at her, as if he truly wanted to meet her. (*My beloved is white and ruddy, the chiefest among ten thousand. Have you seen my love? His head is as the most fine gold . . .*) Her hopes rose, she stretched her step and approached. (*Rise up, my love, my fair one, and come away. For lo, the winter is gone, the rain is over and gone . . .*) She was trembling.

Points of light were darting from the jewels set in his throne, from the eyes of the lions couchant on each of the twelve steps, and bouncing in the sunlight off the water running across the courtyard before his dais. She was bewildered, she wanted to shade her eyes, but formality prevented her and besides she would need to hold up her dress to save it from getting wet. She mustn't show fear, she told herself, she must not hesitate, but go forward, answer his beckoning hand, his open, smiling glance.

Then she saw her own throne, beside the dais, winking with its own constellation of starry stones, and their light, mixed with the shooting flashes from Solomon's dais and the glints dancing on the water in front of her, blinded her. She was unutterably dismayed. But she kept on, answering his greeting; she stepped out of her shoes as there was no bridge and this must be a custom in King Solomon's kingdom, and went towards him, into the water.

The fish beneath her do not school away in a flash of scales; they remain suspended, stock still; the water does not open to her advance. Solomon's eyes meet her confusion. He looks down, she feels his look lick her limbs. She follows the King's eyes and she sees that she is walking on mirror, her white petticoat ruffle looks back at her, she can see her bare legs, and so can Solomon.

Are they hairy?

The Muslim story-tellers differ.

In one tale, the djinns fix the Queen's problem in a jiffy, inventing a depilatory cream on the spot.

But that is a late, bastardized version – obviously by some comedian from the bazaar.

Is she hooved? Maybe.

In other stories, the ones we know better, the Queen is beautiful all over. (*Thou art all fair, my love; there is no spot on thee.*)

Solomon chuckled. The success of his trick was splendid. He felt warmly towards the stranger queen who had so compliantly fallen in with his plans, and a chivalrous pity filled his breast as he saw her discomfiture, her pain. He rose and came towards her, and they embraced as visiting heads of state, right hands clasped, heads bowed in respect, and then she dropped in a curtsey. Close to him, she could smell him, a slightly peppery, bitter smell, sweat in the gold gimp of his robes, ineradicable even by the dry cleaning solvents of the wisest man in the world. He was not as young as he looked from below, but his lips were full, the upper one protruding ripely over the bottom as if ready to be kissed. (*His mouth is most sweet; yea, he is altogether lovely.*)

But now she was there to calm him down, to deflect his intentions on her country, to propose a treaty, to make friends. She must flatter him, she knew how much men like women to admire them; but she also understood that her flattery would mean nothing if she seemed too easy. Already, she had been outwitted, already he had stolen an advantage.

The Queen rose from her curtsey and turned to ask for her shoes; one of her attendants knelt to dry her feet and then slipped them on.

She looked up and forced a smile; Solomon grinned back.

'I've a great many questions to put to you,' she said, 'for I've heard that nothing's hidden from your wisdom.'

The King waved his hands in modest dissent, but then nodded to tell her to proceed.

She showed him two identical roses. One was a true rose, and the other cast in silver by the lost wax process from a rose so that every vein and speckle and delicate rib and curl of the petals and leaves was faithfully reproduced then painted. She asked him how to tell the simulacrum from the real thing.

Solomon considered the roses. Then he clapped his hands and gave an order to a djinn. The servant flitted away through the air, and returned with a hive, buzzing with bees; another ran up with a napkin. When he uncovered it, a donkey's mess inside, flyblown and steaming, released its fetor.

Solomon said to the Queen of Sheba, 'Watch.'

The flies buzzed around, tried the roses one by one and flew back to the dung; the bees circled, rose, and then one tacked in mid-air, reversed and flew down to the rose in her left hand, and bending its abdomen voluptuously to rub the gold dust on the stamens with its tail tip, nuzzled at the honey in the centre of the flower.

'You see,' said Solomon, 'bees can tell the copy.'

Though she had to drop the rose to avoid the bees, the Queen was impressed, and pleased to see Solomon seemed to appreciate her test. 'We're too much slaves of the eye altogether,' she said, 'touch and smell and taste and hearing – these other means of understanding are far too easily overlooked, don't you think, O King?'

And Solomon, amused by the barbarian queen's earnestness, nodded, in complete agreement. (That is the riddle she posed and the fable as told, and if it seems to connect with what I tried to say that night with the boys, then it's none of my doing.)

She tried him again, with another question, dear to her and

more so to me. She was ticking off the number of her riddles on her fingers, schoolmistressy, not to be put off.

'Boys and girls are different in bodies, I know,' she said, 'but how are they different in their minds?'

The stories we have are bent on covering Solomon in glory, and so, immediately, effortlessly, brilliantly, he naturally finds an answer.

Again he whispered a command to a servile djinn and again, when the djinn returned he was carrying something, in a bulging net sack, which he hoisted over to the King, who, shouting to the Queen's train of youths, dipped into it and chucked with boisterous, Santa-like cheeriness a succession of brightly coloured balls, a cascade of sweets and chocolates and cherries, into the group of girls and boys, of boys dressed as girls and girls dressed as boys. One after another his gifts tumbled pell-mell into the company.

The Queen looked on while her servants caught Solomon's scattered largesse, and saw nothing but a mêlée. But Solomon crowed.

'I knew it, I knew it,' he whooped. 'The boys jump for it, they snatch, even if you have togged some of them up like houris, while the girls, well, I'm glad to see that even from your country they're proper little women, aren't they, and thank God for it! They're gathering up the presents from the ground, and putting them in their skirts and if they aren't wearing skirts because for some reason you've got them done up as sentries then they're filling a corner of their tunics with the stuff as if in an apron. You thought you could take me in, but you can't!' He was pink with delight at his success, he was almost breaking into applause, his laughter was making his eyes glisten, when he noticed that the Queen was still standing.

'Come now,' he said, taking her gently by the waist. 'Kneeling shows the female sex, as your little ladies have shown us, but you, you gorgeous thing you, you must be seated.' And he handed her to her own throne. (*He brought me to the banqueting house, and his banner over me was love. His left hand shall be under my head, and his right hand shall embrace me.*)

She was shaking. She had heard that in other countries like Solomon's, women were kept in seclusion as the possessions of their husbands, but she had not experienced their manners before. In Sheba, she knew about women's weakness too, but there, differences between women and men did not mean that one sex ruled or laughed or mocked the other; besides she was sorry he had taken her question so literally, disillusioned that he accepted such a simple solution.

Or at least this is how I see her encounter with Solomon, as her awakening to a society where they throw a woman coloured balls, they throw her sweets, and she kneels to pick them up, like me.

In Ethiopia – and according to many authorities, Sheba lay there, in the Horn of Africa – Solomon marries the Queen and she has a child – Menelek – with him, with whom she returns to Sheba. She raises him to become the first of the Lions of Judah, direct ancestor of the Emperor Haile Selassie and founding father of the Rastafarian cultists today, in their tricolour bonnets over felted cigarillo dreadlocks.

In the chapel of the Ethiopians in Jerusalem, in the whitewashed roof of the church of the Holy Sepulchre, past the beehive cells of the few sable-hued monks who remain, the Queen of Sheba's meeting with Solomon and their ensuing love fill the panels of a painting along one wall. Scarlet, saffron, viridian figures, huge-eyed as nocturnal mammals, move through the frames of a devotional strip cartoon to tell of her magnificent and exalted capitulation to the wisest man in the world, and of the peace she brought to Sheba by her alliance, when she became Solomon's beloved (*My sister, my spouse*), and converted to his faith and thus founded Ethiopian Christianity.

Idyll of Africa, gentle southern parable concealing an ancient surrender, the ending didn't always turn out so sanguine. In Yiddish folklore, the Queen of Sheba metamorphoses into Lilith, demon woman, bloodsucker, child murderer, the woman who defied Adam's authority from the very start, in Eden, just as the Queen of Sheba, in her unattached state, threatened the code by which polygamous

Solomon and his patriarchal descendants live. In this cycle of stories, the Queen returns to Sheba as she came, unmarried, with her store of arcane knowledge, an unseemly thing in woman. She remains childless herself, even hating all children; amulets were made to prevent her preying on babies in their cradles.

But in the median version, the favourite among Muslim story-tellers, the Queen of Sheba receives her trouncing at the hands of the wise King, as is only right, converts to his God – in this case, Allah – and accepts his laws, including the custom – unfamiliar in Sheba – of marriage. Solomon chooses her a husband, and gives her several of his djinns to slave for the pair of them and set them up in their new household. The djinns are tremendously relieved that Solomon does not marry her himself, for the offspring of such a union would inherit powers of sorcery and continue to hold them in subjection; but with this weaker union, the djinns will be free when Solomon dies, like Ariel when Prospero breaks his wand. And indeed, as soon as they hear the news of the King's death, years after the Queen's embassy, down tools they do, and refuse to work for her or her husband ever again.

I was standing on the ramparts of the Old City of Jerusalem, looking across the valley of Kidron, with George H., a most knowledgeable guide and friend – he was born in Jerusalem, in the Armenian quarter. After my paper to the conference that morning, I'd given the others the slip. I didn't much want to face them, after my small but painful collusion and betrayals.

George was pointing towards a shallow hill opposite, its shield-shaped crown fringed by dark green and dense trees, as if it were wearing a cap pulled down on its head. In the boneyard barrenness of the Judaean terrain, such wooded shade was unusual.

'That's where Solomon kept his women, or so they say,' George told me. 'He had to make sure of them, so he kept them at a distance from the city, in a high place, with guards set around.' The disapproval of George, who is a mystic of determined Christian persuasion, sounded clearly in his voice.

*(King Solomon loved many strange women . . . he had seven hundred wives, princesses, and three hundred concubines . . .)* There was henbane bristling in the wall as we looked towards the hill, the hill of Silwan. It had opened its yellow face and purple throat; if the Queen of Sheba had had freckles, she might have decocted the leaves to bleach them.

'I'd like to go there,' I said. We took a taxi up the hill into the wood; there was long damp grass under the pine trees, and golden aconites were in flower, wearing lacy ruffs like the subjects of Dutch portraits. Small blue wild iris pulled leopard-spotted tongues and cyclamen uncurled in the moist shadows with their pink ears folded back; cryptograms were printed on their dark emerald hoof-shaped leaves. Lemon trees were flowering and fruiting at once, and there was a scent of fresh sweetness in under them. Here perhaps Solomon and the Queen exchanged love songs once. (*Thy navel is like a round shining goblet . . . Thy two breasts are like two young roes that are twins.*)

The hill commanded a sweep over the city: the excavations of the City of David, Solomon's son by another woman, were laid out in fretwork under the stacked bleached stone of Jerusalem; Absolom, David's son, was buried under the dagoba-style monolith hewn from the valley floor and cliff-face below; on the other side, the mirror of the Dead Sea, mercury and milk and mother of pearl, shone beyond the stilled ocean of the dunes' rise and fall in the desert.

This is where she opened to her beloved, when she put her hand in at the door and felt her fingers drip with myrrh and her insides turn over for him. (*Honey and milk are under thy tongue.*) And even though I had to disapprove – I wanted her not to concede anything, let alone that 'unpierced pearl' of the story, I wanted her to emerge untouched – I couldn't help feeling pleasure too in that fragrant wood with the valley of Kidron below where the water of Gihon still wells up.

The door of the building that now stands on the hill in the wood of Silwan opened in its turn, and a gaunt woman in the grey habit and veil of a nursing nun hurried down the steps towards us. She was fluttering; there had been a few foreigners murdered recently in Jerusalem, by terrorists of as yet unidentified affiliation, and she was nervous of strangers, it was plain. George explained, 'We are researching the traditions about King Solomon: she –' he pointed at me, 'is a visitor from England, a teacher.' The nun relaxed. Her face was waxy from washing it in water, her posture bent, ingratiating, and she had a gold incisor, which gleamed, and an enamel badge of the Virgin Mary at her throat. She answered, in French, though from her faltering it wasn't her mother tongue, 'Yes, there is a story, but I don't know much about it. That this was Solomon's . . . I don't know the word.' And she twittered.

George, who speaks most languages, supplied it.

'His harem, yes, that's it,' she said. '*Le roi Solomon tenait ses femmes ici.*' She repeated the phrase and peered around short-sightedly. I followed her look; of course it was fixed on nothing but the pines.

There were sounds, though, and scents; above all a song. (*Make haste my beloved; and be thou like to a roe or a young hart upon the mountain of spices.*) I wanted not to hear. Fight back, I said to myself. Resist the longing. Ass's hooves are fine. Hairy legs are fine. Don't let yourself hear the song. And don't listen, when you do.

# Biographical Notes on the Authors

CHRISTOPHER BURNS was born in 1944 and lives in Cumbria with his wife and two teenage children. His novel, *Snakewrist*, and a collection of stories, *About the Body*, were published in 1988. His work has also appeared in *Best Short Stories 1986*, the *London Review of Books*, *Critical Quarterly* and *London Magazine*.

PATRICE CHAPLIN is an author, playwright, journalist and the producer of a BBC radio documentary on 'The Cabbala in Spain'. She has published ten novels – most recently the autobiographical *Albany Park* and *Another City* – many short stories and over a dozen plays for radio and television. She is the author of *From the Balcony* for the National Theatre and Radio 3. She has travelled widely, has lived in New York and Los Angeles and has two sons.

JIM CLARKE was born in Belfast in 1971, the eldest of four children. He started writing at a very early age and has written for a number of diverse Northern Irish magazines. In addition he has contributed a story to the mythology of fantasy author Joe Dever's world of *Magnamund*. He is currently editing his first novel, *Starchase and Shadow Seeking*.

RICHARD CRAWFORD was born in Lisburn, County Antrim, in 1961. He has been a barman, a postman, an art student, a drama student and a busker. He has been employed in a civilian capacity by both the Ministry of Defence and the Royal Ulster Constabulary and is at present working for the DOE in the centre of Belfast. Although he has written widely in both prose and poetry, *Autumn Rain* is his first published work.

RONALD FRAME was born in Glasgow in 1953. He has written five books including the prize-winning novel *Winter Journey, Sandmouth People, Watching Mrs Gordon* and *A Long Weekend with Marcel Proust*. His latest published collection, a novel and fifteen stories, is *A Woman of Judah*. He received the Samuel Beckett Prize for his first television play, *Paris*, and he also won Pye's Most Promising Writer New to Television. He is currently working on a new novel.

SOPHIE FRANK was born in Manchester in 1961. She read English at Oxford and subsequently did a variety of odd jobs in the film industry. Until recently she worked as script consultant for Channel Four. She is currently writing several screenplays. *Birth* is the first short story she wrote. She lives in London.

PENELOPE GILLIATT has been a fiction writer for the *New Yorker* since 1967, also contributing profiles to the magazine of, mainly, film actors and directors. She has written much film and theatre criticism, a number of plays and the screenplay for *Sunday, Bloody Sunday*. Her fifth novel, *A Woman of Singular Occupation*, was published this year, and she has five collections of stories to her name.

NADINE GORDIMER was born and lives in South Africa. She has published nine novels, including the recent *A Sport of Nature*, and *Something Out There* is the latest of her seven collections of short stories. Her first collection of non-fiction, *The Essential Gesture*, is published this year. Among many literary awards, she has received the Booker Prize.

# BIOGRAPHICAL NOTES ON THE AUTHORS

GEORGINA HAMMICK was born in 1939. She has three grown-up children and lives in Wiltshire. She writes the gardens column for *Books* magazine. Her poetry is included in *A Poetry Quintet*. She began writing stories in 1984, and her first collection, *People for Lunch*, was published in 1987.

HANIF KUREISHI was born in South London and studied philosophy at King's College, London. He is currently Writer-in-Residence at the Royal Court where he works with young writers. He has also written two films, *My Beautiful Laundrette* and *Sammy and Rosie Get Laid*. A novella, *With Your Tongue Down My Throat*, was recently published in *Granta*. Faber are to bring out his first novel next year.

JIM MANGNALL was born in Liverpool in 1930. His poetry has appeared in various magazines and anthologies including the *PEN Anthology 1972* and *Arts Council New Poetry 1975*. In 1980 he turned to prose and his short stories have appeared in *Ambit*. In 1985 he won the Donny MacLeod Award presented by the BBC's *Pebble Mill at One*.

ADAM MARS-JONES was born in London in 1954. His first book of fiction, *Lantern Lecture*, won the Somerset Maugham Award in 1981. Since then he has edited *Mae West Is Dead*, a collection of lesbian and gay fiction, and co-written (with Edmund White) *The Darker Proof: Stories from a Crisis*. His story, 'Remission', is included in the second edition of that book.

DEBORAH MOGGACH was born in 1948. She read English at Bristol University but only started writing fiction while living for two years in Pakistan. Her first novel, *You Must be Sisters* was followed by *Close to Home*, *A Quiet Drink*, *Hot Water Man* and *Porky*. Her most recent novel, *To Have and to Hold*, has been dramatized into an eight-part TV serial and was shown in autumn 1986. She also writes for newspapers and magazines. Deborah Moggach lives in London and has two children.

SALMAN RUSHDIE, born in Bombay in 1947, is the author of four novels: *Grimus*, *Midnight's Children* (which won the Booker Prize), *Shame* and *The Satanic Verses*. He lives in London.

GRAHAM SEAL was born in England in 1930. He worked for several years in Canada – as a surveyor for an oil exploration firm, a technical writer, and as an attendant in a mental hospital. His plays have been produced by CBC and BBC and his short stories and poems have appeared in various publications. He now lives in Cornwall.

LIONEL SEEPAUL was born in Trinidad and has taught high school in Trinidad and Canada. He began writing for the BBC and received a literary award in his native island. His stories have been published in *Short Story International* (New York) and *London Magazine*. He lives with his wife and three daughters in Vancouver.

HELEN SIMPSON read English at Oxford, and now lives in London. After winning its talent contest, she worked for *Vogue* as a staff writer for five years. She has written two recipe books on *Afternoon Tea* and *Breakfast*. Recently she went freelance. Her short stories have appeared in various magazines, glossy and otherwise.

WILLIAM TREVOR was born in Mitchelstown, County Cork, in 1928. Among his books are *The Old Boys*, *The Ballroom of Romance*, *Angels at the Ritz*, *The Children of Dynmouth*, *Lovers of Their Time*, *Fools of Fortune* and *The News from Ireland*. In 1976 he received the Allied Irish Bank's Prize and in 1977 was awarded the CBE. He is a member of the Irish Academy of Letters. William Trevor's new book, *Silence in the Garden*, is published this year. He is married and has two sons.

GUY VANDERHAEGHE was born in Saskatchewan, Canada, in 1951. Since leaving university he has worked as a teacher, an archivist and a researcher, but now devotes his time to writing. He has had numerous stories published in literary magazines and anthologies and, among other prizes, has won the *Canadian Fiction Magazine*'s award for short fiction. He has published a novel, *Man Descending*, and a volume of stories, *My Present Age*. He is married and lives in Ottawa.

MARINA WARNER was born in 1946 and brought up in Egypt, Belgium and Cambridge. Her father was a bookseller; her mother teaches Italian in London. She has written on myths about women – on the Virgin Mary, Joan of Arc and *Monuments and Maidens*. Her third novel, *The Lost Father*, is published this year. In 1987–88 she was a Visiting Scholar at the Getty Center for the History of Art.

# Acknowledgements

'Angelo's Passion', copyright © Christopher Burns 1987, was first published in the *London Magazine* December 1987 and is reprinted by permission of the author and Anthony Sheil Associates, 43 Doughty Street, London WC1N 2LF.

'Night in Paris', copyright © Patrice Chaplin 1987, was first published in the *Fiction Magazine* January/February 1987 and is reprinted by permission of the author.

'The Death of the Tribe', copyright © Jim Clarke 1987, was first published in *Passages 1* 1987 and is reprinted by permission of the author.

'Autumn Rain', copyright © Richard Crawford 1987, was first published in *Passages 1* 1987 and is reprinted by permission of the author.

'Fruits de Mer', copyright © Ronald Frame 1986, was first published in the *London Magazine* December 1986/January 1987 and is reprinted by permission of the author and Curtis Brown Ltd, 162–168 Regent Street, London W1R 5TB.

'Birth', copyright © Sophie Frank 1987, was first published in *Ambit 108* 1987 and is reprinted by permission of the author.

'Lingo', copyright © Penelope Gilliatt 1987, was first published in the *New Yorker* 7 September 1987 and is reprinted by permission of the author and A. P. Watt Ltd, 20 John Street, London WC1N 2DL.

'Spoils', copyright © Nadine Gordimer 1987, was first published in *Granta* Autumn 1987 and is reprinted by permission of the author and A. P. Watt Ltd, 20 John Street, London WC1N 2DL.

## ACKNOWLEDGEMENTS

'High Teas', copyright © Georgina Hammick 1987, was first published in the *Listener* 17/24 December 1987 and is reprinted by permission of the author and Curtis Brown Ltd, 162–168 Regent Street, London W1R 5TB.

'The Buddha of Suburbia', copyright © Hanif Kureishi 1987, was first published in the *London Review of Books* 19 February 1987 and is reprinted by permission of the author.

'Vigil', copyright © Jim Mangnall 1987, was first published in *Ambit 107* 1987 and is reprinted by permission of the author.

'Remission', copyright © Adam Mars-Jones 1987, was first published in *Granta* Autumn 1987 and is reprinted by permission of the author and A. D. Peters & Co Ltd, 10 Buckingham Street, London WC2N 6BU.

'Horse Sense', copyright © Deborah Moggach 1987, was first published in the *Fiction Magazine* April 1987 and is reprinted by permission of the author and Curtis Brown Ltd, 162–168 Regent Street, London W1R 5TB.

'Good Advice is Rarer than Rubies', copyright © Salman Rushdie 1987, was first published in the *New Yorker* 22 June 1987 and is reprinted by permission of the author and Aitken & Stone Ltd, 29 Fernshaw Road, London SW10 0TG.

'Stopover', copyright © Graham Seal 1987, was first published in the *London Magazine* December 1987 and is reprinted by permission of the author.

'A Sleeping Pill for the Doctor', copyright © Lionel Seepaul 1987, was first published in the *London Magazine* July 1987 and is reprinted by permission of the author.

'Good Friday, 1663', copyright © Helen Simpson 1987, was first published in the *Listener* 3 September 1987 and is reprinted by permission of the author and A. D. Peters & Co Ltd, 10 Buckingham Street, London WC2N 6BU.

'A Trinity', copyright © William Trevor 1987, was first published in the *New Yorker* 11 May 1987 and is reprinted by permission of the author and A. D. Peters & Co Ltd, 10 Buckingham Street, London WC2N 6BU.

'Home Place', copyright © Guy Vanderhaeghe 1987, was first published in the *London Review of Books* 12 November 1987 and is reprinted by permission of the author and Curtis Brown Ltd, 162–168 Regent Street, London W1R 5TB.

'The Legs of the Queen of Sheba', copyright © Marina Warner 1987, was first published in the *Fiction Magazine* 3 April 1987 and is reprinted by permission of the author and A. D. Peters & Co Ltd, 10 Buckingham Street, London WC2N 6BU.

We are grateful to the editors of the publications in which the stories first appeared for permission to reproduce them in this compilation.

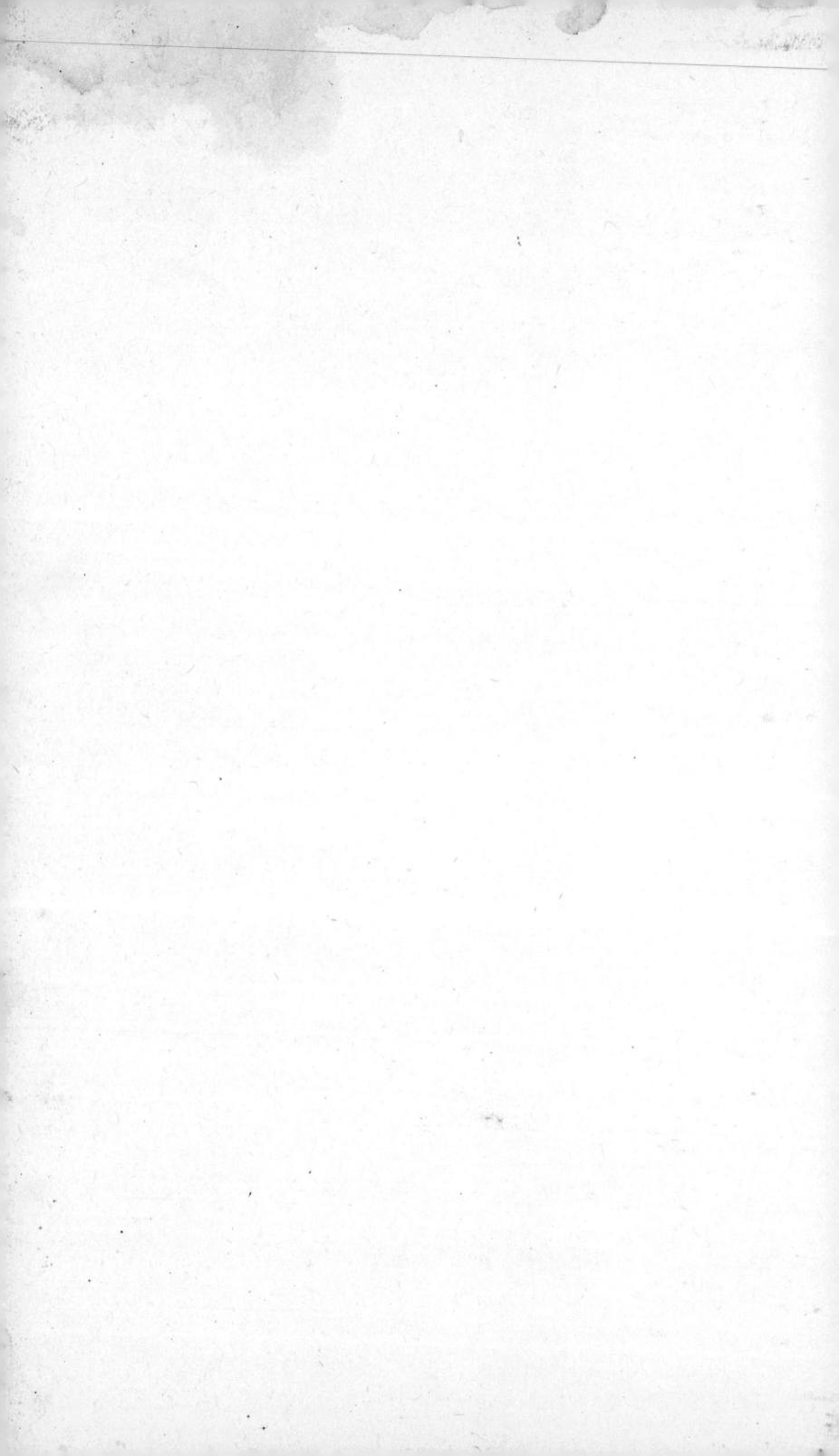